IRON MAIDEN AT 50

DANIEL BUKSZPAN

IRON MAIDEN, LOOKING TOTALLY
'80S WITH A UNION JACK. (L-R)
DAVE MURRAY, BRUCE DICKINSON,
NICKO MCBRAIN,, STEVE HARRIS,
AND ADRIAN SMITH.

CONTENTS

INTRODUCTION 4

ONE
AN AGE-OLD DREAM 9

01. MERRY CHRISTMAS, MR HARRIS 10
BYE-BYE, FOOTBALL; HELLO, PROG

02. THE SOUNDHOUSE TAPES 12
LIMITED MAIL-ORDER EP SELLS OUT

03. HELLO, EMI 14
"THEY WERE FOR REAL"

04. MAIDEN GIVETH, AND MAIDEN TAKETH AWAY 16
"IT HAD ITS OWN EDGE"

05. BURNING AMBITION 18
THE FIRST SINGLE, "RUNNING FREE"

06. NO PRECEDENT, NO EQUAL 20
DEBUT LP RELEASED

07. THE URCHIN REUNION 22
STRATTON REPLACED BY ADRIAN SMITH

08. WHEN RITCHIE BLACKMORE TALKS... 26
"WE WERE REALLY LUCKY TO GET HIM"

09. MAIDEN RELEASES KILLERS 30
THIS IS PERFECT, CHANGE NOTHING

10. DID HE TRY TEA WITH HONEY AND LEMON? 34
MAIDEN PARTS WITH DI'ANNO

TWO
THE DEVIL SENDS THE BEAST WITH WRATH 41

11. THE AIR RAID SIREN 42
BRUCE DICKINSON JOINS

12. GET OUT AND PUSH 46
MAIDEN GETS THEIR FIRST UK NO. 1

13. CLIVE, UNSTOOLED 48
ANOTHER CHANGE IS IN THE AIR

14. REVELATIONS 50
FRANK HERBERT HATES IRON MAIDEN

15. DO OR DIE 56
SONGS ABOUT SWORD FIGHTING

16. FROM WARSAW TO IRVINE 60
MAIDEN WITHSTANDS THE WORLD SLAVERY TOUR

17. IT'S NO TURBO 66
IRON MAIDEN GETS A LUNCH BREAK

18. SEVENTH SON OF A SEVENTH SON 68
AMERICA DISAPPOINTS STEVE HARRIS

19. HEADLINING DONINGTON 72
IT SHOULDN'T HAVE GONE THIS WAY

20. "AGONIZING" 74
A MEMBER OF THE CLASSIC LINEUP MOVES ON

THREE
MEN ON THE EDGE 81

21. BACK TO BASICS, BUT NOT THAT WAY 82
JANICK GERS REPLACES SMITH

22. TOILET GRAFFITI 84
MAIDEN'S ONLY NO. 1 UK SINGLE

23. A RETURN TO FORM... KINDA 88
PLUS, CHANGES AFOOT

24. TIMING IS EVERYTHING 94
BRUCE DICKINSON HAS HAD ENOUGH

25. LET'S GET THIS OVER WITH 96
DAVE MURRAY, LIFE COACH

26. SO LONG, BRUCE BRUCE 98
DICKINSON LEAVES TO PURSUE SOLO CAREER

27. LIVE FAST, DIE FAST 100
MAIDEN GETS DIVISIVE

28. D-I-V-O-R-C-E 102
LOVE STINKS

29. PUT YOUR MASK ON 104
BEST OF THE BEAST COMPILATION

30. COMO ESTAIS, AMIGOS 108
"THERE WAS SOME KIND OF FUNNY VIBE"

FOUR
THE THREE AMIGOS
115

31. "THAT WAS IT FOR ME" 116
EMI PUTS ITS FOOT DOWN

32. "THE WORLD NEEDS IRON MAIDEN" 118
BUT WHAT ABOUT JANICK?

33. "WE ARE ALL SONS OF MAIDEN" 120
THE BAND BECOMES THE MOTHERSHIP

34. RETURN TO RIO 124
AN ABSOLUTELY ESSENTIAL LIVE ALBUM

35. CLIVE AID 126
"WE CALL IT THE CLIVEMOBILE"

36. EDDIE'S ARCHIVE 128
HAMMERSMITH 1982 COMES OUT OF COLD STORAGE

37. NO MORE LIES 130
IT WASN'T AN ACCIDENT

38. THE LONGEST DAY 134
MAYBE THEY'LL STOP AFTER THE EIGHTH SONG?

39. "PLAY CLASSICS" 138
THE BAND FLIES AROUND ON ED FORCE ONE

40. "AFTER 20,000 MILES, YOU RELAX A BIT" 142
BANGER FILMS GOES TO INDIA

FIVE
"WE'LL ALL PROBABLY DROP DEAD ONSTAGE"
147

41. NO, IT'S NOT THE FINAL ALBUM 148
MAIDEN SHARES THE CHARTS WITH TAY TAY

42. TECH FINDS THE FANS . . . 152
. . . ALLEGEDLY

43. "A SUBTLE HINT OF LEMON" 154
MAIDEN CHECKS THE NATION-STATUS BOXES

44. RIP CLIVE BURR 156
TRIBUTES POUR IN FROM MAIDEN NATION

45. THE BOOK OF SOULS 158
DICKINSON TANGLES WITH THE BIG C

46. LEGACY OF THE LOCKDOWN 160
COVID-19 THROWS A CURVEBALL

47. THE WRITING ON THE WALL 164
SECRET UNRAVELED BY ATTENTIVE FANS

48. "I'LL BE FOREVER GRATEFUL" 166
THE BAND HELPS AN OLD FRIEND

49. A MESSAGE FROM NICKO 169
"I CAN'T GET IT"

50. RIP PAUL DI'ANNO 170
"END OF STORY"

DISCOGRAPHY 174
BIBLIOGRAPHY 185
PHOTO CREDITS 186
ACKNOWLEDGMENTS 187
INDEX 188

INTRODUCTION

It feels weird to be writing a retrospective book about Iron Maiden. It's not that they don't deserve one—they've certainly been around for long enough, and you would be hard-pressed to find a more influential band outside of the Beatles, Black Sabbath, or AC/DC. Whatever plaudits this band has received over the years, they've earned.

No, it seems weird because, as of the time of this writing, they're on the globe-hopping *Future Past* tour, which has seen them hit every continent except Africa, Antarctica, and Europe. One assumes they will hit Africa soon enough, and they're hitting Europe during their 2025—2026 *Run for Your Lives* tour. And we still wouldn't bet against Antarctica.

Iron Maiden was formed on Christmas Day 1975 by bassist Steve Harris. While there have never been any slouches in the group, his belief in his vision has been unwavering and uncompromising. While several members came and went, none of them were along for the ride, either. If you look at the band's extensive tour itineraries, you'll see that they would break most other musicians in half. This is true even now, while all the band members are hovering around age seventy.

My experience with Iron Maiden was less an immediate infatuation than a slow seduction. I became aware of them through MTV in the 1980s, and what I saw, frankly, made me take a step back. It's not that the videos for songs like "Run to the Hills" or "The Trooper" were scary—they were more comical than anything else.

What really came through to me was a sort of thuggish energy. Between singer Bruce Dickinson's manic vitality and Harris with his foot on the monitor, pointing his bass at the audience like a machine gun, these seemed like people you didn't want to tangle with. They were for real. You knew they meant business, even if you didn't quite understand what that business was.

Later, I came to understand that along with Judas Priest, Iron Maiden was the archetypal heavy metal band. From the way they dressed—long hair, studs, and lots of leather—to the mastery of their instruments, this was the band you could invoke if you only had a few seconds to explain what "heavy metal" is. They also had a ghoulish mascot named Eddie, whose image would regularly scare children away, which was just gravy.

Fans of the band got zero respect from classmates when I was growing up. They thought the glassy-eyed kids with Iron Maiden back patches who reeked of Marlboro reds were just too icky to approach. There was nothing wrong with them, but just by listening to the band and wearing the regalia, they had separated themselves from polite society. In return, polite society scorned them and their favorite band and treated them with the same welcome you would give a passed-out drunk lying on your front doorstep.

While this band experimented with their sound, sometimes changing it radically, the music we ended up with was always ferocious, savage, and uncompromising. Some albums were dense and progressive, whereas others were more commercial. Either way, they did whatever the hell they wanted to do, and bollocks to anyone who didn't like it.

Certain eras of the band are more beloved than others. I love all of it. A couple of albums, like *No Prayer for the Dying*, didn't do much for me, but that was never enough to dampen my enthusiasm. If they had a new album, I bought it on release day. When I put their music on, it would completely consume me. I have never in my life been in a physical altercation, nor have I ever committed an act of violence against anyone. But when certain Iron Maiden songs come on, I suddenly understand why people riot. The music possesses you before you even know what hit you.

Some eras of the band are held in higher regard than others, but when you look at the entirety of their catalog, you realize it all belongs there. The two records the band made in the 1990s with singer Blaze Bayley were poorly received at the time of their release, and to this day, many people still talk about that era like it was a horrible artistic blunder that never should have happened.

Thirty years later, the band still plays those songs, and those albums have always remained in print. Perseverance is a very Maiden trait, as is total belief in the music. While those albums had the misfortune of being released when metal was thoroughly unhip, the band never backed down from them. They always presented that music the same way they presented their most popular songs. It was all part of a continuum, and the band didn't care if people didn't get it. *They* knew it was good music. It was just the rest of us who needed decades to become receptive to it.

I don't have a favorite era of the band. Whether it's the brash proto–speed metal of *Killers*, the stadium anthems of *Powerslave*, or the complex epics of their twenty-first-century incarnation, this band has always brought the goods, and I have always been there for it. I love this band, and I love their music, and even now, while I'm in middle age, their music gets me going the second it starts playing. I'm immediately seized by it. It makes me act like a crazy person, and I don't want to regain my composure. Nothing about showing decorum beats the sensation of losing my mind to "Aces High."

This book was great fun to write, and I feel lucky that I got to talk about a group that has meant so much to me and brought me so much joy. I'm sure not everyone will agree with all my spicy hot takes about this album or that, but it doesn't matter. What matters is that this band has unwavering belief in itself and the music they've made for us over the years. So sit back, put on your favorite Maiden album at the highest volume your stereo system can withstand, and enjoy the fifty-year ride this band has been on.

IRON MAIDEN FOUNDER STEVE HARRIS HOLDS DOWN THE LOW END AT NEW YORK CITY'S MADISON SQUARE GARDEN IN 1983.

ONE
AN AGE-OLD DREAM

THE LINEUP THAT RECORDED IRON MAIDEN'S SELF-TITLED DEBUT ALBUM HANGS OUT IN THE LONDON DUNGEON. PLEASE PAY NO ATTENTION TO THE CADAVER BEHIND THE BAND. HE WAS LIKE THAT WHEN THEY GOT THERE.

01

MERRY CHRISTMAS, MR. HARRIS

BYE-BYE, FOOTBALL; HELLO, PROG

FAR RIGHT INSET: THE ORIGINAL POSTER FOR 1939'S *THE MAN IN THE IRON MASK*, THE MOVIE THAT DEPICTED THE FICTITIOUS TORTURE DEVICE THAT INSPIRED THE NAME FOR STEVE HARRIS'S BAND.

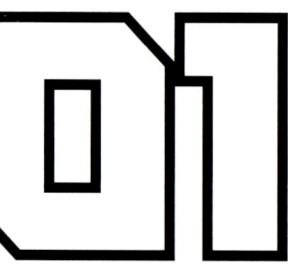

WHILE IRON MAIDEN IS AS METAL AS IT GETS, STEVE HARRIS HAS ALWAYS BEEN A BIG FAN OF PROGRESSIVE ROCK, AND THAT INFLUENCE HAS BEEN A BIG PART OF THEIR MUSIC. SOME ALBUMS THAT SIGNIFICANTLY AFFECTED THE YOUNG BASSIST WERE *NURSERY CRYME* BY GENESIS, *AQUALUNG* BY JETHRO TULL, AND *FRAGILE* BY YES.

Steve Harris was born in the Leytonstone area of East London on March 12, 1956. This made his zodiac sign Pisces, just like Yes bassist Chris Squire.

Whether by coincidence or astrological intervention, he would have more than a few things in common with "The Fish." They were both aggressive, up-front bass players who never took a back seat or supporting role in the music, and they both stayed with their respective bands no matter what.

Harris was the oldest of four siblings, the other three being sisters, and he was raised by a homemaker mother and a truck-driving father who was often out of the house trying to support the family. This left Harris as the only male in the house much of the time, as he lived with his grandmother and four aunts. It was a high-estrogen home, leading him to describe it in Mick Wall's 2004 biography *Iron Maiden: Run to the Hills* as "a house surrounded by women."

Initially, he dreamed of becoming a famous footballer and played for his school and local amateur teams. But after a couple of teenage years spent training for the big leagues, he decided the investment of time it would take to go professional was a bridge too far. It would require a 24/7 commitment on his part, and while he wasn't sure what he wanted to do instead, he knew football wasn't it.

Before trying to play football, he had gotten interested in music, thanks partly to hearing the Beatles and Simon & Garfunkel records his sisters played at home. He liked that music, but what grabbed him was the progressive rock stylings of bands like Genesis, Jethro Tull, and Yes. In 2020, he told *Illinois Entertainer* that it had been a simple decision to strap on his bass and throw himself into the musician's life.

"I actually thought, 'I'd really like to have a go at this myself and try to play music,'" he said. "That was it, really."

He joined the band Smiler in 1974, a few weeks shy of his eighteenth birthday. Some of the music they performed was by the group Wishbone Ash, whose twin-guitar harmonies would have a significant impact on Harris's songwriting.

The bassist wrote songs for Smiler, but they showed little enthusiasm for Harris's intricate prog-influenced compositions. He decided to quit and start his own band, which would play as many intricate, prog-influenced songs as he could write.

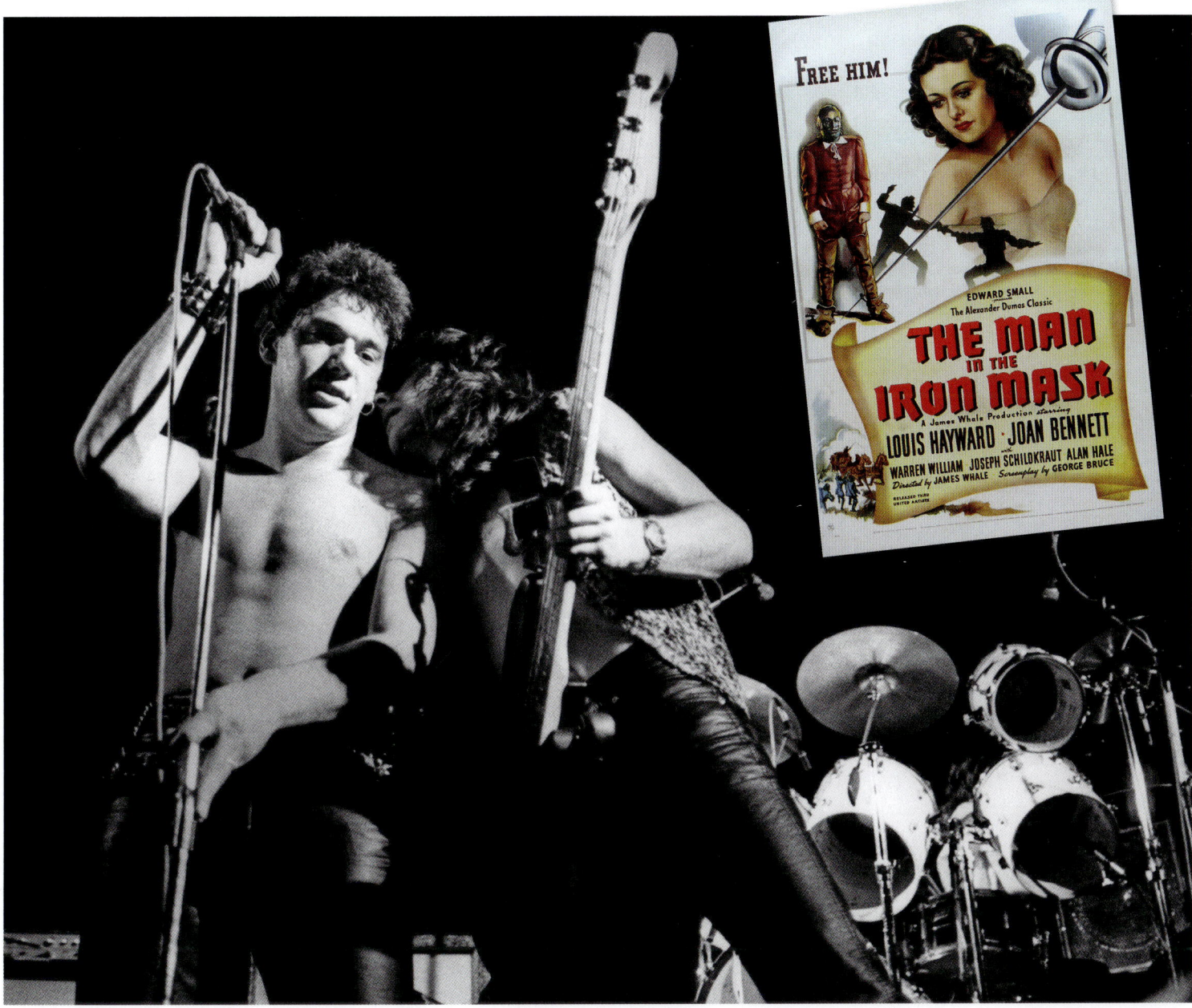

PAUL DI'ANNO AND STEVE HARRIS IN THE MIDDLE OF A HIGH-ENERGY GIG AT LONDON'S LYCEUM ON FEBRUARY 10, 1980.

The embryonic version of Harris's new band came together in 1975. He named it "Iron Maiden" after taking some inspiration from the movie *The Man in the Iron Mask*. The legendary medieval torture device did not appear in the film, and tragically for one and all, it was never even a real thing! It was entirely made up! Boo hiss!

The fictional torture device was a tall iron cabinet with a spiked interior, and many believed it was a real thing used during the Spanish Inquisition to torture heathens into accepting Christ. While heathens certainly got shoddy treatment during that period, no Iron Maiden was involved.

Even if the thing didn't actually exist, it was a great name. The band Steve Harris had assembled on December 25, 1975, was dubbed Iron Maiden, and he even called upon his experience as a draftsman to design its striking and iconic logo, which is still in use.

While it was great that the band had a name, it began hemorrhaging members quickly, including guitarists. Dennis Wilcock, who was fronting the band, knew a great guitarist, Dave Murray, who he felt would fit right in. Fifty years later, Murray and Harris are the only members of Iron Maiden to have appeared on every album.

While Harris, Murray, and drummer Doug Sampson were all in place, Wilcock had lasted only a short time with the band, and the all-important lead singer spot remained vacant. Potential singers came and went without getting the gig until a friend of the band suggested an acquaintance named Paul Di'Anno.

Di'Anno already had the look and the attitude down when he showed up at the audition. But could he sing? After warming up with a little Deep Purple and moving on to embryonic versions of "Iron Maiden" and "Prowler," Harris, Murray, and Sampson were won over. They had their singer.

"There's sort of a quality in Paul's voice, a raspiness in his voice . . . that just gave it this great edge," Harris said. "[Murray and Sampson] thought he was brilliant as well, so I thought, 'Right, this is the boy.'"

THE SOUNDHOUSE TAPES

LIMITED MAIL-ORDER EP SELLS OUT

BRITISH DJ NEAL KAY, WHO MANAGED THE BANDWAGON HEAVY METAL SOUNDHOUSE AND PLAYED DEMO TAPES OVER THE PA BY NEW AND UP-AND-COMING HEAVY METAL BANDS.

Many have wrongly assumed that Iron Maiden was influenced by punk rock. Steve Harris has forcefully denied this at every opportunity. In a 2012 interview with *The Quietus*, he refused to say Iron Maiden shared a DIY aesthetic with the punk bands. Or shared anything, for that matter.

"We hated them, and we hated what they were about," he said.

Part of that hatred was well-earned. In the late 1970s, London's East End clubs were almost exclusively booking punk bands, leaving Iron Maiden few opportunities to perform in front of people. They decided that if they wanted to further their career beyond London's pubs, they should make a demo tape and circulate it far and wide.

They recorded four tracks at Spaceward Studios in Cambridge during the last hours of 1978. While the rest of the world was impairing itself at New Year's Eve parties, the band had recorded four songs: "Invasion," "Iron Maiden," "Prowler," and "Strange World." The demo made it into the hands of disc jockey Neal Kay, who played new heavy metal for rabid fans at the densely packed Bandwagon Heavy Metal Soundhouse.

"It was a club that, when bands were not onstage, would play tapes from unsigned bands," sociologist Deena Weinstein said. "They played Maiden, and that was the start of their career."

Fans came to the club with homemade cardboard guitars to air guitar with—if you were an up-and-coming heavy metal band with a demo tape, this was the crowd you wanted to get it in front of. Di'Anno, Harris, and Murray came by and gave Kay a copy, hoping to secure a gig. He was immediately won over, saying in Garry Bushell's seminal band biography, *Running Free*, that it was "the most impressive demo" anyone had ever handed him.

"Aggressive bands have been a dime a dozen ever since, but no one since has had the tunes, too," Kay said.

The demo went into high rotation at the Soundhouse. One night, Di'Anno and Harris decided to see how their music went down, and when their tape came over the PA system, they saw their effect on the kids who packed the place.

"They put 'Prowler' on, and the next thing there's all these nutters giving it loads down the front, throwing themselves about, headbanging and playing air guitar and all this business," Harris said. "I couldn't believe it, that one of our songs could do that."

Bushell wrote that it was no secret to him why the band was catching on with the public. "Live, they just steam," he said. "They're like men possessed."

It became clear that their demo could do more than just win them gigs. The UK magazine *Sounds* had begun running the Soundhouse charts based on what Kay played most at the club. "Prowler" had reached number one. The band decided to release the demo to the public, dubbing it *The Soundhouse Tapes*.

Weinstein said that in addition to Maiden's furious live sets, they were accepted partially because the public was now ready for them. She said the 1976 Judas Priest album *Sad Wings of Destiny* had created a heavy metal blueprint, and Iron Maiden benefited from following it.

"When Iron Maiden was starting off in '78, '79, there was already a genre with rules for them on what to play, what to say, how to look, et cetera," she said.

Weinstein added that it benefited them that they came from London, which had taken the title of "Heavy Metal Capital of the World" from Birmingham, the hometown of Black Sabbath and Judas Priest.

"London was the center of the UK, and the rock press there was very influential," Weinstein said.

"Iron Maiden," "Prowler," and "Strange World" all got rerecorded for the eventual debut album, and all three newly recorded versions are superior to the demo versions. Still, the band's energy on the demo comes through, even when the equipment doesn't. It's also worth mentioning that "Invasion," the one *Soundhouse* track not to be rerecorded for a studio album, has almost Neanderthal violence to it, especially during the bit where Di'Anno repeatedly informs us that "the Norsemen are coming." That bit makes you want to throw hands! It was used as the B-side of the band's 1980 single "Women in Uniform," but it deserved much better.

AN EXTERIOR SHOT OF THE CART AND HORSES PUB IN EAST LONDON TAKEN IN 2024. IN THE 1970S, IT WAS WHERE A VERY YOUNG AND HUNGRY IRON MAIDEN PLAYED SOME OF THEIR EARLIEST GIGS, WHEN THEY WERE FULL OF BRAVADO AND DEFIANCE.

IRON MAIDEN'S DEBUT EP, THE SOUNDHOUSE TAPES, RELEASED ON NOVEMBER 9, 1979. IT SOLD 3,000 OF ITS 5,000 COPIES IN ONE WEEK.

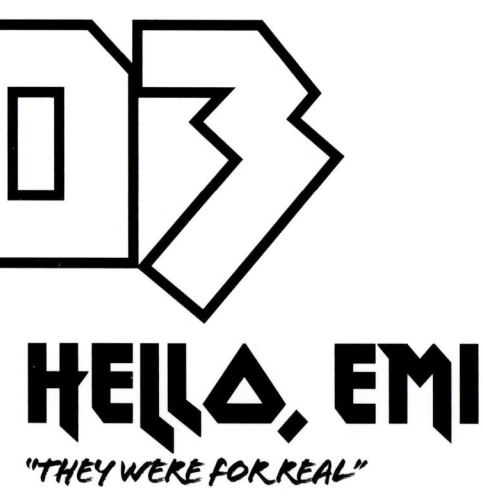

03
HELLO, EMI
"THEY WERE FOR REAL"

Iron Maiden pressed 5,000 copies of the Spaceward demo, now officially dubbed *The Soundhouse Tapes*, and released it on their own Rock Hard Records label in November 1979. At first, there was some concern about whether they needed to press that many since the band sold them only by mail order and only to the faithful. When 3,000 sold in the first week, it was clear that somebody was listening.

All 5,000 copies sold out in just a couple of weeks, entirely because of the music. The band had a buzz going for them since topping the Soundhouse charts, but buzz alone won't sell 5,000 demo tapes by mail order. Audiences loved the music and greedily ate it up.

The tape came to the attention of Rod Smallwood, a man who was so disgusted by the experience of artist management that he had stopped doing it, intending to maybe go to law school instead. Despite turning his back on the music industry, the demo tape was so compelling that he reconsidered.

Smallwood contacted the band and agreed to see them perform at Hammersmith's Swan, but there was a snag. Di'Anno had been standing outside the venue when he was subjected to a random search for drugs by two police officers. He wasn't carrying any, but he was carrying a switchblade, which landed him in the hoosegow. Rather than cancel the gig, Smallwood encouraged the band to take the stage anyway and let Harris perform vocal duties in his singer's stead.

Even with twenty-five percent of the band sitting in the pokey, Iron Maiden managed to impress Smallwood enough that he agreed to help them get a record deal. In *Running Free*, he said the band exceeded his expectations. "They had a good built-in attitude, a lot of integrity, and the vitality and the charisma onstage just from Steve and Davey was very, very powerful," he said. "I think it was their honesty that impressed me most. They were for real."

While Smallwood still wasn't sure he wanted to manage another band, he and Maiden began to build trust in each other. They saw eye-to-eye on many things, even things that might have seemed the wrong move at the time. Large retail music stores like HMV and Virgin had wanted to order 20,000 copies of *The Soundhouse Tapes* based on the hubbub the band was getting. Both the band and Smallwood said no.

"It would have been selling out the kids who'd gone to all the trouble to send in for one of the original 5,000 copies," Smallwood said in *Run to the Hills*. Harris cosigned on the sentiment, if somewhat artlessly: "It would have totally destroyed the magic of having one of the original 5,000 copies, so we said, 'Bollocks to that!'"

Smallwood secured a five-album deal for the band with EMI, with a clause written into the contract stating that the label couldn't drop the band until after its third album. Getting EMI to agree to three albums gave Maiden time to keep building an audience through word-of-mouth, always the best publicity.

All parties signed the EMI contract in December 1979, then promptly retired to a local pub to consume many adult beverages. Di'Anno said that the day after the signing, he felt the whole thing had been a little anticlimactic.

"I don't know what I expected to happen," he said. "But there I was the next night, watching telly, thinking, 'Well, this is it, then, I suppose.'"

IRON MAIDEN HAS NEVER BEEN A PUNK ROCK BAND, AND ANYONE WHO COMPARES THEIR MUSIC TO PUNK ROCK MIGHT FIND THEMSELVES ON THE RECEIVING END OF A STERN TALKING-TO FROM STEVE HARRIS. HAVING SAID THAT, HERE'S ORIGINAL SINGER PAUL DI'ANNO LOOKING VERY MUCH LIKE SID VICIOUS.

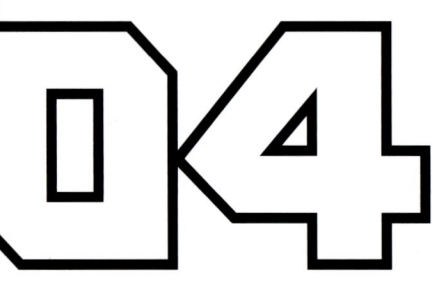

04

MAIDEN GIVETH, AND MAIDEN TAKETH AWAY

"IT HAD ITS OWN EDGE"

As 1980 dawned, Iron Maiden was a well-known local band with a sold-out demo and a deal with EMI Records. The deal led to two weeks of nightly gigs and an appearance on the *Friday Rock Show* at BBC studios. Those November 1979 performances eventually saw wide release in 2002 on the two-disc compilation *BBC Archives*, which was part of the *Eddie's Archive* box set.

The arrangements and performances were already locked in. Even at this early stage, they sounded like themselves, and the energy was undeniable.

Most bands would look at that, pat themselves on the back, and declare it a job well done, but Maiden was still struggling to find a second lead guitarist to spar and harmonize with Murray. Many had already come and gone, some after lasting just a couple of months. Something permanent was needed.

The band ran an ad in *Melody Maker*, specifying that they wanted a heavy metal diehard no older than twenty-two. Dennis Stratton was twenty-seven. He wasn't a heavy metal diehard either. But he had a lot of experience, had done a bit of touring, and was an excellent guitarist. He also had a wife and kid to support, so joining a band on its way up seemed the right move.

Stratton has said that he found the complex compositions crafted by Iron Maiden to be a real challenge. He was a burgeoning journeyman musician, so it wasn't that he couldn't cut it—rather, he found that the material was written in a way that defied conventional songwriting wisdom.

"I'd done a fair bit of session work by then, and it wasn't really like anything I was used to playing, but it had its own edge, its own identity, and I respected that," he said in *Run to the Hills*. "It was kind of a challenge for me, but as a musician who reckoned he could handle most things, I started getting into it on that level."

While adding Stratton to Maiden's ranks was a stabilizing influence, there was another issue. Drummer Doug Sampson was having health problems related to the band's lifestyle, and it was too much for him. A quick look at their itinerary shows it would be too much for almost anybody. Even before getting signed, the band had played nearly fifty club gigs in five months, all while living out of the back of a van.

"You'd come offstage sweating like a pig and then go straight into this draughty old van and on to the next gig, and it was like I was ill all the time," Sampson said. "I suppose it must have affected my playing."

He was heartbroken but understood why he had been shown the door. The band wanted to play every night for the rest of their natural lives. If his health buckled under the strain of playing ten gigs a month, how would he hold up to thirty-one per month, twelve months a year?

Sampson remembered being called into a "band meeting" at Smallwood's office, but only Harris and the manager were there when he arrived. He knew what was up, as surely as anyone knows what's up when they walk into a meeting with their manager and the head of HR is sitting there.

"They were worried I wouldn't be able to fulfill all the commitments they had coming up—really big stuff, like the Judas Priest tour, which they were already in the frame for," he said. When Iron Maiden spent the next three years touring nonstop, he conceded that the decision had probably been the right one.

ORIGINAL IRON MAIDEN GUITARIST DENNIS STRATTON COULD PLAY HIS ASS OFF BUT WAS ASKED TO LEAVE THE BAND BECAUSE, IN HIS OFF-HOURS, HE LISTENED TO STEELY DAN. ALSO, HE'S PHOTOGRAPHED HERE SMILING, WHICH IS NOT HEAVY METAL.

05
BURNING AMBITION
THE FIRST SINGLE, "RUNNING FREE"

Iron Maiden released their debut single, "Running Free," on February 8, 1980. While it's a great tune and an ideal choice for a first single, it's notable for another reason: the sleeve marked the first appearance of the band's mascot, Eddie, albeit in silhouette form. The undead ghoul, designed by artist Derek Riggs, would appear on every official album the band released, as well as on T-shirts, back patches, and every other bit of branded merchandise.

As for the song itself, it's short by Iron Maiden standards at three minutes and eighteen seconds, and despite their reputation for complex compositions, this song benefited from its simplicity. The lyrics, penned by Di'Anno, were inspired by his days as a juvenile ne'er-do-well, an attitude he brought to his tenure as Iron Maiden's frontman. The band may never have set out to emulate punk, but Di'Anno projected unadulterated hooliganism nonetheless.

The B-side, "Burning Ambition," was recorded in 1979 at London's Wessex Sound Studios by the four-piece lineup, which saw Murray handling all the guitar duties and featured drumming from Doug Sampson.

The song dates to Harris's tenure in his first band, Gypsy's Kiss, and it's easy to hear why it was relegated to B-side status. It's just much too chirpy and cheerful to fit an Iron Maiden record. In fairness, it must be said that the guitar solo is absolutely top-flight stuff. During the roughly thirty seconds in which it occurs, the song is completely brought up to code as a furiously headbanging Iron Maiden classic. Unfortunately, once Murray is back to power chords to finish the song, it immediately goes back to "please turn that off" status.

Rather than let the song fade into complete obscurity, Iron Maiden eventually released it as part of *Best of the B-Sides*, a two-disc compilation that appeared in 2002's *Eddie's Archive* box set. But only completists will want to listen to it, and it will probably only get played by said completist once.

There were some problems with the A-side too. Both the French and German pressings of "Running Free" used the wrong recording of the song. Those territories mistakenly used the version recorded at the Wessex sessions that "Burning Ambition" came from. The band didn't like how the recording turned out, and it should never have appeared on an official Iron Maiden release.

"Running Free" also featured the work of new drummer Clive Burr. Stratton had known him casually from the local music scene and recommended him as a replacement for the just-ousted Doug Sampson. Burr was as hungry for a music career as everyone else in Iron Maiden and didn't mind putting in the hard work to make it happen. He was also a spectacular drummer with a great groove and feel, and even people who didn't know there was a new drummer probably noticed a difference.

DRUMMER CLIVE BURR AND BASSIST STEVE HARRIS PLAY UNDER THE WATCHFUL EYE OF A SOMEWHAT LOW-RENT ITERATION OF EDDIE THE HEAD. IT WOULD GET BETTER.

06

NO PRECEDENT, NO EQUAL
DEBUT LP RELEASED

ADRIAN SMITH, PAUL DI'ANNO, CLIVE BURR, STEVE HARRIS, AND DAVE MURRAY IN 1981 LINED UP IN A QUITE ORDERLY FASHION.

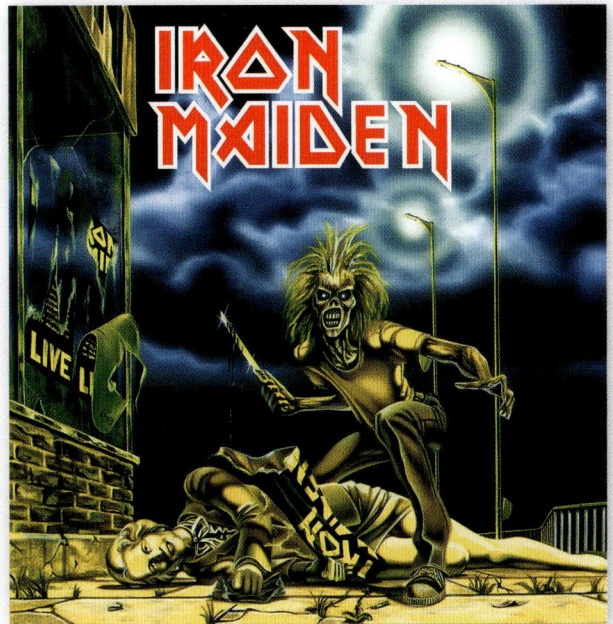

Some bands take a couple of albums to hit their stride. Iron Maiden's 1980 self-titled debut had no such issues. It entered the world fully formed without a weak track to be found anywhere in its thirty-eight minutes. In 2013, journalist Geoff Barton put it at the top of his list of the top ten New Wave of British Heavy Metal albums of all time.

"In comparison with the sleek prog-metal machine the band evolved into, *Iron Maiden* sees them as a bunch of scruffy East End herberts with a powerful point to prove," Barton wrote. "*Iron Maiden* is just an aggressive metal album, and as raw as an open wound."

It was helmed by British producer and arranger Wil Malone (credited as "Will" Malone, with two L's). He was hired at the suggestion of their label, EMI, but the band found him uninterested in the project—in fact, some accounts allege that he spent a good portion of the studio time reading magazines.

The band gave the debut's sound low marks, attributing this directly to Malone. At the same time, this forced the band to step in and handle much of the production, which would come in handy in the future. Hey, if you want something done right, do it yourself.

They may have been dissatisfied with the final mix, but their hard-won fans didn't complain. The album is aggressive as hell and gets right in the listener's face from the opening guitar chords of "Prowler." Songs with more dynamics, such as "Remember Tomorrow" and "Strange World," might have benefited from a little more spit and polish, but the lack of more pristine production doesn't negatively affect either. It just makes them sound consistent with the rest of the record.

Even if you feel those songs are missing something, it's not enough of a problem to detract from the album. The music is simply too good to write off. "Phantom of the Opera" is an absolutely savage tune that predicts the frenetic rhythms and abrupt tempo changes of speed metal, which would emerge a couple of years later. Speaking of speed metal, during the guitar solo in "Transylvania," the bass playing sounds like Cliff Burton, before there was even a Cliff Burton to sound like. It's forward in the mix and drives the song, and there's an almost carefree lack of concern on Harris's part that he might be overplaying a bit.

After "Strange World" comes "Charlotte the Harlot," whose lyrics do not conform to the standards of the #MeToo movement. It depicts a lovelorn young man whose beloved Charlotte shares her affection with a bunch of other dudes, something we learn in the bridge section has broken his heart. Luckily, the song careens along at such a breakneck pace that you'll be too busy jumping up and down on your sofa and shouting "HELL YEAH!!!!!" to cancel them.

The album ends with "Iron Maiden," another fast tune that suggests thrash metal is only a couple of years off. There's no better or more anthemic way to end the album. Honestly, there's not a bad song anywhere on this LP, and short of taking an X-Acto knife to its playing surface, *Iron Maiden* is impossible to ruin.

Interestingly, the only time the track listing was ever messed with was in the 1990s when the LP was reissued in North America with the non-album B-side "Sanctuary" shoehorned into it as the second track. Some believed the sacrosanct integrity of the original eight-song running order had been ruined, but luckily for them, it was removed from the subsequent reissue in the 2010s. Some fans didn't like that either, but too bad.

Iron Maiden is belligerent and urgent. It's the sound of a band that had taken the time to hone their craft and had come up with something utterly original. Eventually, its sound would catch on and spawn countless forgettable imitators, but in 1980, it had no precedent or equal.

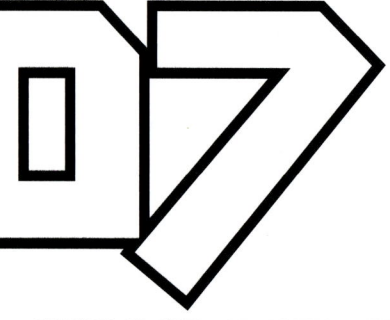

07 THE URCHIN REUNION

STRATTON REPLACED BY ADRIAN SMITH

By any standard, the self-titled *Iron Maiden* debut LP was a rousing success. Journalist Geoff Barton of *Sounds* praised it in glowing terms.

"*Iron Maiden* is deadly," he wrote. "Heavy metal for the '80s, its blinding speed and rampant ferocity making most plastic heavy rock tracks from the '60s and '70s sound sloth-like and funeral-dirgey by comparison."

The album reached number four on the UK albums chart, which is fantastic for a debut album, particularly one made in just thirteen days. Still there was trouble in paradise: guitarist Dennis Stratton was finding himself the odd man out, for numerous reasons.

In 2023, he told *Ultimate Guitar* that Smallwood had started to have issues with him after the band's 1980 performance at the Reading Festival. It got worse when the band secured the support slot on tour with Kiss.

"It was a shame because on the Kiss tour was when Rod started talking about the sort of music I listened to," Stratton said. "We had constant arguments about what I listened to in my hotel room, and it was a shame because it started to affect his thinking about me in the band."

Based on Geoff Barton's description of the band's performance at a 1980 concert in Leiden, Netherlands, on the Kiss tour, it's hard to believe anyone thought a change to the band's personnel was in order.

"I've seldom seen Maiden better," Barton said. "They're playing at such a fast pace, they're in danger of starting their second number before they've finished their first . . . your old hard rock albums from the 1970s have been made redundant by the freshly forged, still-scalding speediness of the Iron Maiden sound."

He also observed that there were already Iron Maiden fans here and elsewhere outside London, and they made their presence known.

"A banner unfurls," he wrote, describing the band's arrival at the venue. "The kids holding it are screaming and pointing. It depicts the contorted face of Eddie, the band's mascot, copied from the cover of their debut album . . . it reads in screaming great big capital letters: 'IRON MAIDEN GO OVER THE TOP.'"

Maiden played the Reading Festival on August 23, 1980, and six songs from their set list were released as part of *BBC Archives* in 2002. The band seems to have excess adrenaline coursing through their systems on these recordings as they take these songs at speeds that defy the human brain. There is not a single complaint to be had with the band's performance, and if Smallwood began having problems with Stratton after this show, it's hard to see why.

When the tour was over, Stratton was called into Smallwood's office, and just as with Doug Sampson in 1979, the only people in the office were the manager and Harris. They were concerned about the music Stratton chose to listen to in his downtime, like the Eagles, and there was some concern about that influence slipping into Maiden's music. Having said that, it would have been hilarious to hear Paul Di'Anno singing "Peaceful Easy Feeling."

Relations became chillier during the Kiss tour when the guitarist preferred hanging out with that band's crew rather than his bandmates. This and his

THE ORIGINAL PRINT ADVERTISEMENT FOR 1980'S READING FESTIVAL. RECORDINGS FROM THIS CONCERT EVENTUALLY ENDED UP ON THE BBC ARCHIVES ALBUM, WHICH WAS PART OF THE 2002 BOX SET EDDIE'S ARCHIVE.

IRON MAIDEN'S KILLERS LINEUP, LOST AMID A SEA OF CLIVE BURR'S CYMBALS. KILLERS IS ONE OF THE GREATEST HEAVY METAL ALBUMS EVER MADE, AND WE HAVE THESE FIVE DUDES TO THANK FOR IT.

STEVE HARRIS LEVERAGES HIS CORE COMPETENCY DURING A CONCERT. HE'S PLAYING BASS VERY WELL, TOO.

1981 PROMO PHOTO OF IRON MAIDEN'S *KILLERS* LINEUP: (L–R) STEVE HARRIS, CLIVE BURR, PAUL DI'ANNO, ADRIAN SMITH, AND DAVE MURRAY.

love for FM rock led to his ouster, surprising some who had worked with the band. Wil Malone, who had helmed the debut, called Stratton "a valuable member of the band—musically," while Tony Piatt, who produced the band's third single, "Women in Uniform," also thought getting rid of him was a strange decision.

"I've always said that Dennis was 'the musician,'" Piatt said. "He really could play."

With that, Stratton won the dubious distinction of being the only person in Iron Maiden history to play on just one studio album. He was replaced by Adrian Smith, whom Murray had played with in a group called Urchin. When they broke up, Harris and Murray asked him to join after bumping into him in the street.

His first job with Iron Maiden was an appearance on the West German television show *Rockpop in Concert*, just days after Stratton had left the group. Harris said in *Run to the Hills* that while he meant no disrespect to Stratton, having Smith in the band felt right.

"You just know if someone's into it, and Adrian was," Harris said. "You could feel the difference straightaway."

Iron Maiden closed out 1980 by doing a string of UK dates with their new guitarist. Before the first gig, he went outside to mingle with the crowd and learned firsthand how intense Maiden fans were. He was recognized by one who asked him if he was the new second guitarist. Smith answered in the affirmative and was told by the fan, "You better be good!"

ONE: AN AGE-OLD DREAM | 25

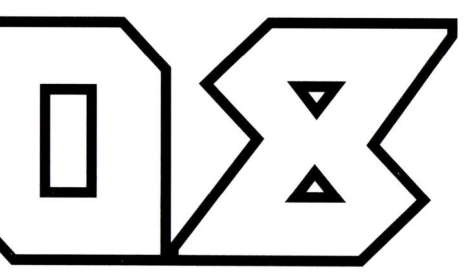

WHEN RITCHIE BLACKMORE TALKS...
"WE WERE REALLY LUCKY TO GET HIM"

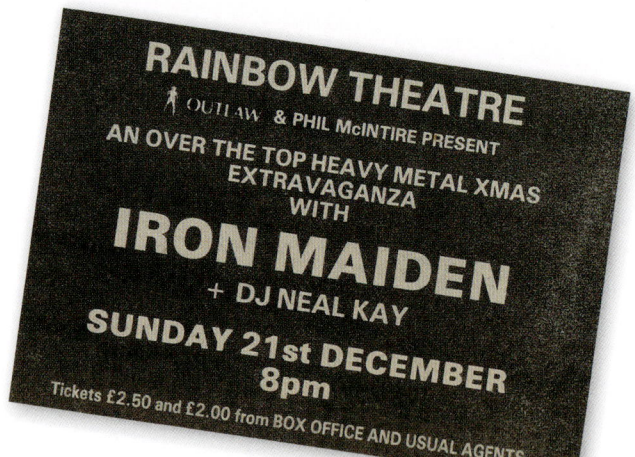

In *Run to the Hills*, record producer Martin Birch recalled visiting the home of guitarist Ritchie Blackmore. The pair had worked together in the past, with Blackmore playing on landmark albums by Deep Purple and Rainbow that were crucial to the development of heavy metal. He said Blackmore played him the Iron Maiden debut, which he had been enjoying immensely, and suggested that Birch produce them.

"It was right up my street, exactly the sort of thing I enjoyed," Birch said. "I just felt I understood what they were about, straightaway."

Birch went to see the band at London's Rainbow in December 1980 and declared their performance "ten times better" than the LP. When he and Harris spoke afterward, the bassist confessed that they wanted him to produce their debut but were too intimidated by his impressive track record to ask him. He had produced Deep Purple's *Machine Head* and Rainbow's *Rising*, influential heavy metal records that a young Steve Harris spun when he was still an aspiring footballer during the 1970s.

Before producing those records, Birch had served as engineer on a trio of albums by Wishbone Ash, whose harmonizing twin guitars were hugely influential to the Iron Maiden sound. It would have been professional, musical, and astrological malpractice for the band and producer not to work together. Still, Murray said he understood that the opportunity hadn't just fallen into their laps.

"We were really lucky to get him," the guitarist said. "He turned down some pretty big bands to do us."

The band and Birch recorded the group's second record at Battery Studios, which was released in February 1981, a little over one year after the "Running Free" single had announced the band to the world. While it was the same studio where the Dennis Stratton lineup had recorded the Skyhooks cover "Women in Uniform," the experience was very different. In 1980, Maiden's publishing company Zomba wanted the producer, Tony Piatt, to make the song a 45-rpm hit. When he took the band-approved mix and sweetened it with radio-friendly secret sauce behind their backs, Harris was livid and remixed the whole thing himself.

"[Piatt] was trying to pull us in a more commercial vein," Harris said in *Run to the Hills*. "The original mixes were much heavier than that."

Even if they had left the mix alone, there was still no way the song would ever become a radio hit. Di'Anno said the band had seen to it.

"I've changed the words around a bit," Di'Anno told journalist Geoff Barton in 1980. "The original was pretty sexist, but our version is *really* sexist."

As it turned out, Birch's approach couldn't have been more different from Malone's or Piatt's. He understood their strength was as a live band, so he had them record the songs as if they were at a gig.

"I had always been interested in getting the natural sound a band produces themselves onstage, and with Maiden I tried to capture that as much as I could," Birch said. "We just concentrated on capturing their natural sound and put little overdubs on afterwards."

The resulting album captured the band's sound in all its maniacal glory. Looking back today, it's hard to see it as anything but a triumph, but at the time, it debuted lower on the UK charts than the first album, and they found themselves being written off by journalists as the last gasp of the dying New Wave of British Heavy Metal movement. In fact, the album they made with Birch would end up being a work of such high quality that it guaranteed the band would outlive every external fad that came or went.

LEGENDARY RECORD PRODUCER AND ENGINEER MARTIN BIRCH IN NOVEMBER 1974 ON THE LOS ANGELES SET OF THE KUNG FU TELEVISION SHOW. HE PRODUCED SEMINAL ALBUMS FOR BLACK SABBATH, DEEP PURPLE, AND, YES, THE MIGHTY IRON MAIDEN.

DAVE MURRAY, PAUL DI'ANNO, CLIVE BURR, STEVE HARRIS, AND ADRIAN SMITH, ALSO KNOWN AS THE LINEUP THAT GAVE THE WORLD THE KILLERS LP.

09

MAIDEN RELEASES KILLERS

THIS IS PERFECT, CHANGE NOTHING

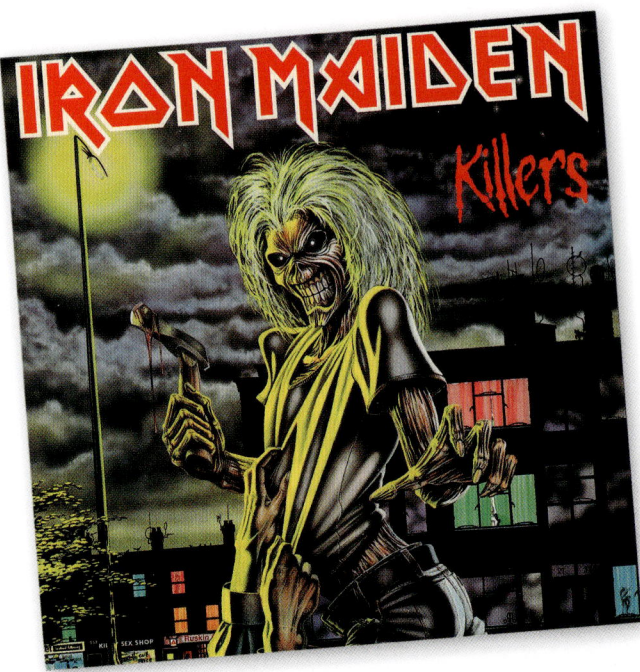

Iron Maiden's sophomore album, *Killers*, was released in the UK in February 1981. It's their best album of the two recorded with singer Paul Di'Anno and remains a high-water mark of their catalog. However, when it was first released, *Sounds* gave it a scathing one-star review, with critic Robbi Millar calling it "more of a failure than a triumph."

In *Run to the Hills*, Harris said that the bad review resulted from Di'Anno engaging in intimate physical relations with Millar, only to turn up his nose at further opportunities to do so. While the truth of this fascinating story may never be known, one thing is undisputable: *Killers* is a masterpiece from start to finish without a single bad song.

The songs on *Killers* are as strong as those on the debut. At times, they exceed them. From Harris's opening bass notes to the instrumental breakdown before the guitar solo, "Wrathchild" simply will not be denied. It features one of Di'Anno's best vocal performances and segues perfectly into "Murders in the Rue Morgue," which mysteriously is not one of Maiden's most popular songs. Other, less celebrated tracks, like "Another Life" and "Innocent Exile," fare well. They're only less celebrated because they're overshadowed by songs that ace the exam with flying colors and even get the extra-credit questions right.

"Genghis Khan," the second instrumental, starts with a minute of music at a normal pace, then completely pulls the rug out from under you and launches into a high-speed battery that's nothing less than a sustained beating with barbed wire on your bare back. Other bands would come along in the ensuing years to create heavier, faster, and more abrasive music, but in 1981, the fast section of "Genghis Khan" didn't have a lot of competition in that department. They had cornered the market.

The title track is notable for being an early example of the patented Iron Maiden "gallop." If you went to music school, you'll understand what it means to say it's a repeating rhythmic figure comprising two sixteenth notes and an eighth note. For those without a background in music, the Maiden "gallop" is that thing they do that sounds like galloping. You're welcome.

The biggest surprise is "Prodigal Son," a significant stylistic departure from the furious rage surrounding it. It's more musically adventurous than anything the band had yet done, with bits that recall some of the classic rock sounds that inspired Harris to pick up a bass in the first place.

It's followed by "Purgatory," taken at the fastest tempo the band had yet attempted. Even though it was only 1981, it's a stylistic building block of

IRON MAIDEN—JUST A BUNCH OF CHILL DUDES WHO LIKED SITTING ON AMPS, MAXING, AND RELAXING. THEIR SINGER PAUL DI'ANNO ALSO ENJOYED TAKING SONGS LIKE SKYHOOKS'S "WOMEN IN UNIFORM" AND MAKING THEM EXTRA SEXIST.

ADRIAN SMITH AT SHINJUKU KOHSEINENKIN HALL IN TOKYO IN MAY 1981, ON IRON MAIDEN'S TOUR OF JAPAN.

what would soon become thrash metal. Iron Maiden may never have set out to inspire that movement, but it's hard to listen to "Purgatory" and come to any other conclusion.

Also hard to do while "Purgatory" is playing is remaining seated, remaining calm, and not gesturing wildly with one's fist for the entire duration. It leads into the less fast but no less furious "Drifter," and the whole thing is over in less than thirty-nine minutes. Not one note should be changed. It's perfect.

Sadly, not everyone in the band saw it that way. While Di'Anno thought the album sounded great thanks to Martin Birch's production, he was still partial to the debut, sonic warts and all. "It didn't have as much impact on me as the first album," he told *Eon Music* in 2019. "I still think that on the first album the songs are much stronger."

While Di'Anno may have had mixed feelings about *Killers*, the album only grows in stature the further it gets from its 1981 release date. The press may not have had much use for it, but today, it's impossible to listen to it and see it as anything but a highly influential masterpiece. To this day, heavy metal bands trace their DNA back to this record.

Unfortunately, this lineup didn't last. Iron Maiden and Paul Di'Anno parted ways afterward, and to a certain subset of fans, the band was never the same street-level gang of musical thugs. All of them are right: the band never was the same after Di'Anno, but their next move would turn them into the unit Harris had always intended.

ADRIAN SMITH, CLIVE BURR, PAUL DI'ANNO, DAVE MURRAY, AND STEVE HARRIS WEAR KENDO UNIFORMS ON IRON MAIDEN'S FIRST TOUR OF JAPAN, IN CASE THEY GOT INTO ANY CLOSE-QUARTER HAND-TO-HAND COMBAT.

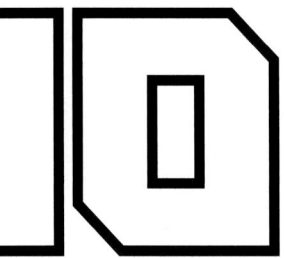

DID HE TRY TEA WITH HONEY AND LEMON?

MAIDEN PARTS WITH DI'ANNO

Paul Di'Anno played his last gig with Iron Maiden in Copenhagen on September 10, 1981. Earlier in the year, he had begun to complain of problems with his singing voice, leading to the cancellation of a string of German dates. According to *Run to the Hills*, Harris's mind was made up after that: their singer, who had graced their first two albums and came up with them when they were an unknown club band, had to go.

Harris said that the cancellation of those German dates resulted from some choices that Di'Anno had made when he was offstage. The bassist said the singer was engaging in behavior known to adversely affect the human singing voice, and the problem continued to snowball.

"He wasn't really looking after himself, physically," Harris said. "Someone who's singing has got to look after their voice, and you can't be staying up all night smoking yourself stupid and taking speed and what have you . . . we ended up canceling gigs because of his problems, and that's one thing, if you know me, I just can't tolerate it."

Smallwood echoed Harris's take.

"He smoked like a chimney, he drank brandy and, you know, now he's doing a bit of coke and speed, too, and he was missing gigs," the manager said. "It's always been a Maiden thing that they've never wanted to let the fans down, and these things were starting to hurt us. We lost the whole German tour."

Di'Anno did not contradict Harris or Smallwood, and he admitted to enjoying the occasional judgment-impairing substance in his day. However, he also said that he could see that this band would only get more popular, and he didn't know if he was up for it.

"Maiden had become so big by then that the band had commitments piling up that went on for months, years, and I just couldn't see my way to the end of it," he said. "I knew I'd never last the whole tour. . . . They had all these plans and, the way I was, I was starting to stick a spoke into them, I could see that."

BACKSTAGE DURING THE KILLER WORLD TOUR IN LYNWOOD, ILLINOIS, ON JUNE 26, 1981. (L-R) CLIVE BURR, DAVE MURRAY, PAUL DI'ANNO, ADRIAN SMITH, AND STEVE HARRIS. ONWARD TO CLEVELAND!

When Di'Anno was asked to leave the band, Harris said that he thought their now-former frontman felt freed by the decision. As it turned out, he was right.

"I was relieved," the singer said. "They had so many ambitions, I couldn't keep up, and I think, in the end, they made the right decision."

While Di'Anno agreed that things went the way they had to go, he never expressed any bitterness about the experience. Of course, there was that one time in 2009 when he compared Harris to failed visual artist and architect of the Third Reich, Adolf Hitler, but he told *Metal Hammer* in 2022 that he was only talking about how efficiently Harris ran the band.

"I did call Steve 'Hitler' once, because of the way he runs things," the singer said. "It's like a fucking army, Iron Maiden. Steve's so focused. And I couldn't think of another person . . . I said 'Hitler.' I didn't mean it in that way."

All fine and good. After Maiden, Di'Anno continued to play music, fronting bands like Gogmagog, Battlezone, and Praying Mantis, as well as his own solo band. He continued to have a music career right up to his passing on October 21, 2024. Friends and fans alike would ask him about the band he once fronted, which at that point was packing stadiums worldwide.

"People say, 'Don't you wish it had been you?'" he said. "I say, 'It was me! I just didn't want it.'"

THE BAND'S FIRST LIVE EP, MAIDEN JAPAN, WAS PROMOTED ON AT LEAST ONE VERY LARGE BILLBOARD, BUT THE ORIGINAL COVER HAD TO BE REPLACED AT SHORT NOTICE. THE ORIGINAL VERSION DEPICTED THEIR MASCOT, EDDIE, HOLDING UP THE BLOODY HEAD OF A JUST-DECAPITATED PAUL DI'ANNO, WHOM THE BAND WAS THEN LOOKING TO REPLACE. AWKWARD!

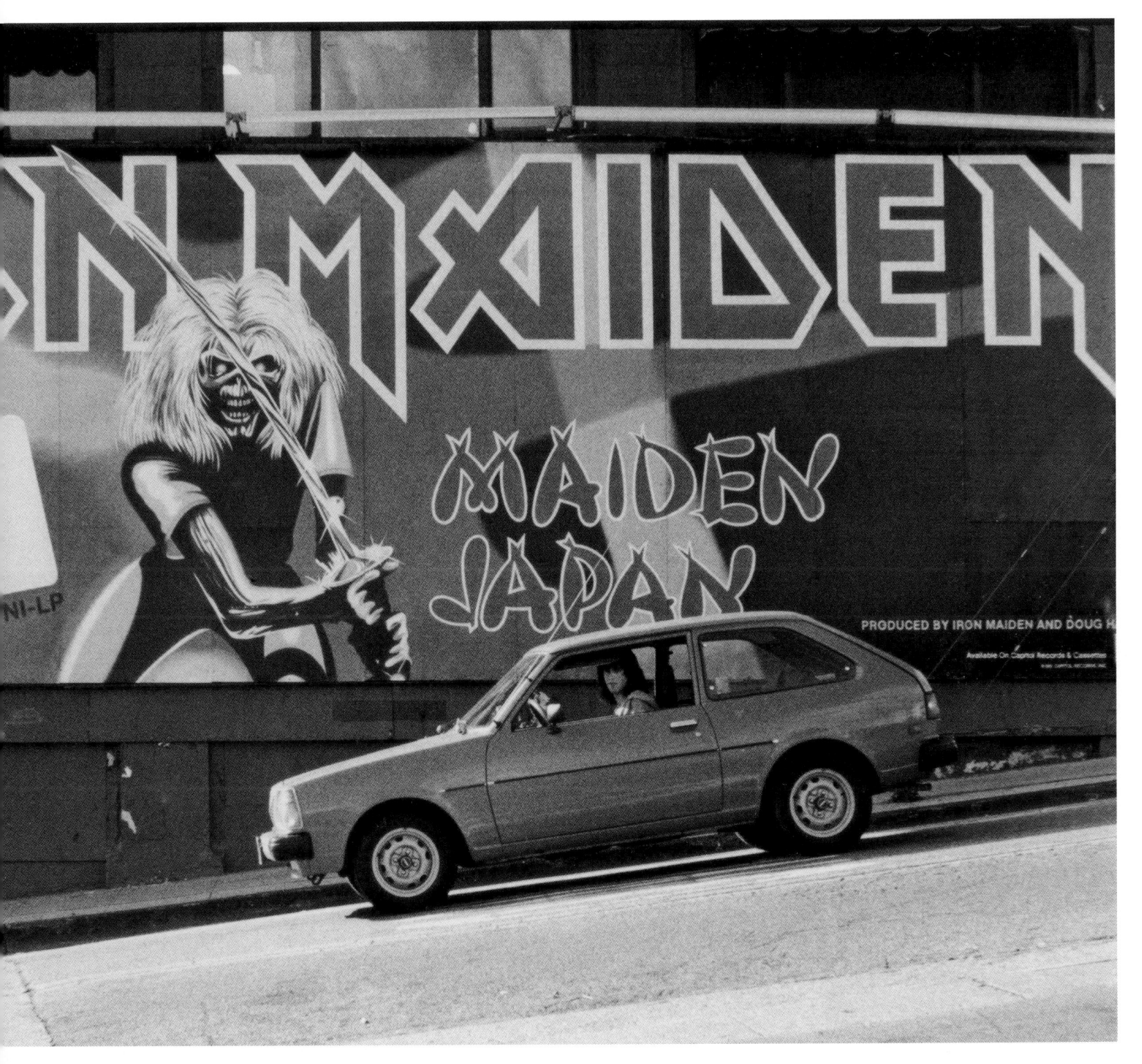

EDDIE THE HEAD

It's tempting to start an entry about Iron Maiden's mascot Eddie by comparing him to the many other band mascots out there and discussing the relative longevity and market penetration of each. However, this would be stupid: no other band has a mascot as iconic and well-known as Eddie, or Eddie the Head (his full name as it would appear on his driver's license and Costco membership card).

Eddie, presumably some heavy metal ghoul, first appeared onstage behind the band during their club days. Back then, Eddie was just a papier-mâché mask molded on the face of David Beazley, better known to the band as "Dave Lights." That mask was part of the band's backdrop, including the lights Beazley operated and the logo Harris had designed.

During those heady club days, the band would close their sets with the song "Iron Maiden," at which time fake blood would squirt from the mask, usually onto the back of drummer Doug Sampson's head. As the band's fortunes improved, the setup grew, and the slightly larger Eddie contraption that they used graduated from a papier-mâché construction to fiberglass. It even emitted red smoke and had flashing eyes.

The idea to turn the stage prop into a mascot came about when Smallwood visited the office of John Darnley, an artists and repertoire (A&R) executive at EMI. A poster of pianist Max Middleton gracing Darnley's office wall caught Smallwood's eye. In *Run to the Hills*, he said it "was just so striking you couldn't miss it. Your eyes just went to it as soon as you walked in the room."

Darnley told Smallwood that the artist was Derek Riggs, so he arranged a meeting to see more of his work. During the meeting, while sifting through Riggs's work, he found a pile of drawings and struck metaphorical oil.

"It was this sort of cartoon of this mad-looking sort of punk monster, but as soon as I saw it, I knew," Smallwood said. "The only change we asked Derek to make was to make the hair a bit longer, so it was less obviously like a punk."

Riggs obliged, and with that extra bit of unkempt hair, the cover of the first Iron Maiden album was born. The choice was solidified when he brought Riggs's portfolio to the band, brought out all the drawings therein, and asked them to choose the perfect one for the album cover. The same picture was the immediate and unanimous choice, and a mascot was born.

Eddie would appear on the cover of every Iron Maiden record, to say nothing of every T-shirt, baseball cap, and back patch. Teenagers began not just wearing the merch bearing Eddie's likeness but also went on to deface their school binder covers

IF WE IGNORE THEM, WILL THEY GO AWAY? DAVE MURRAY, CLIVE BURR, DENNIS STRATTON, STEVE HARRIS, AND PAUL DI'ANNO ARE PUBLICLY MENACED BY SOME EDDIES.

with multiple attempts at the band's angular logo and zombie mascot. When they did, all the normals sitting next to them got up and sat somewhere else. Eddie's image and likeness were exceptionally effective at repelling anyone who was not into the band while at the same time helping fans find one another and connect.

Riggs created the album sleeves for every Iron Maiden album up to 1990's *No Prayer for the Dying*. While Eddie remained a fixture of the band's artwork, in 1992, the group decided to let other artists take a crack at their covers, provided Eddie was still in the mix. One who did that was graphic artist Hugh Syme, who had created all but two album covers for Canadian rockers Rush. At Iron Maiden's behest, he designed the cover for 1995's *The X Factor*, the first of two Maiden albums with Blaze Bayley on vocals.

"They were motivated to deliver something more palpable, tactile to their fans," Syme said. "They opted to venture into a more photorealistic realm with *The X Factor*, citing how I had created 'Vic Rattlehead' for Megadeth on their recent covers."

In 1995, as in 2025, the only way to get a photorealistic image was to take a photograph of a real-life subject. Syme went old school in achieving that.

"To make Eddie look real—this is all pre-CGI—I was charged with creating something that could be photographed, under controlled lighting, to look very real," he said. "So sculpture was my only solution. I immediately started digging in to produce Eddie as a three-dimensional sculpture using armature wire for the limbs, hands, and torso, packed with foil for support and form, and Sculpey [clay] for his outer layer."

While *The X Factor* cover remains one of the more striking in the Iron Maiden catalog, not everyone was thrilled with having to look at it, especially in real life.

"Following the two-week photo session, the sculpture remained in my basement," Syme said. "My young daughters grew up with that horrific, eviscerated torso and torture table within view of their playroom . . . for years!"

If Iron Maiden had never had Eddie the Head as their mascot, they likely still would have had similar success. However, having him gives all their albums a throughline that has helped the band's catalog remain a single, unified work. You always knew what you were getting when you saw Eddie on the cover.

Sociologist Deena Weinstein said that Eddie also helped smooth the way during the band's various lineup changes. No matter who was in the band, Eddie was a constant, and he was arguably the biggest celebrity in the band.

"Eddie is an icon for the band itself," she said. "Instead of having one member stand for the rest of the band, Eddie stands for the band. Clever move on their part."

DAVE MURRAY PLAYS GUITAR UNDER THE WATCHFUL EYE OF EDDIE THE HEAD. ASK YOUR DOCTOR IF A LOBOTOMY AND A STRAITJACKET ARE RIGHT FOR YOU.

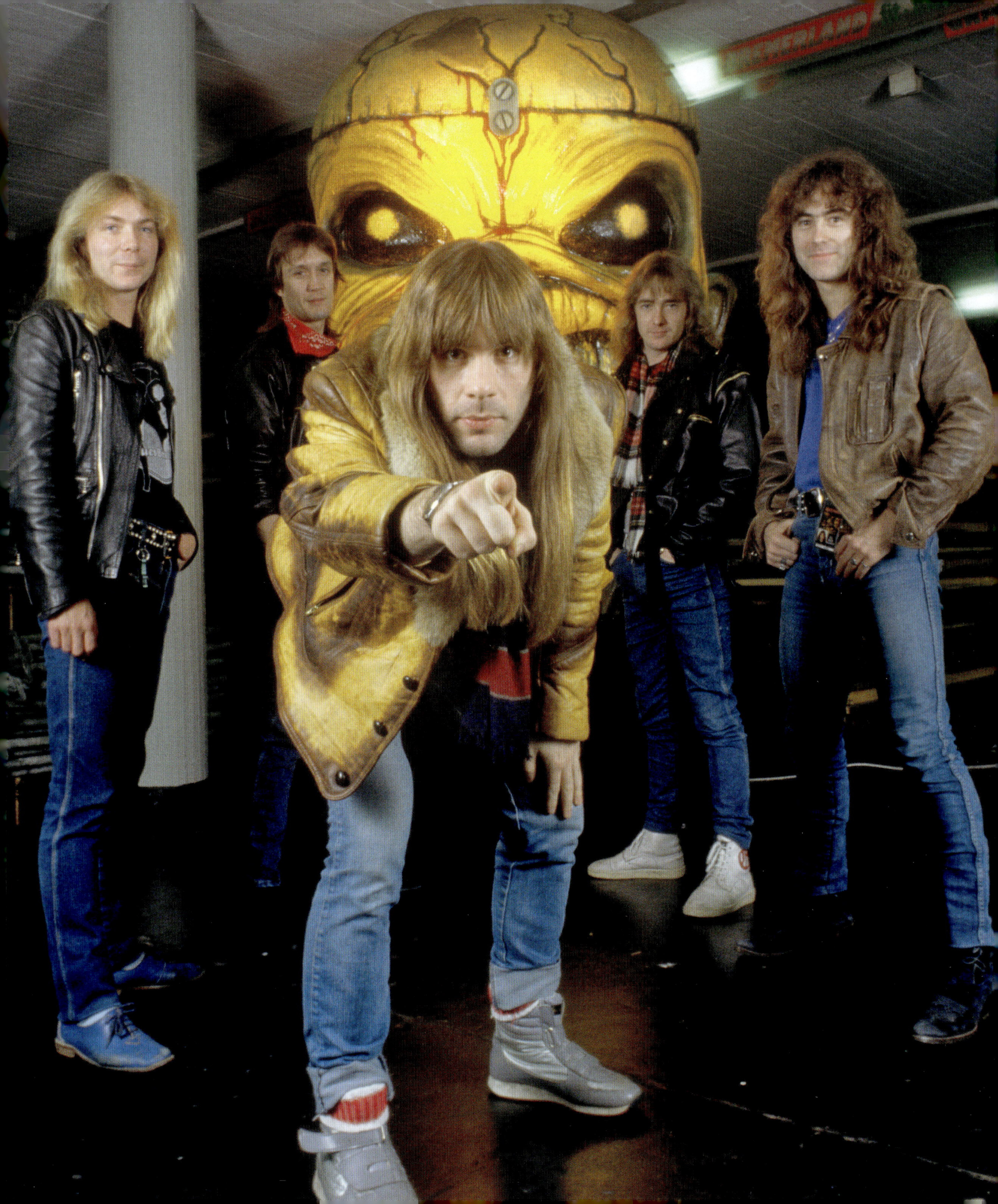

two

THE DEVIL SENDS THE BEAST WITH WRATH

11

THE AIR RAID SIREN

BRUCE DICKINSON JOINS

Bruce Dickinson had been interested in music since convincing his grandfather to buy him the Beatles' "She Loves You" single. He joined several groups as lead singer, but it wasn't until performing one night with a local band called Shots that he learned he was no mere singer—he was an entertainer.

One night during one of their many pub gigs, he stopped a song halfway through to address individuals in the sparse audience. Each time, he participated in the act of "roasting" the audience member. This had the effect of galvanizing the attention of the rest of the patrons. Suddenly, people who had previously been gazing into their pints of lager were looking at the band. Mission accomplished.

"That was when I first started to get the hang of not just being a singer but being a frontman," Dickinson said in *Run to the Hills*. "A lot of people can sing, but ask them to get up onstage and handle a crowd and they can't."

In 1978, he was poached by a local heavy metal band called Samson. Drummer Barry "Thunderstick" Purkis and guitarist Paul Samson had seen him at a Shots gig and were impressed enough to offer him a position as lead singer. After a first rehearsal at which the sedative Mandrax had so impaired Purkis that he had to be propped up against the wall behind him to keep playing, Dickinson went on to record two studio albums with them: 1980's *Head On* and 1981's *Shock Tactics*.

The singer, who went by the stage name "Bruce Bruce" when he fronted Samson, had his first contact with Iron Maiden when they opened for his band in 1980. He watched them perform one night and was so impressed with how good they were that he wished he was onstage with them. But just a year later, the tables had turned—Samson was now scheduled to open for Iron Maiden, but the label, Gem, closed shop and couldn't finance the tour. So when Samson played its final show at the Reading Festival, and Smallwood approached Dickinson with a chance to audition, there was no reason to turn it down.

The audition took place the next day, and Dickinson ran down four songs from the debut LP: "Prowler," "Sanctuary," "Running Free," and "Remember Tomorrow." Suitably impressed with his live performance, the band hurriedly took Dickinson to a recording studio to hear how that sounded. It sounded great.

"That was it," Dickinson said. "We all went out and got roaring pissed and I was in Iron Maiden."

The first thing the band did with their newly minted singer was play five dates in Italy in October 1981. A recording of "Remember Tomorrow" from one of these dates was used as the B-side for the 1982 single "The Number of the Beast." While Dickinson had just barely joined the band, this version reveals that he was already at a different level than the singer who preceded him. It would be safe to say he was at a different level than almost any other singer on earth.

Dickinson could reach really high notes and sustain them for more time than was probably physically healthy, but the music benefited immensely. He sings the absolute crap out of "Remember Tomorrow," and at its highest pitch, his voice bypasses the human eardrum and goes directly into the brain. In *Running Free*, the singer said he was just helping finish the song.

SAMSON SINGER BRUCE BRUCE JUST MONTHS BEFORE JOINING IRON MAIDEN AND BECOMING BRUCE DICKINSON, BETTER KNOWN TO AT LEAST ONE IRATE FAN AS "THE AIR RAID SIREN."

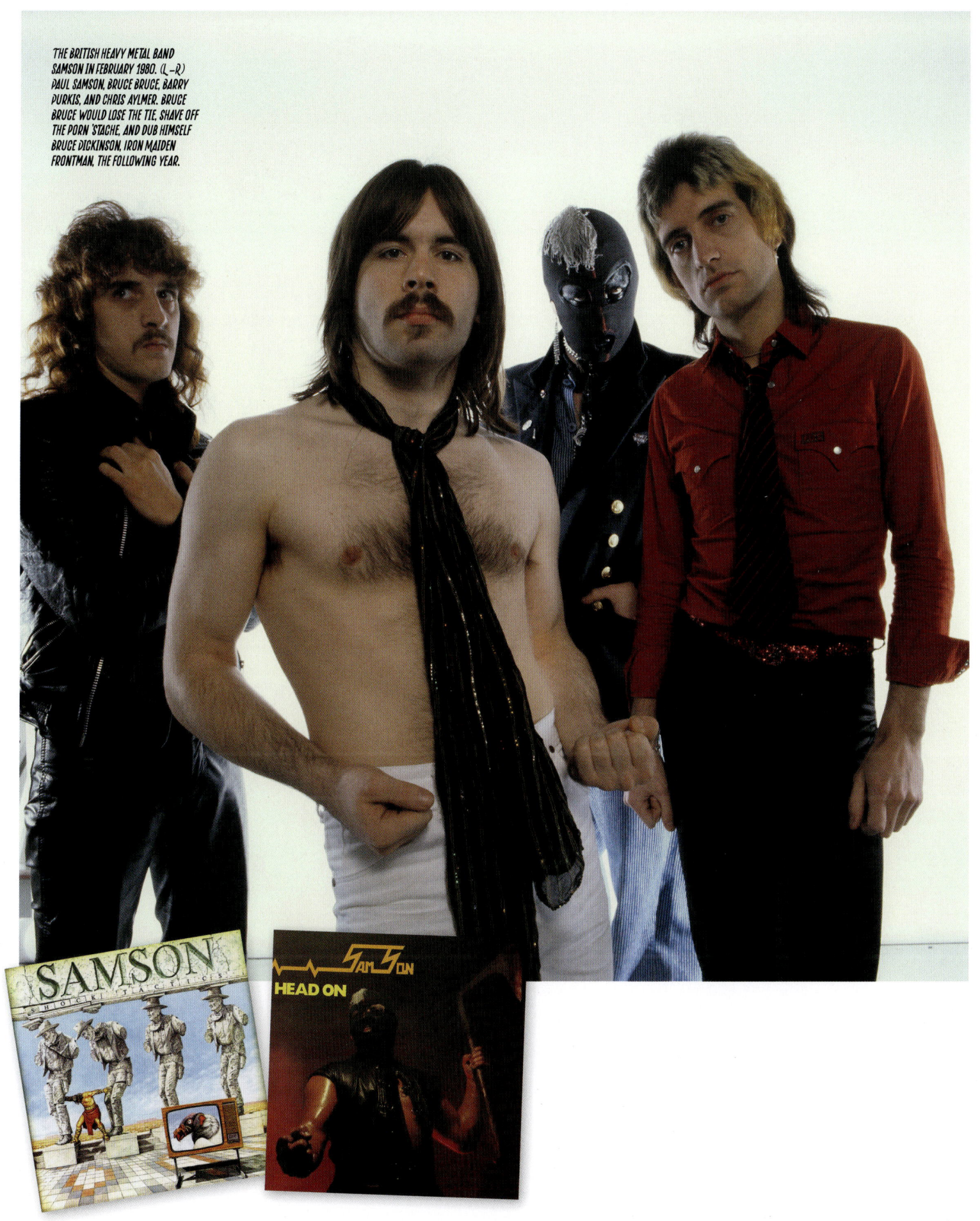

THE BRITISH HEAVY METAL BAND SAMSON IN FEBRUARY 1980. (L-R) PAUL SAMSON, BRUCE BRUCE, BARRY PURKIS, AND CHRIS AYLMER. BRUCE BRUCE WOULD LOSE THE TIE, SHAVE OFF THE PORN 'STACHE, AND DUB HIMSELF BRUCE DICKINSON, IRON MAIDEN FRONTMAN, THE FOLLOWING YEAR.

TWO: THE DEVIL SENDS THE BEAST WITH WRATH | 43

DAVE MURRAY, BRUCE DICKINSON, STEVE HARRIS, CLIVE BURR, AND ADRIAN SMITH DEMONSTRATE THEIR GREAT RESPECT AND ADMIRATION FOR THE BRITISH SCHOOL SYSTEM BY CONGREGATING IN A DISORDERLY FASHION OUTSIDE LONDON'S HANOVER PRIMARY SCHOOL IN 1982.

"I added a few things to songs like 'Remember Tomorrow,' but they were just things that should have been there anyway," he said.

As well as the Italian dates had gone, there was still a date at London's Rainbow coming up, and as far as Dickinson was concerned, that was the real test. London was the band's hometown. If the change in vocalists didn't work here, there would be problems.

"I wasn't worried about doing the job," Dickinson said in *Run to the Hills*. "I felt I'd proved in Italy that I had that side of things already pretty much sorted. It was just more a question of whether their fans would actually accept me."

The band received a rapturous reception from their hometown audience. Bands can change drummers and bass players with casual fans not noticing, but getting in a new singer is a much more dicey proposition. Not this time. There were a few people in the audience clamoring for the return of Paul Di'Anno, but not enough to make a dent in the overwhelmingly positive response to Dickinson.

"There's no doubt the majority of punters took to him like a duck to orange sauce, colorfully christening him 'The Air Raid Siren,'" Bushell wrote. In 2017, Dickinson told radio host Eddie Trunk that the nickname was initially used to insult him. He had been compared unfavorably to an air-raid siren by a disgruntled fan at the Rainbow who hadn't cared for Dickinson's vocal approach to the songs from the first two albums. He wrote management a letter of complaint to address his grievances with the singer: "I hate this new singer," the letter read, per Dickinson. "It's like listening to all my favorite songs being played through an air-raid siren!"

In a 2004 interview with *Rock Hard*, Paul Di'Anno said that Dickinson had been a good choice, considering where Harris wanted the band to go stylistically. He still believed he was the right singer for the band's first two records, but he couldn't deny that Dickinson was the right choice for what came after.

"He was, and still remains, a gigantic singer, and there's no doubt that he was the best vocalist Maiden could ever find," Di'Anno said.

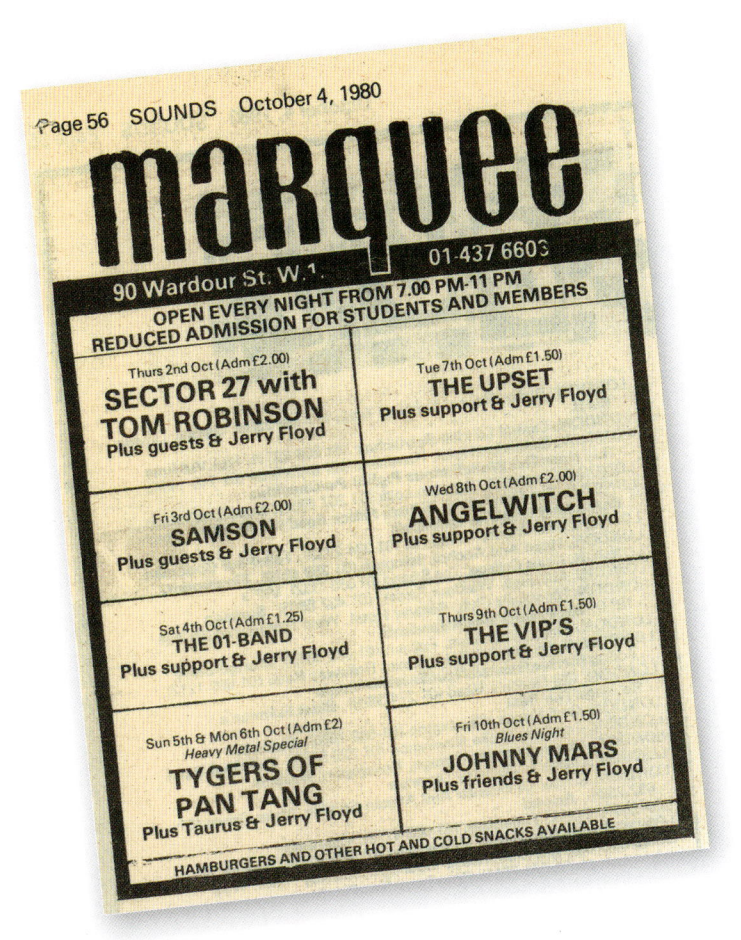

12

GET OUT AND PUSH

MAIDEN GETS THEIR FIRST UK NO. 1

When you make a good decision, it just feels right. Dickinson expressed this sentiment in *Run to the Hills* when describing getting acclimated to his new band.

"I felt at home straightaway," he said. "It just felt like one big family that I'd suddenly become a part of."

His new bandmates felt the same. When Smith said the singer was a natural, he wasn't just talking about the guy's voice. He also meant that the singer appeared completely comfortable onstage and unintimidated by the responsibilities of being a frontman for the baddest band in the UK.

"If he had nerves, he certainly didn't show it," Smith said. "He just came onstage and sang like he'd been in the band since day one."

The band returned to Battery Studios with Martin Birch. While there had only been one personnel change since *Killers*, he immediately noticed it was a big one. He knew that Harris wanted to write more complex music but privately doubted whether Di'Anno was the right fit. He had no such worries about Dickinson.

"He had a much bigger range, and he could carry melodies," the producer said. "It opened up the possibilities for the new album tremendously."

Birch decided to push the singer to produce a perfect scream for the song that would become the album's title track. It took some doing, and there was take after take, somewhat vexing the new singer, but Birch knew that the artist formerly known as Bruce Bruce had it in him and kept pushing.

The scream that Dickinson produced after much prodding appears in the song "The Number of the Beast." When you listen to it for the first time, it's hard to imagine any other vocal laid over the track. The scream that Birch coaxed out of Dickinson brings the song and the band to an entirely new level.

Almost all the material on 1982's *The Number of the Beast* is at the same high level as the title track. "Invaders," which starts the album, shares a little DNA with "Invasion" (they even go off about Norsemen!). But whereas "Invasion" was dirty and aggressive, "Invaders" has an operatic grandiosity that wasn't possible before, and not just for technical reasons—all of Dickinson's performances were full of theatricality and showmanship, turning every Iron Maiden song into something colossal.

"Children of the Damned" is an ideal opportunity for Dickinson to flex his vocal muscles, which he does like crazy. Clive Burr really shines on "The Prisoner," thoughtfully filling pauses while going absolutely nuts on the kick drum at the same time. But it's side two where the band really shines. It opens with the title track, which starts with a twenty-four-second oration taken from the Bible's Book of Revelation:

WOE TO YOU, OH EARTH AND SEA, FOR THE DEVIL SENDS THE BEAST WITH WRATH, BECAUSE HE KNOWS THE TIME IS SHORT. LET HIM WHO HAVE UNDERSTANDING RECKON THE NUMBER OF THE BEAST FOR IT IS A HUMAN NUMBER. ITS NUMBER IS SIX HUNDRED AND SIXTY-SIX.

With that bit out of the way, the band launches into one of their best-known songs. It's still a fixture of their live set, in which they even play back the recitation at the beginning. Then comes "Run to the Hills." If you had less than four minutes to explain the music of Iron Maiden to somebody, this song is the best candidate for the job. It has everything we expect from the band, from the operatic, sing-along chorus to the rhythm guitar "gallop" and the virtuoso, bravura drumming of Clive Burr.

The third undisputed classic on side two is "Hallowed Be Thy Name," which closes the record with the story of a man who's going to be sent to the gallows, narrated by the condemned himself. Its gloom reinforces the notion that the governor will not be calling for a stay of execution. Our humble narrator is going down.

With that performance behind them, the only question was how the new album would be received. They would find out on tour, between dates in Switzerland and France, that the album had gone to number one on the UK chart, but they didn't get a chance to celebrate because the coach taking them to the next gig had broken down, meaning they all had to get out and push. Congratulations, boys!

DAVE MURRAY PLAYS GUITAR BESIDE SINGER AND NEW GUY BRUCE DICKINSON IN MERRILLVILLE, INDIANA, DURING THE BEAST ON THE ROAD TOUR ON MAY 25, 1982. AS FOR THE NEW GUY, THEY LIKED HIM.

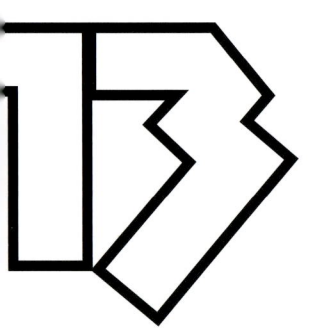

13
CLIVE, UNSTOOLED
ANOTHER CHANGE IS IN THE AIR

On the eve of the release of *The Number of the Beast*, Iron Maiden played in friendly territory: the Hammersmith Odeon in London. Documented on *Beast over Hammersmith*, the highlight of this performance full of highlights is "Hallowed Be Thy Name." Each band member left everything on the field with that performance, which may well be the definitive rendition of the song. Then they played seven more songs.

Clive Burr, sadly, never recorded with the band again. Even though *The Number of the Beast* had topped the UK charts, he parted ways with Iron Maiden after the tour, and while his replacement would occupy the drum stool for the next 41 years, Dickinson felt like the band had lost something when they lost Clive Burr.

"Clive had incredible feel, and you can't learn that," he said.

Accounts vary as to why Burr and Maiden parted ways. Adrian Smith said in *Run to the Hills* that Burr's live performances were becoming inconsistent, and the number of "off nights" was increasing. Harris said that he couldn't stand for it.

"It upsets me when we're not at our best, and on that tour we were really struggling, some nights, because Clive just couldn't hold it together," he said.

Burr didn't see it that way. He said that his father passed away while the band was touring the United States, and the understanding was that the drummer for the band Trust, Nicko McBrain, would fill in for him on the remaining dates. Burr would then resume his duties when he got back to the band after grieving with his family. However, Burr said that when he returned, the band had already decided to continue with McBrain.

"I knew Nicko," Burr told *Classic Rock* in 2011. "He loved the band; he loved being part of it all. And the rest of the band liked him."

After McBrain joined, the band experienced its first period with no lineup changes between albums. This stability would only last for a few years, but for a band that had lost blood after every album, it was nice to have a few in a row with no changes.

As for Burr, he said that his ouster had nothing to do with his conduct on tour. Furthermore, he flatly denied the stories of him being shown the door for being too impaired to play. "I've heard the stories—that it was because of drugs or too much drink," he said. "It wasn't anything like that."

The band's performance at the August 1982 Reading Festival that's on *BBC Archives* dates to Burr's last bit of time with the band. If his playing was subpar or in any way compromised, it doesn't show on this performance. Burr doesn't miss a step, and it makes you wonder what deficiencies in his performances drove his bandmates to kick him out.

Whatever the reasons, Burr was not happy. However, he was never publicly bitter about it either. As painful as it was to find himself on the outs with this band that he had given his all to for years—especially on the heels of his father's passing—he took it in stride and busied himself with playing in other bands. One was Gogmagog, which featured former Iron Maiden singer Paul Di'Anno and future Iron Maiden guitarist Janick Gers.

Despite the sad circumstances, you can do much worse in life than play on the first three albums by one of the greatest heavy metal bands of all time, especially when those three are considered pillars of the genre. But just as he didn't dwell on what had gone wrong, Burr never rested on his laurels either. He simply moved on.

"There was a grieving period," Burr said. "I grieved for my dad and I grieved for my band—and then I brushed myself down and got on with it."

ADRIAN SMITH, DAVE MURRAY, STEVE HARRIS, BRUCE DICKINSON, AND CLIVE BURR SUN THEMSELVES AT LONDON'S READING FESTIVAL ON AUGUST 28, 1982.

14

REVELATIONS
FRANK HERBERT HATES IRON MAIDEN

Clive Burr's dismissal from Iron Maiden for alleged excess partying had an undeniable effect on the rest of the band. In *Run to the Hills*, Adrian Smith said that the experience made him less likely to have that one last drink on the road.

"I started to take things that little bit more seriously on the next tour," Smith said. "Besides, I was tired of coming onstage with a headache."

Ironically, the drummer who replaced Burr was known to be a hearty partier. However, Harris said that any hijinks McBrain engaged in never affected his drumming.

"No matter what he's been up to, it's never affected his gig," the bassist said. "I know he'll be right on it the minute we step onstage."

Performing live and being able to bring the goods every night has been crucial to the band's success. Sociologist Deena Weinstein said that the band's epic road journeys, along with tape trading, were pivotal to spreading the word.

"The band toured relentlessly," she said. "They played everywhere and anywhere and built up a very large audience everywhere they went. They did not depend on the usual mediators for their popularity—radio and MTV were not particularly in love with Maiden at all. That meant those who came to see them were more committed to metal than casual listeners."

With this lineup in place, the band recorded the next studio album outside London for the first time, decamping to Compass Point Studios in the Bahamas. They recorded nine songs and released the album track "Flight of Icarus" as the first single for the US market. In *Running Free*, Garry Bushell pulled no punches in assessing the song.

"My integrity forces me to say I thought it was as weak as Clark Kent laden with Kryptonite," he wrote. "Plodding rather than powerful, it seemed universally unpopular with hardcore British metallurgists whose worst fears were bolstered by the number's release as the first American single."

While the album has a bit of filler, it also sees the band stretch out and create some genuinely ambitious stuff. With "Revelations," the band gets its prog on, and "The Trooper" is one of the best songs they ever recorded.

Unfortunately, the making of *Piece of Mind* was not without its tragedies. Initially, the band wanted to record a song about Frank Herbert's *Dune*, and they intended to name it exactly that. The response they got from Herbert's agent when asking for permission had to be a little upsetting.

"Frank Herbert doesn't like rock bands, particularly heavy rock bands, and especially bands like Iron Maiden," came the

BRUCE DICKINSON AT LONDON'S HAMMERSMITH ODEON ON MAY 26, 1983. SCREAM FOR HIM.

FRANK HERBERT'S 1965 BOOK DUNE, WHICH INSPIRED A SONG ON THE PIECE OF MIND ALBUM. HERBERT DENIED THEM PERMISSION TO NAME IT AFTER THE BOOK, SO THEY HAD TO CALL IT "TO TAME A LAND" INSTEAD.

response from Herbert's camp. The band had to call the song "To Tame a Land" instead, although all the references to sandworms, the Kwisatz Haderach, and the Gom Jabbar might have given away the source material a bit.

Piece of Mind missteps mainly in the lyrical goofiness department, and in the case of "Quest for Fire," responsibility rests squarely with Harris, who wrote every word of it. You know you're in for it when a song starts with the line, "In a time when dinosaurs walked the Earth." Still, all the music is solid, and in cases where the album works, such as "Still Life" and "Sun and Steel," it *really* works. However, two things solidify this album's status as a classic more than anything else: the cover and "The Trooper."

The album cover depicts Eddie chained up and straitjacketed in a rubber room. Close inspection reveals that malicious doctors have attempted to lobotomize him by opening his skull, removing the objectionable bits of his brain, and installing a clasp so that the organ can be easily accessed in the future. However, Eddie's demeanor on the cover is aggressive, indicating the lobotomy didn't work. The striking image remains one of their most iconic album covers.

"The Trooper" is the strongest song on the album and one of the best things the band ever

BASSIST AND MAIDEN FOUNDER STEVE HARRIS DURING THE WORLD PIECE TOUR AT THE ALPINE VALLEY MUSIC THEATER IN EAST TROY, WISCONSIN, ON AUGUST 6, 1983. THE BAND'S LINEUP WOULD REMAIN STABLE THROUGHOUT THE REST OF THE DECADE.

recorded. It stays in their set lists for a reason, even while other songs from the same album have fallen by the wayside. Again, that darn "gallop" sells the song more than the melody or lyrics.

By this time, the perception of Iron Maiden as Satanists had taken root in the United States, partly thanks to the title of their previous album, *The Number of the Beast*. The band decided to wind up people who believed they sacrificed goats. McBrain, under the influence of a drink or three, did an impression of Ugandan dictator Idi Amin, unaware that he was being recorded. The fifteen seconds of inebriated McBrain was grafted in backward form to the beginning of "Still Life." One can only hope that the morally upstanding ladies from the Parents' Music Resource Center listened to it repeatedly in search of demonic speech when, in reality, it was the drummer having a laugh.

DAVE MURRAY AT LONDON'S HAMMERSMITH ODEON ON MAY 26, 1983. MURRAY REMAINS THE ONLY MEMBER OF IRON MAIDEN BESIDES BAND FOUNDER STEVE HARRIS TO PERFORM ON EVERY ONE OF THE GROUP'S ALBUMS.

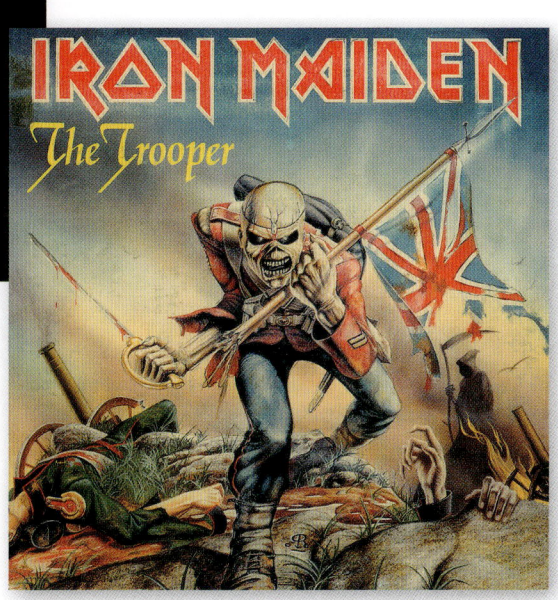

LIVE & HEAVY EXPRESS
IRON MAIDEN
World Piece Tour'83
SPECIAL GUEST
THE MICHAEL SCHENKER GROUP
4.12. Philipshalle
DÜSSELDORF
Einlaß: 19.00 Uhr
Beginn: 20.00 Uhr
Tel. Kartenbestellservice Theaterkasse im Hause Saturn, (0221) 121912

IRON MAIDEN

IRON MAIDEN
MICHAEL SCHENKER GROUP
LE COMBAT HARD DE L'AUTOMNE
ROUEN
MARDI 15 NOVEMBRE. 21 H.
PARC DES EXPOSITIONS
Nº 1610 60 F

avec RTL
IRON MAIDEN
MICHAEL SCHENKER GROUP
ROUEN
MARDI 15 NOVEMBRE
PARC DES EXPOSITIONS. 21H.
PARIS
JEUDI 17 NOVEMBRE
ESPACE BALARD. 20H.
BESANÇON
VENDREDI 18 NOVEMBRE
PALAIS DES SPORTS. 21H.
CLERMONT-FERRAND
SAMEDI 19 NOVEMBRE
MAISON DES SPORTS. 21H.
LYON
DIMANCHE 20 NOVEMBRE
PALAIS D'HIVER. 18H.
LE COMBAT HARD DE L'AUTOMNE

DAVE MURRAY, STEVE HARRIS, AND ADRIAN SMITH IN 1983 AT NEW YORK CITY'S MADISON SQUARE GARDEN, THE WORST-SOUNDING CONCERT VENUE IN THAT FAIR CITY UNTIL BARCLAYS CENTER CAME ALONG.

15
DO OR DIE
SONGS ABOUT SWORD FIGHTING

There's a persuasive case to be made that 1984's *Powerslave* is Iron Maiden's greatest studio recording. It contains some of their most rousing and anthemic tunes, some of which can withstand 800 consecutive plays without the listener tiring of them. "Aces High" and "2 Minutes to Midnight," the first two cuts on the album, are such songs. Indeed, the band still plays them live, lest the townsfolk start rioting.

"Aces High" is more than just a strong opening track—it's Iron Maiden at its absolute peak, with every band member in perfect balance. Dickinson's soaring delivery shows why he's considered one of the greatest heavy metal vocalists of all time. Murray and Smith trade off leads that complement and rival one another. Harris's bass is aggressively forward in the mix, and McBrain's drumming keeps everything simultaneously chaotic and cohesive.

It's followed by "2 Minutes to Midnight," an antiwar song written by Dickinson and Smith about nukes, a frequent song topic back in the day. It's taken at a slightly less frenetic tempo than the previous song but doesn't lose energy. It has an addictive prechorus section, and Dickinson's delivery makes the song, especially when he tells us not to pray for his soul anymore.

"Flash of the Blade" jacks the tempo back up and features some truly inspired guitar, both of the chugging rhythm kind and the weedly-weedly-wee kind. It's also one of two songs on the album about sword fighting, and it has an extraordinary guitar solo that climaxes with the other instruments dropping out while

EN GARDE! *AVID FENCER BRUCE DICKINSON KEEPS HIS PARRYING AND FEINTS UP TO PAR IN LJUBLJANA, YUGOSLAVIA, ON AUGUST 19, 1984.*

Murray and Smith guitar-fight each other. That bit is so overdriven that you can hear someone's guitar pick scraping against the strings in a manner that recalls someone keying your car.

The other song about sword fighting, "The Duellists," is followed by "Back in the Village," another high-tempo stomper written by Dickinson and Smith. The two had created a formidable songwriting partnership and could produce material that worked well alongside Harris's songs.

The proceedings take a turn for the epic on the seven-minute title track, penned by Dickinson. Its riffs and melodies sound Middle Eastern, or at least Middle Eastern enough to suggest he had listened to Rainbow's "Gates of Babylon" a few times.

The song ends decisively enough, and they could have gotten away with ending the album right there. But what fun is that? Everything has been leading up to "Rime of the Ancient Mariner," the thirteen-minute magnum opus that rounds out the album. The track is based on Samuel Taylor Coleridge's 1798 poem of the same name. This eighteenth-century British poet was so metal

JUST AS CANADIAN ROCKERS RUSH HAD ADAPTED THE SAMUEL TAYLOR COLERIDGE POEM "KUBLA KHAN" TO CREATE "XANADU," IRON MAIDEN ADAPTED HIS POEM "RIME OF THE ANCIENT MARINER," THEREBY MAKING HIM THE HARDEST-ROCKING POET OF THE EIGHTEENTH CENTURY.

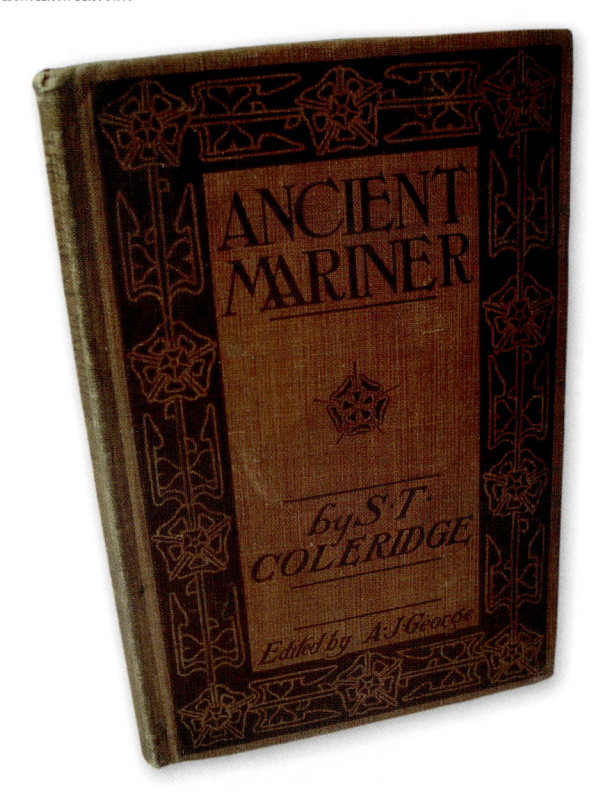

STALKING PEOPLE IN THE WORKPLACE IS WRONG. HAVING SAID THAT, WHAT ONE PRESUMES IS A MUMMIFIED EDDIE IS SEEN HERE STALKING BRUCE DICKINSON ONSTAGE IN LJUBLJANA ON AUGUST 19, 1984.

that he also provided Rush with the poem "Kubla Khan" so they could make "Xanadu," an epic track exceeding ten minutes to call their very own.

At about the five-minute mark, "Rime of the Ancient Mariner" disappears into a moody sequence in which the poem is whispered over volume-swelling guitars and an ostinato bassline. While it's unfortunate that it sounds very much like the beginning of "Stonehenge" by Spinal Tap (and came out in the same year!), it doesn't make any difference. Not only is it thoroughly listenable, but it's also admirable. This band stuck to its guns and remained true to its vision. They had earned the right to have songs of any length based on the works of whatever poet they wanted.

The fans were certainly on board with it, as demonstrated by the fact that *Powerslave* hit number two on the UK charts and stayed on the US *Billboard* chart for thirty-four weeks. Decades later, songs from this album have remained in the band's live sets, and indeed, some concert attendees might feel ripped off if they don't at least play "2 Minutes to Midnight."

Powerslave was so magnificent that Garry Bushell spent an entire paragraph in *Running Free* explaining how good the record was.

THIS SOUNDS MORE LIKE A SAVAGE STAMPEDE OF BUTCHERING BUCCANEERS, A SOUPED-UP CITY-LEVELING HURRICANE, OR A BARROOM BRAWL OF BRAIN-BRUISING BELLIGERENCE. RHYTHMS SO FAST THEY'D SCORCH THE ARSE OF ANY PUNK BAND YOU COULD NAME.... *POWERSLAVE* ACTUALLY TOPS EVERYTHING THIS BAND HAVE RECORDED BEFORE.

Powerslave was also a big deal in that it marked the first time that the lineup on the previous album had stayed intact and recorded the next one. Maiden had replaced a member on every prior release, and this was the first time that hadn't happened.

Unfortunately, this would eventually cease to be—there were changes on the horizon. But this lineup remained stable for the rest of the 1980s and would record some of Iron Maiden's best-known music.

16

FROM WARSAW TO IRVINE

MAIDEN WITHSTANDS THE WORLD SLAVERY TOUR

Iron Maiden's *World Slavery* tour began in Warsaw on August 9, 1984. Almost eleven months later, it ended in Irvine, California—a punishing 189 gigs over 331 days. Oh, and one of the dates was January 11, 1985, when they played the Rock in Rio festival to an audience of 300,000 people.

On paper, this was all a rousing success, but the marathon tour of the world's stadiums had caused some trauma for the band members. Dickinson said he started to suffer from tunnel vision about the tour's end, particularly when Smallwood kept adding dates to keep up with demand. "I never thought it was going to end," he said in *Run to the Hills*. "I guess it was the first time I really thought about leaving. I don't just mean Iron Maiden. I mean quitting music altogether."

McBrain seconded his singer. Even the youngest and hungriest band would have wilted in the face of their punishing itinerary. "I'm really surprised we got through that tour," he said. "We were at the height of our success, especially in America, and we were doing four shows on the trot, then one day off, four shows on the trot, one day off . . . there were a couple of times we did five shows running on that tour."

Smith said that the rigors of such a long tour also take a toll on a musician's private life. If you had any interests other than being on tour constantly, you probably wouldn't make it. "You're gone for a year and your whole life goes out the window," he said. "As for keeping long-term relationships going—whether it's with friends or lovers or whoever—I mean, forget it . . . I remember I went to see my parents when I got home and I knocked on the wrong door."

Eventually, the band ganged up on Smallwood, who had made them the biggest band in the land and made their wildest rock star dreams come true. *Please*, they entreated him, *for the love of God, we beg you, stop scheduling more dates on the World Slavery tour*.

Smallwood relented.

So, was it worth it? The 1985 album *Live After Death* says yes. Culled from recordings made at London's Hammersmith Odeon in October 1984 and California's Long Beach Arena in March 1985, this album was described by Greg Prato of *AllMusic* as "easily one of heavy metal's best live albums." In Sputnikmusic, Mike Stagno called *Live After Death* "by far, one of the best live albums I have ever listened to." Stagno cited the palpable energy from both band and audience on this record, even on longer songs like "Rime of the Ancient Mariner."

Listening to *Live After Death*, nothing in the band's performance indicates that the songs on the album's first three vinyl sides were recorded in the middle of a grueling world tour,

Dave Murray, Bruce Dickinson, and Steve Harris bring the decibels and the pain to Ljubljana on August 19, 1984. None who saw it were ever the same again.

TWO: THE DEVIL SENDS THE BEAST WITH WRATH | 61

the length and scale of which the band members had never experienced before. Nothing suggests anyone was less than 100 percent committed, and nothing reveals anyone on the record was considering quitting music. This is because Iron Maiden always pulled it together and gave every performance everything they had, no matter what was happening offstage.

They were not an improvising band, so what you got on their live records, and the reason fans bought them, were note-perfect versions of the studio songs performed with more energy and abandon. In that sense, *Live After Death* is an almost perfect compilation of the band's biggest "hits" up to that point. It finds them operating like a machine that does nothing but spit out one highly energetic live take after another, and they don't miss a step anywhere.

DAVE MURRAY AND ADRIAN SMITH
AT THE HOLLYWOOD SPORTATORIUM
ARENA IN PEMBROKE PINES, FLORIDA,
ON FEBRUARY 15, 1985.

Budweiser KING OF BEERS
"YOUR CONCERT CONNECTION"

IRON MAIDEN

WORLD SLAVERY TOUR

SPECIAL GUEST **ACCEPT**

JUNE 18 — 7:30 PM
PEORIA CIVIC
CENTER

Tickets: $12.50 Reserved
at Peoria Civic Center Box Office and all
Ticketmaster Ticket Centers including Bergner's
in Peoria, Pekin, Bloomington, and Galesburg,
and Video Sound Warehouse in Peoria
By Phone: 309/676-8700 with Visa/MasterCard

"I NEVER THOUGHT IT WAS GOING TO END." BRUCE DICKINSON IN NOVEMBER 1984, IN THE MIDDLE OF THE INTERMINABLE (FOR HIM) WORLD SLAVERY TOUR. DESPITE THE MASSIVE SUCCESS OF THE TOUR, IT PUT A SIGNIFICANT STRAIN ON HIM.

THE LOUD, SWEATY, RAUCOUS, AND VERY MALE CROWD AT THE IRON MAIDEN CONCERT IN LJUBLJANA ON AUGUST 19, 1984. IF YOU HAD THE TASK OF ENTERTAINING THESE GUYS, YOU WOULDN'T WANT TO LET THEM DOWN, EITHER.

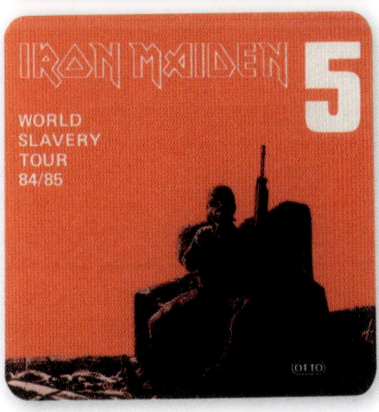

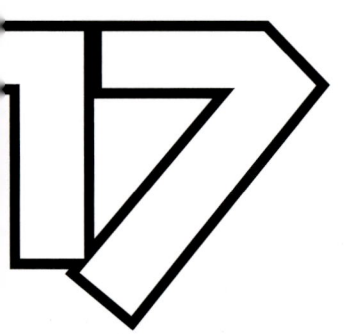

17
IT'S NO TURBO
IRON MAIDEN GETS A LUNCH BREAK

After the *World Slavery* tour came to its oft-delayed end and *Live After Death* became the next Iron Maiden album in the pipeline, the band found themselves with two things that had always been in short supply when they recorded in the past: time and money.

The band took four months off to do things like sleep in a bed, remain at one fixed address, and live the civilian life. Dickinson was far from the only band member completely fried by the end of the tour, and everyone benefited from the time off.

Harris did not give exact figures, but he said in *Run to the Hills* that their next album was the most expensive they had ever made. They used three separate studios to make it. Bass and drums were recorded in the Bahamas, guitars and vocals were recorded at Wisseloord Studios in the Netherlands, and Birch mixed it at Electric Lady Studios in New York City.

"We went a bit crazy," Harris said.

Harris, Murray, and Smith also experimented with guitar synthesizers, a concept that would have been anathema to this band just a year or two earlier. The album that emerged, *Somewhere in Time*, was the most slickly produced and ornately arranged thing the band had ever done, and it paid off. It peaked at number three on the British charts and sold two million copies in the United States.

Steve Huey of *AllMusic* gave the album a so-so review, saying they had nailed side one. Indeed, it's front-loaded with songs like "Caught Somewhere in Time," "Wasted Years," and "Heaven Can Wait," so it's easy to cosign that part of his assessment. However, on side two, he said it all went horribly wrong, singling out "The Loneliness of the Long Distance Runner," "Deja Vu," and "Alexander the Great (356–323 B.C.)" as subpar offerings.

Furthermore, he compared the album's use of synthesizers to Judas Priest doing the same on their *Turbo* album, which is worse than calling someone a sex offender. However, he acknowledged that Maiden had done a better job of it than Halford et al.

"The production does have more of that typically '80s studio sheen, but Maiden makes the new instrumentation serve their existing sound, rather than trying to hop on contemporary trends," Huey said. "Their ferocity hasn't gone anywhere either."

Dickinson has no songwriting credits on *Somewhere in Time*. He revealed that he had written some acoustic material that he thought would expand their sound and prevent them from falling into a creative rut. All of it was rejected.

While many musicians would have taken an "if it ain't broke, don't fix it" attitude toward their formula after three successful records, Dickinson felt the opposite. He thought this was the time to take creative risks, lest the band settle for churning out the same old thing every year.

"I felt we had to come up with our *Physical Graffiti* or our *Led Zeppelin IV*, or whatever, that we had to get it onto another level or we'd stagnate and just drift away," he said. "I just thought the time was right for us to do something audacious, something vast and daring, and I didn't feel that we did that with *Somewhere in Time*. We just made another Iron Maiden album."

It was left to Birch to tell Dickinson that the band wouldn't use any of the songs he had written. To him, it was nothing personal and not meant as a slight against the singer. He simply felt the songs didn't match the project.

"They were all acoustic and they just didn't fit," he said. "They had to go."

Dickinson said the rejection wounded him a bit, which affected his enthusiasm for the band. It wasn't immediate, and the band carried on, but the seeds of resentment had been planted.

EVEN IRON MAIDEN, THE BADDEST BAND IN THE LAND, COULD NOT RESIST THE DAY-GLO TEMPTATIONS OF LOS ANGELES CIRCA 1986.

TWO: THE DEVIL SENDS THE BEAST WITH WRATH

18

SEVENTH SON OF A SEVENTH SON

AMERICA DISAPPOINTS STEVE HARRIS

To many longtime fans, 1988's *Seventh Son of a Seventh Son* is the best album Iron Maiden ever recorded. If they were going through a bad period behind the scenes, it stayed behind the scenes. As far as anyone outside the band and its inner circle knew, Iron Maiden was going from strength to strength and creating one classic album after another. The idea that anyone would quit was the last thing on any fan's mind.

The new release was a concept album based on the book *Seventh Son* by science fiction writer Orson Scott Card, and musically, it was the most progressive thing they had yet released. *Seventh Son of a Seventh Son* also features several writing contributions from Dickinson, who said that the entire process of making this album was much more to his liking than the experience of making *Somewhere in Time*.

Harris had not set out to make a record based on the novel and even said in *Run to the Hills* that he started with no ideas for the album other than the fact that it was their seventh. Once he read the 1987 book, he called Dickinson to discuss turning the concept into their next record. Dickinson said that being asked for his input by Harris made him more enthusiastic about the album overall, and the feelings of alienation faded for a while.

Seventh Son of a Seventh Son debuted at the top spot on the UK albums chart, and the lead single, "Can I Play with Madness," reached number three on the UK singles chart. The entire album was full of solid material, including "The Evil That Men Do," "The Clairvoyant," and the title track, which sure doesn't feel like it goes on for ten minutes. This band could sometimes get long-winded, but you never feel it on this album. Every song seems to be there for a reason and is well thought-out. It ends perfectly with "Only the Good Die Young," and when the stylus hits that runoff groove, it's hard to see the album as anything but a triumph.

The album went platinum in the United States, but to Harris, it should have gone platinum-er. The problem in the States, it turned out, was a problem that the band had indirectly caused. They were no longer young upstarts who shoved pure metal down listeners' throats and alienated everyone else. They were established now. Furthermore, the role of baddest band in the land didn't belong to them anymore, at least not in the United States. America had become utterly infatuated with speed metal and its practitioners, such as Metallica, Slayer, and Anthrax.

These were the newest baddest bands in the land, and Iron Maiden had heavily influenced them. They also took the full-throttle, aggressive sound of early Maiden and gave it performance-enhancing drugs, resulting in extreme music that made Maiden sound mainstream. So, while *Seventh Son of a*

BRUCE DICKINSON SERENADES THE PUBLIC IN HIS ONE-OF-A-KIND CHAINMAIL TANK TOP.

Seventh Son sold very well everywhere else, it sold less than its predecessors in the United States, and Harris couldn't get past it.

"I thought it was the best album we did since *Piece of Mind*," he said in *Run to the Hills*. "I loved it because it was more progressive—I thought the keyboards really fitted in brilliantly—'cause that's the influences I grew up with, and I was so pissed off with the Americans, because they didn't really seem to accept it."

On tour, Harris started traveling in his own bus so that he could bring his family along. He said the change initially caused some concern, as there had been a long tradition in rock music of band members traveling separately when a breakup loomed.

Luckily, Iron Maiden was not at that point, and the other members followed Harris's lead, finding time alone on the road to pursue their own interests. Dickinson took up fencing, and McBrain learned how to fly a Cessna. Drugs and alcohol were also starting to fade from the band members' interests, but they got into a much more tragic addiction that few have beaten: golf.

"We'd learned from the *Powerslave* experience, and from all the previous tours, that we had to build in some space for ourselves where we could just get away from it all for a day or two and do something completely different," McBrain said. "Steve had his soccer and Adrian liked to go fishing. . . . There was a lot of escapism on that tour."

Despite introducing self-care into the Iron Maiden touring regimen, the band would soon fracture. They had made a string of excellent records, and as far as anyone could tell, all was well. Unfortunately, it didn't last.

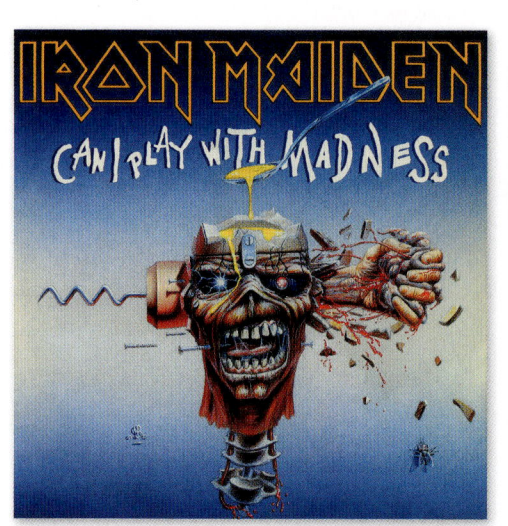

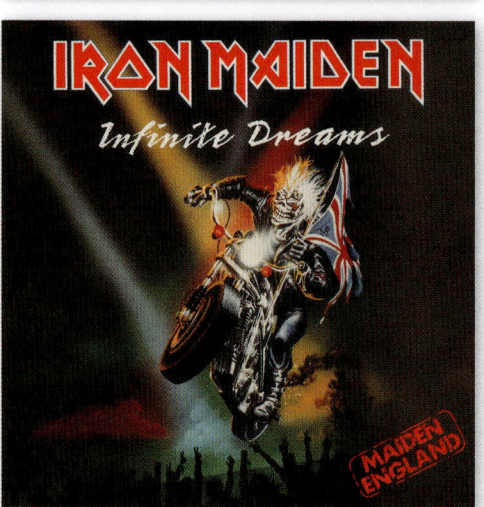

DAVE MURRAY, BRUCE DICKINSON, AND ADRIAN SMITH DURING ONE OF IRON MAIDEN'S ETERNAL WORLD TOURS IN THE 1980S.

1988 SAW IRON MAIDEN RELEASE FOUR SINGLES OFF THEIR SEVENTH SON OF A SEVENTH SON *ALBUM*. ALL OF THEM WERE BANGERS, JUST LIKE THE ALBUM THEY CAME FROM.

TWO: THE DEVIL SENDS THE BEAST WITH WRATH | 71

19

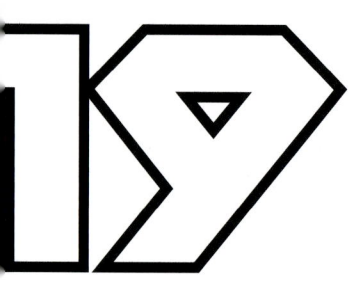

HEADLINING DONINGTON
IT SHOULDN'T HAVE GONE THIS WAY

Iron Maiden brings the goods to a vast and enthusiastic crowd, just as they did when they were a struggling club band with something to prove. That attitude never went away.

In 1988, Iron Maiden got some great news. Their tour to promote the *Seventh Son of a Seventh Son* album would feature a headlining engagement at Castle Donington as part of the Monsters of Rock festival.

It was their first time playing there, and despite turning down the gig in the past, they said yes this time because they would be headlining. Despite opening for them years before, they would even have Kiss as a support act. Things had changed.

"Like everything with Maiden, we wanted to wait until the time was absolutely right, and 1988 was it, absolutely, without a doubt," Smallwood said in *Run to the Hills*. "It should have been their crowning glory."

Certainly, the band was ready. Playing to an audience of 100,000 was old hat for them since they'd played to three times that number in Rio just a few years earlier. Furthermore, "The Evil That Men Do" from *Seventh Son of a Seventh Son* peaked at number five on the UK singles chart. The band was flying high, and the crowd rapturously received their marathon set. By any standard, it was a triumph.

It wasn't until the band came offstage that they learned the horrible news: two fans near the front of the stage had been trampled to death. It had been raining, turning the dirt field at the front of the stage into mud. Both fans slipped, fell, and couldn't get back up.

It happened during Guns N' Roses' afternoon set, hours before Maiden took the stage. Nobody knew that the two fans had been killed until long after. This performance was supposed to be a massive triumph for the band, but Smith said it was impossible to see it that way in the face of those two deaths.

"When we did Donington that year, it felt like the cap on all our achievements," Smith said. "But my main memories now are pretty tragic, because the deaths of those two kids just overshadowed everything."

Smith remembered the performance as a good one and said the band and the crowd really enjoyed themselves.

"The crowd were incredible," he said. "We turned the lights on at one point and as far as you could look out you could see people. All Maiden fans. It was an unbelievable thing to stand there and see."

Booking agent John Jackson had been watching Guns N' Roses from offstage when the incident took place. He said he could immediately tell that something was wrong, although the density of the crowd made it impossible to see.

"You could tell fairly quickly that there was a major problem," he said. "When a band's onstage, there's always a lot of swirling around, and because it was so muddy the kids just lost their footing and went down. It's impossible, looking down from stage, to see if people are actually on the floor, but I knew something was going on."

Guns N' Roses would gain a lot of notoriety for walking offstage after a forty-five-minute set in Montreal in 1992, which sparked a riot during their tour with Metallica. In 1988, Jackson said they were much more cooperative.

"They were fifteen minutes into a storming set, second band on, and suddenly they were told to stop, which they did," he said. "They couldn't have had any idea what was going on, but they cooled the set down completely."

After the concert, there were calls from the press for all outdoor music festivals to be banned. That never happened, but future festivals in the UK were required by law to cap attendance at 72,500 people.

Eight songs from this performance were released on *BBC Archives* (which, if you haven't figured it out by now, you should go out and buy). The band is enthusiastic and tears through the songs at the same high energy level that was now customary at every performance. During the song "Seventh Son of a Seventh Son," the audience sings along to the chorus football chant style. From all the evidence on the recording, it was a purely celebratory performance for all parties concerned. There's nothing to indicate that there had been any loss of life.

That year's tour ended on December 12, 1988, at Hammersmith Odeon. What no one knew at the time was that one of the band members had just played his last show with the group.

20

"AGONIZING"
A MEMBER OF THE CLASSIC LINEUP MOVES ON

Iron Maiden's classic 1980s lineup ended in December 1988 after a tour-ending performance at Hammersmith Odeon in the band's hometown of London. No one knew it yet, but the lineup was about fracture.

The band had decided, wisely, to take 1989 off. For Harris, taking a year off from Maiden meant locking himself in an editing room while he assembled the footage for the *Maiden England* video. Murray, meanwhile, went to Hawaii with his wife. This left the rest of the band to shift for themselves, and they didn't like sitting around.

Smith formed a side project to get songs he had written out to the listening public. The material was too commercial for Maiden, and it had been piling up. He dubbed it "Adrian Smith and Project."

Some bands do not look kindly on members having side projects. It became a massive bone of contention for Metallica when bassist Jason Newsted formed his own side project, and the ill will was a factor in his decision to leave the group. Smallwood thought it was an excellent idea for Smith to record this stuff.

"I didn't see it as a challenge to Maiden at all, because it was so different from what Maiden would do," he said in *Run to the Hills*. "It would also allow Adrian to get some of his more commercial leanings off his chest."

A full ASAP album was released in September 1989 but didn't sell. Smith felt the music wasn't metal enough for Maiden fans, and if it was supposed to appeal to new markets, it didn't do that either.

Dickinson was also thinking about activities outside of the band. He had been approached to contribute a song to the soundtrack of *A Nightmare on Elm Street 5: The Dream Child*, and he came up with "Bring Your Daughter . . . to the Slaughter." Guitarist Janick Gers, who had played with Deep Purple's lead singer Ian Gillan in the band Gillan, contributed to the recording. He and Dickinson had been friends since the singer was a member of Samson, and he was a good choice for a guitarist when Dickinson wanted to get away from the Maiden sound. It was a good thing, too, because just before Dickinson asked him to participate, he had been so demoralized by his career misfortunes that he contemplated selling off his gear.

"Bruce called me and I went 'round to see him and he brought out this song that sounded AC/DC-ish," Gers said. "He was trying to get away from the Maiden sound, so he was very open to ideas. And we went in, we recorded it in a day, two days, whatever, and it was great."

Dickinson decided to abscond with Gers and make a solo album. After about two weeks, the album *Tattooed Millionaire* was in the can. Dickinson and Gers embarked on a short tour of America with bassist Andy Carr and drummer Fabio del Rio in tow. They played zero Iron Maiden songs.

"Bring Your Daughter . . . to the Slaughter" did not appear on *Tattooed Millionaire* despite being the song that got the ball rolling. Surprisingly, Harris had asked Dickinson not to use it because he loved it and wanted it for the next Maiden record. Dickinson gladly obliged.

"I wandered back into Maiden to start the new album a very happy-go-lucky little leprechaun, so there was no intention whatsoever of leaving at that stage,"

ADRIAN SMITH AT BRENDAN BYRNE ARENA IN EAST RUTHERFORD, NEW JERSEY, ON JULY 8, 1988. HE DIDN'T KNOW IT YET, BUT HE WOULD SOON PART WAYS WITH THE GROUP.

76 | IRON MAIDEN AT 50

he said. "If anything, the joy of doing my own album had made me sure I was happy where I was."

One person, however, was not happy: Adrian Smith. The material for the next album was shaping up to be a more stripped-down affair, and if the idea was to embrace something a little more down and dirty that recalled their first couple of albums, he didn't want any part of it.

"The vibe was, 'Let's go back and make a really raw-sounding album like *Killers*,' and I didn't want to do that," he said. "I thought we were heading in the right direction with the last two albums. I thought it was a step backwards to strip it all down again."

Smith confided in Harris that he was not pleased with the music's direction. During their discussion, the bassist reminded him it wasn't just about making the new record—it would be followed by a year of touring. The prospect of spending a year on the road to promote music he didn't like was something Smith did not want to do. He was out.

"It all happened over a couple of agonizing days," he said. "There were lots of long phone calls. It was all very emotional. Maiden had been my life for ten years. It had become like a family to me . . . but at the same time it felt like it was a weight off my shoulders."

JANICK GERS PLAYS GUITAR ALONGSIDE BRUCE DICKINSON ON THE TATTOOED MILLIONAIRE TOUR AT LONDON'S ASTORIA THEATER ON JUNE 27, 1990.

TWO: THE DEVIL SENDS THE BEAST WITH WRATH | 77

SCREAM FOR ME, POZNAŃ

In August 1984, Iron Maiden began their *World Slavery* tour. This excursion saw them go all over the world, including markets like Japan and Australia.

Bands had played in those places before. Indeed, Iron Maiden played four Japanese dates as early in their career as 1981. But visiting those countries was economically burdensome, causing some Western bands to pass them by. The cost-benefit analysis made it look like a boondoggle, so bands generally limited touring to countries that were a safer bet.

Iron Maiden was different. Throughout their career, they played in countries many other artists skipped, such as Croatia, India, and the United Arab Emirates. This practice helped make them the internationally renowned group that they are today. But well before that, they began laying the groundwork for it by going where the fans were instead of waiting for the fans to come to them.

This tradition gained traction when they played five dates in Poland. At the time, it wasn't just a matter of visiting an exotic destination most bands didn't get to. In 1984, Poland was part of the Communist Bloc, making it sketchy territory for Westerners. The decision to go and play before Polish fans in their own country was unprecedented for a Western heavy metal band.

Along for the ride was nineteen-year-old journalist Howard Johnson, who tagged along to cover the historic string of dates. He said it was clear that wherever they went, the walls had ears.

"The level of government paranoia is an eye-opener," he said. "With Polish security personnel provided to accompany us 24/7 as a nonoptional extra. . . . This kind of shit only happens in North Korea, doesn't it?"

Maiden played gigs in Warsaw, Lódz, Poznań, Wroclaw, and Katowice. Their fifth album, *Powerslave*, would not be released in Europe for a few more weeks, but that didn't matter. Almost no Western music got an official release there anyway, and any Polish citizen who wanted a personal copy of a band's record had to buy a bootleg version, which Johnson said cost "half a month's wages." But promoting a single record wasn't the point. The fact that the band went there was all that mattered.

If anyone was worried that the trip might be a bust, they didn't need to be. On the first night, the band played to an audience of 6,000 at Warsaw's Torwar Sports Hall, and Johnson described the scene as joyful mayhem. Or, as he put it, the crowd was "going apeshit."

He added that soldiers in full military regalia were there, but rather than monitor the crowd, they threw off their hats and shirts and were as much a part of the chaos as anybody. The visit had significant political and cultural importance, but Harris told Johnson in a tour bus interview on the way to Katowice that they weren't doing it for those reasons.

"We're providing entertainment for the kids," he said. "They're seeing something new, and if our playing here opens the doors for other bands to come here, then the visit will have served a purpose."

Maiden's Polish performances did more than establish them as the first Western heavy metal band to play in the Communist Bloc. It benefited the heavy metal subculture as a whole. When the Iron Curtain fell, the repressive regime's citizens could move freely throughout the area, and many of them made their way to what was once West Germany to visit record shops. Hard rock and heavy metal records flew off the shelves.

Sociologist Deena Weinstein said Poland was the correct Eastern Bloc country to choose as an entry point. Government censorship existed, but it wasn't quite as draconian as in parts of the USSR. This allowed a more hospitable environment for a subculture to form. She said that tape trading was crucial to Maiden's success on this trip, just as the practice had helped create a buzz about the band before they were signed. While the slogan "Home taping is killing music" found its way onto many of the major musical releases of the 1980s, that same practice created crucial word of mouth for the British band.

"Maiden played in Poland because of tape trading," she said. "Loads of Polish young boys were trading tapes . . . tapes and albums were smuggled in and rerecorded and passed around, so when Maiden came to Warsaw, there were tons of kids who were metalheads at the time who went to see them and form their own bands."

She added that one of the people who saw Iron Maiden perform in Poland was a young man named Piotr Wiwczarek, who would go on to form the death metal band Vader. He was inspired to create his own group after seeing Maiden, and she said he got help from an improbable source: the Catholic church.

"The church was against the communist system because the communists were not fans of Christianity or any religion other than their own," she said. "Other communist countries did not have as strong a Catholic church as they did in Poland, so Poland was a lot more open to rock music in general and metal in particular. Friends of mine who lived in Moscow, Bulgaria, and St. Petersburg would tell me how they snuck into Poland to see metal concerts and get albums."

Iron Maiden's decision to play in Poland helped create a heavy metal underground in Eastern Europe when it was still under communist rule. The thirty-minute documentary *Iron Maiden: Behind the Iron Curtain* consists of footage from this trip and was expanded to almost an hour and included as the bonus disc on the 2002 DVD reissue of *Live After Death*.

Watch it in all its sweaty glory.

MAIDEN'S 1984 POLISH PERFORMANCES DID MORE THAN ESTABLISH THEM AS THE FIRST WESTERN HEAVY METAL BAND TO PLAY IN THE COMMUNIST BLOC— THEY CREATED A PRECEDENT FOR THE BAND TO PERFORM IN NEW MARKETS THAT OTHERS BYPASSED. DROZNY!

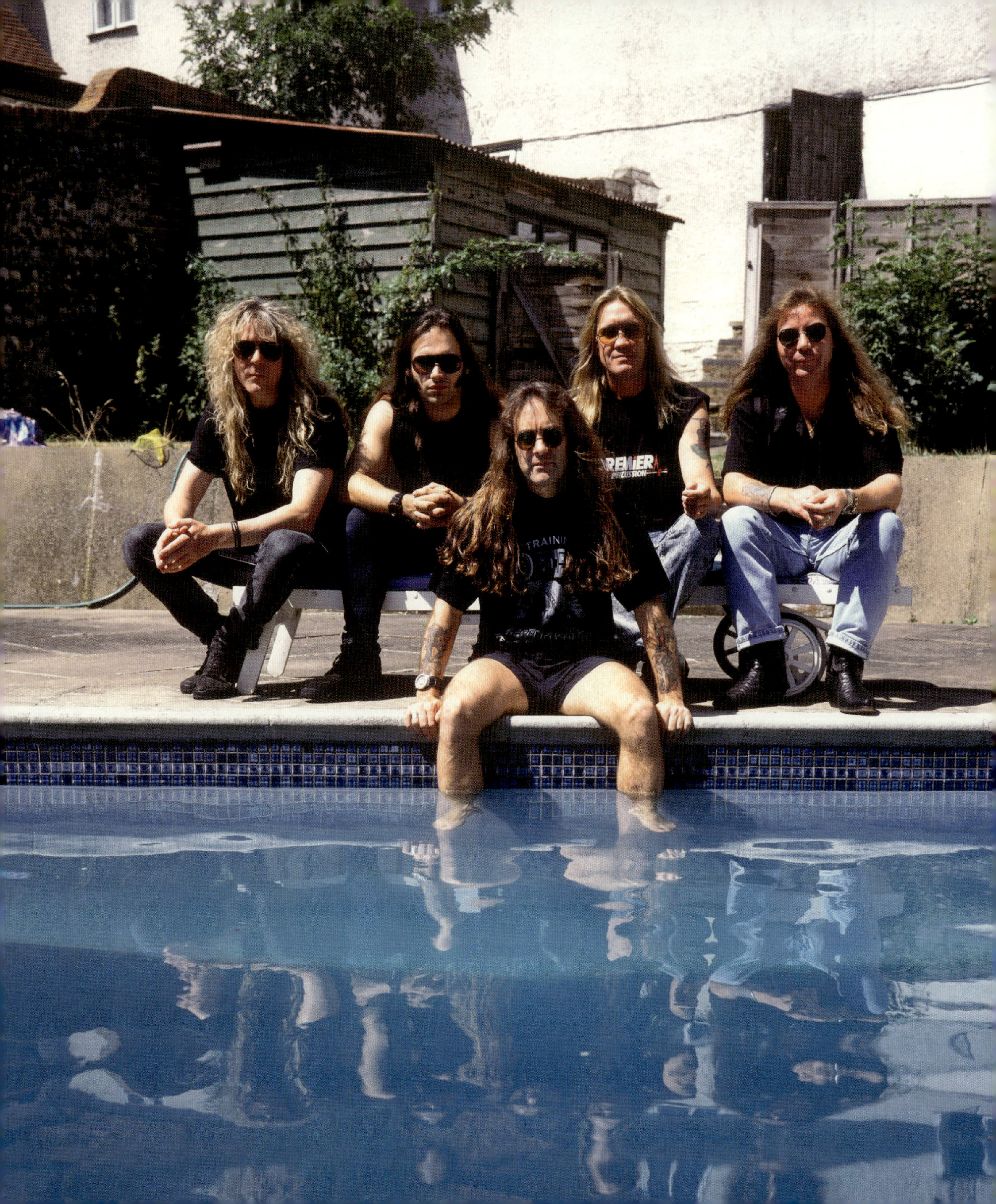

THREE
MEN ON THE EDGE

JANICK GERS, BLAZE BAYLEY, STEVE HARRIS, NICKO MCBRAIN, AND DAVE MURRAY HANG OUT AT THE SWIMMING POOL AT THE BASSIST'S HOUSE, WHERE BARNYARD STUDIOS IS LOCATED.

21
BACK TO BASICS, BUT NOT THAT WAY
JANICK GERS REPLACES SMITH

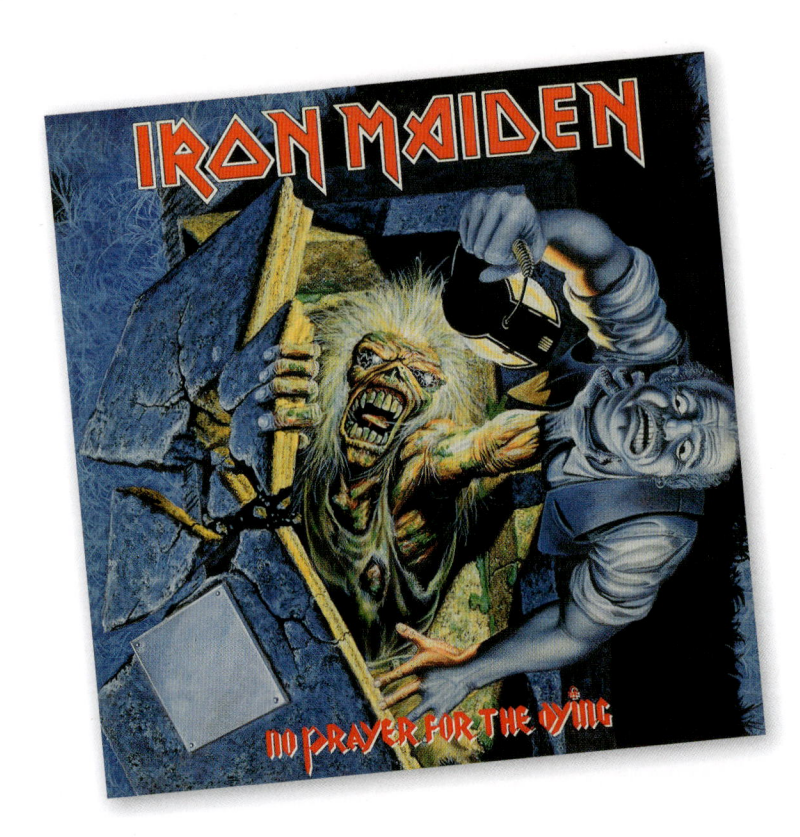

When Janick Gers received a phone call from Bruce Dickinson asking him to audition for Iron Maiden, he did not expect it. He knew most of the band members casually, but he didn't know anything had happened to affect the lineup until he got the phone call. Even then, he didn't quite catch on at first.

Dickinson asked Gers if he would be interested in coming down to play some Iron Maiden songs, and the guitarist couldn't understand why—they had already decided that Dickinson's solo band would never perform Maiden material. Dickinson clarified that the intention was to see if Gers wanted to replace the just-departed Adrian Smith in Iron Maiden.

"I was really shocked," he said in *Run to the Hills*. "My girlfriend said I was as white as a sheet when I got off the phone. She thought someone had died or something."

Gers met up with the band and ran down some classics with them, to impressive effect. He was informed that not only was he in the band, but they would start recording the new album the next day.

The album that resulted, *No Prayer for the Dying*, marked a significant change from the ones preceding it. Gone were the synthesizers and long songs—in fact, at five minutes and thirty-two seconds, "Mother Russia" is the longest song on the album, with the other nine songs hovering around the four-minute mark. If the intention had been to go back to basics, strip down to the essentials, and rip away all the finery, the record was a rousing success.

Unfortunately, the music itself kind of stinks. It's not the performances or the Martin Birch production that kill it, though—the songwriting is simply not up to par, and the album is full to bursting with mediocrities that make you think Adrian Smith left at exactly the right time.

It has some good bits—"Tailgunner," "Fates Warning," and "Mother Russia" all have engaging moments—but nothing manages to cross over into "at least fifty-one percent good" territory. Some songs show promise but have titles like "Public Enema Number One," which sounds like a placeholder name for a song that doesn't have lyrics yet. Strangely, at the same time, the band plays with consistent confidence that suggests they thought they really had something here. Well, at least they enjoyed themselves.

The universe's cruelest joke was that this album full of two-star songs hit number two on the UK albums chart. Furthermore, "Bring Your Daughter . . . to the Slaughter" topped the UK singles chart, making it the band's first and only visit to that ranking. It was like the Oscars ignoring *Raging Bull*, *Taxi Driver*, and *Goodfellas*, only to give Martin Scorsese a statuette for *The Departed*. Wrong, wrong, wrong.

As with their previous album, the band experienced another dip in sales in the United States with this one. Thrash metal was still flying high, and worse yet, another musical trend known as "grunge" was bubbling under the surface. Eventually, every metal band would have to contend with these market forces, including Maiden, but at this point, they could still write it off as some geographical anomaly. This dip in sales was happening only in the United States. The rest of the world was still on board.

Gers made his live debut with Iron Maiden at the Milton Keynes Bowl in Buckinghamshire on September 19, 1990. The stage was conspicuously free of the massive sets that had graced their appearances for the last few years.

"We thought the *Seventh Son* stage show just got a bit out of hand," Harris said. "The giant icebergs and stuff were a bit naff, I think, and we just wanted to get away from all that and turn everything into like a massive club gig again, which we really managed to do."

IN 1990, AFTER THE DEPARTURE OF GUITARIST ADRIAN SMITH, JANICK GERS BECAME IRON MAIDEN'S NEWEST NEW GUY, A GIG THAT SAW HIM PLAY AT LONDON'S WEMBLEY ARENA ON DECEMBER 18, 1990.

SHOOT THAT FU*KER IRON MAIDEN TAILGUNNER

22

TOILET GRAFFITI
MAIDEN'S ONLY NO. 1 UK SINGLE

When Iron Maiden hit the top of the charts for the first time with "Bring Your Daughter . . . to the Slaughter," it wasn't just their first visit to the top of the UK singles chart. It was the first chart-topping single in the UK by *any* metal band. Other metal bands had visited the UK singles charts before, as in the cases of the Scorpions' "Rock You Like a Hurricane" and Quiet Riot's "Cum on Feel the Noize," but none of those songs hit number one. Iron Maiden did, even with minimal radio play.

While you'd think fans would be happy to see the band kick down this door, time has been unkind to the song that did it for them. In 2022, Theo Page wrote in *Metal Hammer* that the song's only problem was that it was "a bit shit." Not exactly a small problem. He pulled no punches in describing the song's deficiencies: "It's not only that the title and chorus sound like it came from the *My First Rhyming Couplet* book—it's the *whole damn song*. In fact, it's not so much a song as it is some toilet graffiti someone has superglued a verse and solo onto."

After pointing out that the lyrics are moronic and, worse yet, that there are no trademark Iron Maiden galloping guitars, Page wrote that the song reaching the top of the charts was attributable to the band's fans—specifically, their hatred of pop singer Cliff Richard.

"Metalheads love an underdog and sticking two fingers up to the boring old farts who clog up airwaves and TV time," Page said. "In this case, it was one Cliff Richard. The permatanned heaven enthusiast was heading for Christmas number one with 'Saviour's

IRON MAIDEN AT CIRCUIT PAUL RICARD IN TOULON, FRANCE, ON SEPTEMBER 21, 1991. BRUCE DICKINSON IS BACK FROM HIS FIRST SOLO OUTING AND CRYING TO THE HEAVENS.

EDDIE THE HEAD TRIES TO INTIMIDATE STEVE HARRIS FROM ON HIGH, LIVE AT CIRCUIT PAUL RICARD IN TOULON, FRANCE, ON SEPTEMBER 21, 1991.

Day,' so Maiden released 'Bring Your Daughter . . .' to try and out-do him—despite the BBC refusing to play the song on Radio 1."

While the band was getting accustomed to its high chart placement, they were also breaking in a new member, and Janick Gers was up to the challenge. His stage act consisted of jumping all over the place (and still does!), making a high-energy spectacle of himself. This was worth more than a fiberglass Pyramid of Giza at any show. The man believes in the power of cavorting, and hopefully, he does lots of stretching and cardio before each performance.

The band greatly appreciated their new addition's stage conduct. Rather than stand in the back draped in shadows, Gers turned every concert into a gymnastics event, and the enthusiasm was contagious. A cheerfully animated new band member was just the thing for a band that was now more than a decade into its history.

"Having Janick in the band gave everybody a much-needed kick up the arse," Harris said in *Run to the Hills*.

In 2017, a writer calling himself Vince Neilstein wrote a spirited defense of Gers's stage antics in *Metal Sucks*. The fact that Gers is enjoying himself up there is not METAL, a genre in which no one is allowed to smile. However, Neilstein insisted there was a method at work.

"That's him up there onstage left (audience right), prancing and dancing around the floor like a fucking goon, allegedly making a mockery of everything metalheads hold so dear," he wrote. "He moves like a ballet dancer in a genre rife with macho posturing."

23
A RETURN TO FORM... KINDA
PLUS, CHANGES AFOOT

Fear of the Dark was Iron Maiden's ninth studio album. It had the same lineup as the one that preceded it, but if anyone thought it meant the band was heading toward a new era of stability, they were wrong. The band would lose a crucial member after the release of this album, and it would be a while before they would regain their footing.

The album went to the top of the UK album charts upon its release, so even though metal was on the wane and grunge was gearing up to send a wrecking ball through the entire scene, Maiden hadn't lost their fandom. Enough people still saw them as the ultimate metal band that they could maintain their popularity.

It didn't hurt that *Fear of the Dark* was a bit of an improvement over *No Prayer for the Dying*. It didn't hold a candle to the band's classic albums, but it had to be good to know that the years of hard work the band had spent establishing themselves had not been for naught. Since their earliest days playing clubs, the band had always given the audience everything they had, and the investment was still paying off.

The group also decided to allow other artists to design their album covers. Derek Riggs had held the job since their first single was released, and the band felt it was time to change things up for the new decade.

"We wanted to upgrade Eddie a bit for the '90s," Smallwood said in *Run to the Hills*. "We wanted to take him from this sort of comic-book horror creature and turn him into something a bit more straightforward so that he became even more threatening."

The design the band used for their 1992 album was made by Melvyn Grant, an unknown artist up to that point. Honestly, it was hard to tell that there was a new illustrator since most people coming to record stores to pick up the album saw the band's logo and Eddie sitting in a tree. That was all most of them needed to see. It wasn't until they looked at the liner notes that they learned there was a change.

Another difference was the album's length. The first Iron Maiden records were short and nasty affairs that delivered the goods in under forty minutes. Now, it was the compact disc age, and the band could fit twelve songs on a single disc, totaling almost an hour.

Some of it is great, such as the opening track, "Be Quick or Be Dead," and the title track that closes it out. The fake Middle Eastern textures of "Fear Is the Key" are pretty cool, as is "The Apparition," despite its riff-against-drumbeat structure sounding like it had been shoplifted from Led Zeppelin's "Kashmir."

Unfortunately, the album falls victim to the same syndrome that plagued so many songs on *No Prayer for the Dying*: lots of

STEVE HARRIS AT VORST NATIONAAL, BRUSSELS, BELGIUM, ON AUGUST 17, 1992. IRON MAIDEN WOULD PLAY A TRIUMPHANT SET AT DONINGTON A FEW DAYS LATER.

good bits, but the band seems to have a hell of a time transforming those bits into thought-out ideas that can sustain an entire song. It's also impossible to deny that quite a few tracks are filler. Several simply don't cut it, and while it's not the total washout that *No Prayer for the Dying* was, the listener will spend a lot more of the album's duration waiting for weak songs to end than being happy when a good one starts.

Fear of the Dark marked another change for the band. Martin Birch, who had been producing their records since *Killers* in 1981, decided to retire. It had nothing to do with the band or any ill feelings between parties because there weren't any. Birch simply had had enough and didn't want to twiddle knobs anymore. It was sad news, but Harris understood. He felt Maiden had been lucky to gain his services in the first place, and he couldn't blame the journeyman producer for wanting to stop.

"I think he just got to a point where he wanted to do his own thing and play golf," Harris said.

When the tour kicked off, the first part included a return to Castle Donington. Unlike the band's experience in 1988, there was no horrific news to greet them after they came offstage. It was a great show from top to bottom (you can enjoy it on the 1993 release *Live at Donington*).

The band believed in their material and didn't want to obscure what they were doing at the time by turning the concert into a nostalgia session. However, the time for nostalgia came at the very end of the set. Someone was in the audience watching them who described the experience as surreal: Adrian Smith.

"The first time I saw the band play after I left was at Donington, in 1992, and they were so good it felt bad, it really did," he said. "To see the songs I used to play, that I had written, being played and I wasn't there with them onstage . . . I felt torn in two."

At the band's invitation, Smith joined them onstage for the encore, "Running Free." He was happy to have the opportunity for some closure, as his departure from Maiden had been somewhat abrupt.

"It was great," he said. "It kind of rounded things off nicely and showed there were no bad feelings between me and the band, and it gave me a chance to say goodbye to the fans, which I hadn't had, because of the way things turned out."

BRUCE DICKINSON AND JANICK GERS LAY WASTE TO LONDON'S WEMBLEY ARENA ON MAY 17, 1993. TEN GIGS LATER, DICKINSON WAS A SOLO ARTIST, AND IRON MAIDEN WAS MISSING A SINGER.

OSSY HOPPE & MAREK LIEBERBERG PRESENT
IRON MAIDEN
LIVE 1993
Fender
ACHTUNG NEUER TERMIN
Sonntag, 11. April 1993 – 21.00 Uhr
Huxley's Neue Welt
Örtliche Durchführung: concert concept Veranstaltungs GmbH
Tourneeleitung: Marek Lieberberg Konzertagentur GmbH
Kartenvorverkauf: KaDeWe 218 10 28, Hertie-Wilmersdorf 312 87 95,
Wertheim-Steglitz 792 99 43, Wertheim-Kudamm 882 53 54,
Hertie Blücherplatz 251 63 67 und an allen bekannten Vorverkaufsstellen.
Telefonischer Kartenservice 301 99 99 und 312 94 97.
BERLIN TICKET
concert concept
The Entertainment Company
EMI
MAREK LIEBERBERG
KONZERTAGENTUR GMBH

Phil McIntyre by arrangement with Fair Warning presents

IRON MAIDEN

plus Special Guests

WOLFSBANE

SEPTEMBER
20th	Southampton Mayflower	0703 229771
21st	Oxford Apollo	0865 244544
23rd	Dublin The Point	0001 366777
24th	Belfast Kings Hall	0232 329666
26th	Newcastle City Hall	091 261 2606
27th	Edinburgh Playhouse	031 557 2590
28th	Aberdeen Capitol	0224 583141
30th	Ayr Pavilion	0292 280544

OCTOBER
1st	Preston Guild Hall	0772 58858
2nd	Leicester De Montfort Hall	0533 544444
4th	Liverpool Royal Court Theatre	051 709 4321
5th	Hull City Hall	0482 226685
7th	Newport Centre	0633 259676
8th	Cambridge Corn Exchange	0223 357851
9th	Sheffield City Hall	0742 735295/6
11th	Derby Assembley Rooms	0332 255800
12th	Manchester Apollo	061 273 3775
14th	Torbay Leisure Centre	0803 522240
15th	Poole Arts Centre	0202 685222
16th	Hanley Victoria Hall	0782 214641
18th	London Hammersmith Odeon	081 748 4081/2

Tickets are available from Venue Box Offices only.
The Box Offices open from 10.00am on
SATURDAY JULY 14TH

24

TIMING IS EVERYTHING
BRUCE DICKINSON HAS HAD ENOUGH

In the gap after the first leg of the *Fear of the Dark* tour, the band took a brief break while Harris worked on compiling the band's next live album. During that time, Dickinson said in *Run to the Hills* that he had become "bored and desperately looking for other things to do." This feeling was compounded when Sony, which released *Tattooed Millionaire*, asked him if he wanted to do another solo album.

Singing for Iron Maiden had been a life-changing experience, but now he wanted to see what else he could do. Staying with Maiden might have been the safer choice, but as an artist, he felt he had to move along.

His timing could have been better. The band's second leg of tour dates was booked for the rest of 1992 and going into 1993, making it an awkward time to announce he was leaving. This left an open question: should they cancel all the remaining tour dates or play everything they had scheduled? It was one thing for Harris to handle vocals for a single club gig when Paul Di'Anno was picked up by police, but what if Dickinson decided he'd had enough and left the band without a singer for forty stadium dates?

Dickinson agreed to fulfill the commitments and stay with the band for the rest of the tour. Crisis averted. At least, that was how it seemed. Harris said that as much as he hadn't liked hearing the news, he wasn't that surprised that Dickinson should want to move on to other things.

"We all knew the reasons," Harris said. "It was obviously the solo albums, and he's into just about everything else you can think of—I mean his books and his TV stuff and everything else—and we knew that, well, something had to give sooner or later." Dickinson had even learned how to fly an airplane, which would come in handy down the line.

The real problem was the upcoming tour dates. To Harris, it was not enough to know that Dickinson would show up for work. He was worried that the singer might phone it in, a cardinal sin for Iron Maiden live performances.

Smallwood had said Dickinson wanted to go out with a bang. That said, the bassist decided the tour should go as planned, hoping Dickinson would be 100 percent committed at every gig.

"Of course, I totally regret it now," Harris said.

The touring was a boon in that it provided the recordings used on the *A Real Live One* album released in March 1993 and then on the *A Real Dead One* album released months later. The releases covered two eras, with the former featuring material from *Somewhere in Time* on, and the latter featuring their material prior to that. In 1998, both albums were packaged as a single two-disc set called *A Real Live Dead One*.

Both discs are mixed bags. On *A Real Live One*, it's not that the band sounds bored so much as hesitant. The songs are executed flawlessly, but there's something off the whole time, and extensive listening will reveal that it's the vibe. It's impossible to guess what was going through the band members' minds during those performances, but once you get it in your head that something is off, it's impossible to un-hear.

As for *A Real Dead One*, it consists of several songs from the Di'Anno era. Dickinson never sang Di'Anno's songs as well as the original singer did. In a way, it's an "Ozzy vs. Dio" situation, where one singer is clearly technically much better than the guy he replaced, but the guy he replaced had a unique vibe that can't be replicated. Dickinson sings them with the ease that one would sing "The Alphabet Song," but in terms of pure attitude, the prize goes to Di'Anno.

Bruce Dickinson in 1992, apparently jumping for joy at the prospect of moving on from the Maiden mothership for a solo career.

25
LET'S GET THIS OVER WITH

DAVE MURRAY, LIFE COACH

If all you ever listened to by Iron Maiden were *A Real Live One*, *A Real Dead One*, and *Live at Donington*, you would have difficulty believing that trouble was brewing in the band. This is because all those releases were recorded before Dickinson announced his departure.

Okay, actually, nine of the twelve tracks on *A Real Dead One* were recorded after he announced his departure. But most of the live Iron Maiden product released in 1993 featured a fully invested Bruce Dickinson on vocals.

Behind the scenes, it was a different story. The typically determined Harris said in *Run to the Hills* that when Dickinson gave his notice, he considered ending the band, and he had *never* considered ending the band before, even when there were plenty of good reasons. He said that at a band rehearsal at which Dickinson was absent, he got a pep talk from Dave Murray, who was usually pretty soft-spoken and not the sort of person to tell you to snap out of it.

"I suddenly just got fed up talking about it and went, 'Look, why the fuck should we give up just 'cause he is? Bollocks to him. Why should he stop us playing?'"

The band decided to soldier on. However, this was easier said than done when the band returned to the road in 1993 with Dickinson to finish the tour as promised. Before going back on the road, the band held a press conference where Dickinson announced his decision to leave after the tour. Not long after that, shows in certain cities began to suffer. According to Harris, if the tour stopped in a major city with lots of press, Dickinson would perform as expected. But if they were somewhere less high-profile, he said Dickinson's performance was "fucking terrible."

1975
Steve Harris starts Iron Maiden
DECEMBER 25

1978
The Soundhouse Tapes
DECEMBER 30

1979
Maiden signs to EMI
NOVEMBER

1980
Debut album lineup is finalized
JANUARY

1980
"Running Free" single is released
FEBRUARY 8

1980
The mighty debut LP is released
APRIL 14

1980
Adrian Smith joins Maiden
AUGUST 23

1980
Producer Martin Birch is enlisted
OCTOBER 27

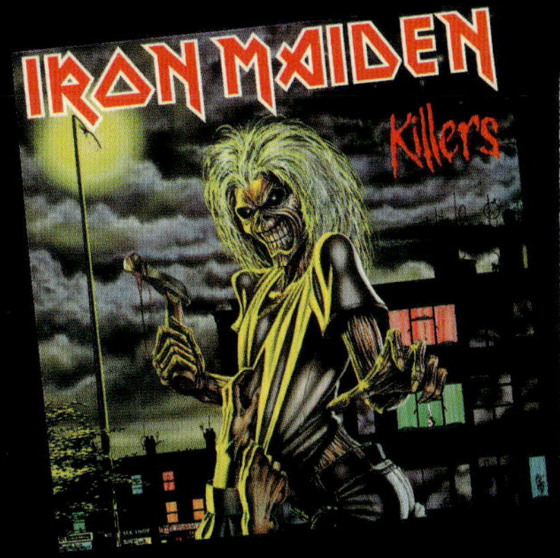

1981
Killers is released, and it still slaps
FEBRUARY 16

1981
The band parts ways with Paul Di'Anno
SEPTEMBER 10

1981
Bruce Dickinson joins
OCTOBER 26

1982
Maiden gets their first UK No. 1
MARCH 22

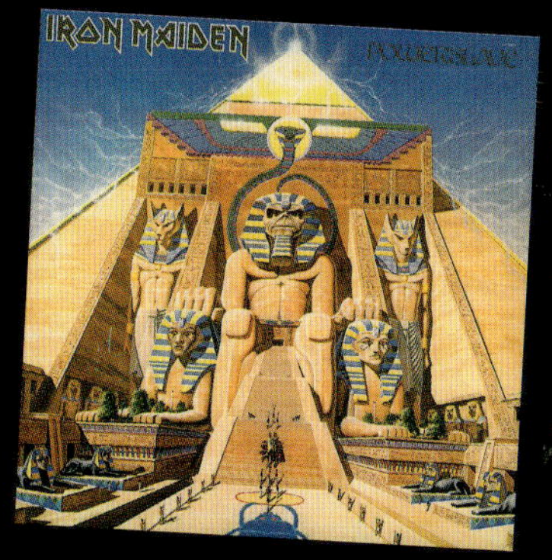

1982
Maiden loses Clive Burr
AUGUST 28

1983
"Classic" lineup makes *Piece of Mind*
MAY 16

1984
The glorious *Powerslave* is released
SEPTEMBER 3

1985
Maiden withstands the *World Slavery* tour
OCTOBER 14

1986
Release of *Somewhere in Time*
SEPTEMBER 29

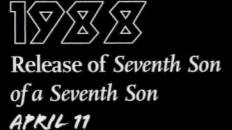

1988
Release of *Seventh Son of a Seventh Son*
APRIL 11

1988
Tragedy at Donington
AUGUST 20

1990
Guitarist Janick Gers joins
OCTOBER 1

1990
Adrian Smith quits... or perhaps is fired
DECEMBER

1992
Fear of the Dark is released
AUGUST 22

1992
Maiden visits the top of the UK singles chart
DECEMBER 24

1993
Bruce Dickinson goes solo
MARCH 22

1993 — Maiden decide to carry on without Dickinson
JUNE 4

1993 — Dickinson's last performance with Maiden
AUGUST 28

1993 — Blaze Bayley becomes the new singer
DECEMBER 24

1995 — *The X Factor* is released
OCTOBER 2

1996 — Maiden tours during metal's lowest point
SEPTEMBER 7

1998 — Release of *Virtual XI* album
DECEMBER 12

1999 — Blaze Bayley steps aside
JANUARY

1999 — Six-man Iron Maiden lineup forms
FEBRUARY 10

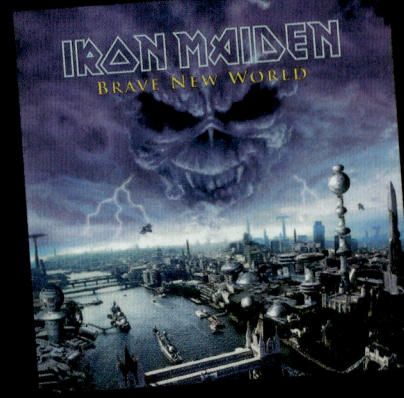

2000 — *Brave New World* is released
MAY 29

2001 — *Rock in Rio* live album is recorded, smokes
JANUARY 19

2002 — Band plays Clive Burr MS Trust Fund
MARCH

2002 — *Eddie's Archive* box set released
NOVEMBER 16

2003 — *Dance of Death* is released
SEPTEMBER 2

2006 — Release of *A Matter of Life and Death*
AUGUST 25

2008 — Touring the world in Ed Force One
FEBRUARY 1

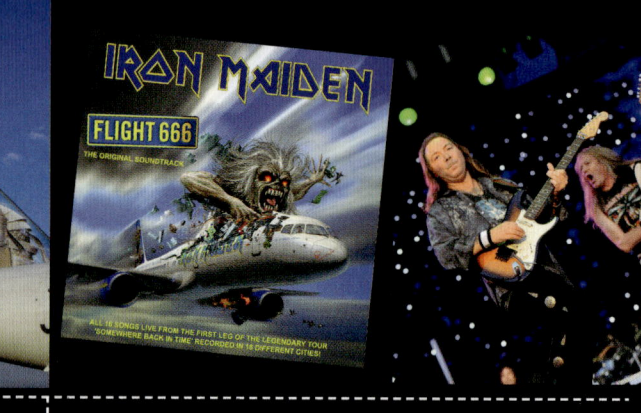

2009 — *Iron Maiden: Flight 666* documentary premiers
APRIL 21

2010 — *The Final Frontier* released—isn't final
AUGUST 13

2011 — The live souvenir *En Vivo!* is recorded
APRIL 10

2013 — Maiden releases Trooper beer
MARCH

2013 — Clive Burr passes away
MARCH 12

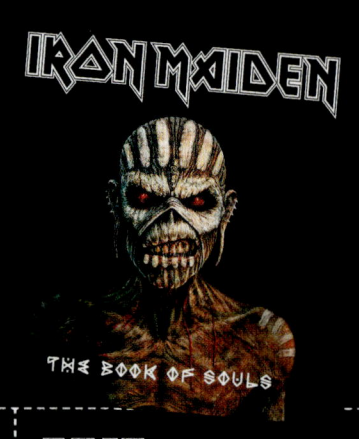

2015 — *The Book of Souls* released, recorded while Dickinson deals with cancer
SEPTEMBER 4

2020 — *Nights of the Dead* live album released during lockdown
AUGUST 9

2021 — *Senjutsu* is released, recorded in secret
SEPTEMBER 3

2022 — Maiden helps Di'Anno pay medical bills
SEPTEMBER

2023 — Nicko McBrain recovers from a stroke
AUGUST 3

2024 — Paul Di'Anno passes away
OCTOBER 21

WHAT'S WRONG WITH THIS PICTURE? IT'S 1993, AND DAVE MURRAY, NICKO MCBRAIN, STEVE HARRIS, AND JANICK GERS CAN STAND AROUND WITH THEIR ARMS CROSSED ALL THEY WANT, BUT THEY'LL STILL NEED TO FIND A NEW SINGER.

"He was mumbling, hardly singing at all," the bassist said.

Dickinson vehemently denied conducting himself in that way. However, he said the feeling onstage wasn't conducive to the big, happy Irish wake he and the band hoped for.

"It wasn't a good vibe at all," he said. "When we walked onstage . . . it was like a morgue. The Maiden fans knew I'd quit, they knew these were the last gigs . . . every single person in that audience must have felt pretty ambivalent about the whole situation, as I did and as the band did."

In retrospect, Dickinson admitted that he hadn't really understood what it would be like up there night after night when he agreed to do the tour. He admitted to some naiveté in hoping it could all work out somehow. Live and learn.

Finishing out the tour under those circumstances took a toll on the band's relationship with its singer. Harris, McBrain, and Murray were all on the same page as far as bitterness was concerned, and the drummer said that at the time, the three of them were so mad at Dickinson that it had a lingering effect on their collective relationship.

"By then we couldn't wait to get rid of the guy," said McBrain.

Despite the unpleasant ending, Dickinson said he never doubted that his former bandmates were decent people. He believed it had simply been a case of the ravages of time and pressure. He had been in the band for a decade, which is usually more than enough time for situations to reach their expiration date.

"I think things just do get worn out after a while, especially in something like a band," the singer said.

THREE: MEN ON THE EDGE | 97

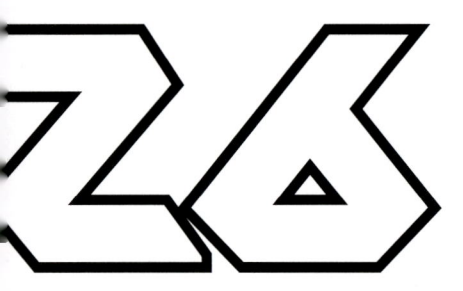

26
SO LONG, BRUCE BRUCE
DICKINSON LEAVES TO PURSUE SOLO CAREER

Bruce Dickinson played his last show with Iron Maiden on August 28, 1993, at Pinewood Studios in London. It was broadcast live via pay-per-view, that relic of the cable television era, and released in September 1994 on home video under the name *Raising Hell*.

It featured a seventeen-song set lasting almost two hours and spanning the band's entire career up to that point. It ends with the song "Iron Maiden," and after Dickinson introduces the band, demonic minions acting at the behest of illusionist Simon Drake abscond with the singer and put him in a prop iron maiden, giving him a mock execution to symbolize the end of his time with the group. Dave Murray also suffered the gruesome mock dismemberment of both of his hands.

Not everyone was thrilled with the unique nature of the show. Specifically, there was some grousing among the fans that a magic show had been grafted onto this final performance. Per the copy on the back of the VHS box, the intention was to present "the most macabre event of all time . . . [the] first and only live rock concert with a horror movie setting." Alice Cooper might have something to say about that, but whatever.

Overall, it's a good performance, but when you watch it, you can tell the band is preoccupied, making the proceedings seem a bit tentative. Being the consummate professionals that they were, they got through the show admirably and without seeming like they were going through the motions, but you can tell that there's a little uncertainty in the back of everyone's mind.

On the Fan Club Iron Maiden Bulgaria website, a review of the video said that Bruce Dickinson "looks somehow bored." Worse yet, the reviewer had to sit through a magic show, which seemed to cause him more displeasure than Dickinson's performance.

"Rather than having an actual plot, as logic would have dictated, it is mainly just a Maiden show with magical tricks performed between the songs," the review said. "Most of [Simon Drake's] 'magic' involved killing his beautiful assistants and even members of the audience in extremely grotesque ways for various trivial offenses such as offering a lighter that didn't work or shouting for more Iron Maiden music."

While there have certainly been more ignominious final performances by bands (see Addiction, Jane's), it was not the best note to go out on. At the same time, giving the band any stick for it is probably a little unfair. The heavy metal genre had entered a state of commercial decline, and some of its biggest names didn't know how to approach the change in the musical marketplace. Rob Halford had left Judas Priest to pursue a solo career, and the band didn't reemerge with a new singer for a few years. It was rough going.

Iron Maiden would have none of that. They set about finding a new singer to pick up where they had left off and keep the machine running. While it's impossible to fault their work ethic or desire to keep bringing the music to the fans, it was a difficult period for the group, just as it was for every other heavy metal band during the Collective Soul years.

They would carry on as always, but it was a steep uphill climb.

SOLO ARTIST BRUCE DICKINSON POKES OUT OF A TINY AIRCRAFT IN STOCKHOLM, SWEDEN, ON MAY 24, 1994. THE PLANES WOULD GET SIGNIFICANTLY LARGER IN THE COMING DECADES.

27
LIVE FAST, DIE FAST
MAIDEN GETS DIVISIVE

Blaze Bayley, born Bayley Alexander Cooke in 1963, started his musical career in earnest as the lead singer of the UK band Wolfsbane. They formed in 1984, and by 1989, they had secured a deal with Def American Recordings for their album *Live Fast, Die Fast*, whose production was overseen by none other than Rick Rubin.

Despite having all that going for them, the band didn't sell records the way the label hoped they would, and they were dropped in 1992. It was a taste of what many heavy metal bands would experience during that decade. However, in the handful of years they spent as Def American recording artists, they shared stages with a number of high-profile artists, including Motörhead, Ozzy Osbourne, and Alice Cooper. Iron Maiden, too, as it happened.

When word got out that Dickinson had left the group, Maiden received countless tapes from aspiring singers who wanted to step into the void he had left behind. Bayley was one of them. He hailed from Birmingham, home of Black Sabbath and Judas Priest, and saw every heavy metal band that came through town. He said that he was fortunate to be a heavy metal fan at the time when he was because he got to see a lot of bands in an intimate setting and not in a football arena.

"Bands played theaters back then," he told *Rolling Stone* in 2022. "The theater in Birmingham was the Birmingham Odeon. It was 1,500 seats . . . I saw Iron Maiden twice there."

When it came time to open for Iron Maiden in 1990, Bayley confessed that Wolfsbane always tried to upstage whatever band they were opening for. Iron Maiden was no exception, and on those nights, Bayley et al. tried mightily to outdo them. Rather than get angry about it, he said Harris told him he liked having a band like Wolfsbane open for them because it pushed Maiden to perform at a higher level.

Bayley was welcomed into the Iron Maiden fold at that point, even joining the band's football club. When Dickinson announced his departure, Bayley was already in the band's inner circle, so auditioning made sense. However, he clarified that just because he knew everybody, it didn't guarantee him Dickinson's vacant slot. He still had to audition like everybody else, and there were 1,500 of them, by his estimation.

That number got whittled down to twelve finalists, and Bayley was one of them. Each aspiring frontman had to sing ten songs with the group that were the foundations of their set, and after singing them live alongside the group, he also had to record the songs in a vocal booth. Many performers are great onstage, but when the time comes to record, it can reveal weaknesses that sometimes get missed in the mayhem of a live performance.

Bayley received the call that he had won the gig singing for Iron Maiden on Christmas Eve of 1993, just one day shy of the band's eighteenth anniversary. He described the experience as utterly surreal, one that didn't sink in until he was writing songs with the group. One of the first songs to emerge from the writing sessions was "Man on the Edge," and it was during that time that he began to feel like he was really becoming a part of this thing.

"Writing and knowing that your ideas are good enough to be on an Iron Maiden album, that was when it really started," he said.

Bayley added that during this period, he unlocked some of the potential in his singing and learned he could do things vocally that he hadn't known he could do. It was also when he realized that if you want to write a good song, it doesn't just appear out of nowhere. It's a craft, and you have to hone it.

"Songwriting is not luck," he said. "This is experience, skill, and work."

Looking back on the experience in 2019, Bayley told *Rockfiend Publications Scotland* that he was surprised he had gotten the gig in the first place. His deep, raw singing voice was very distinct from the operatic shriek of his predecessor, but he said when he was invited to join, the band had been looking for something different anyway, so picking him made sense.

"I was very, very surprised that they chose me to be the singer," he said. "My voice is so different to Bruce."

Again, that was the point. The band wanted to go in a new direction, and while Bayley's tenure with the group has remained polarizing, they got the change they wanted. This iteration of the group was an embryonic version of what the band would become in the new millennium.

"The albums that I did, *The X Factor* and *Virtual XI*, that was the real start of the progressive era of Iron Maiden," he said. "The music that we came up with was just fantastic, I think."

IRON MAIDEN SINGER BLAZE BAYLEY IN 1995, THIS TIME HAVING HIS TURN AS THE NEW GUY. HIS TENURE WITH THE BAND LASTED FIVE YEARS AND YIELDED TWO ALBUMS THAT MORE PEOPLE NEED TO LISTEN TO.

28

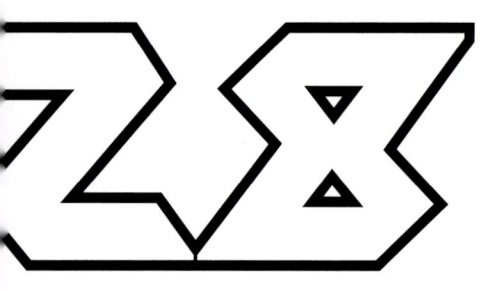

D-I-V-O-R-C-E

LOVE STINKS

The X Factor was released on October 2, 1995, and for longtime fans, it was a significant change. Its dry sound was far removed from the studio polish of the band's 1980s output, and Bayley's baritone contrasted sharply with Dickinson's tenor. Furthermore, Harris's marriage was unraveling, and he used the experience as fodder for his lyrics. Divorce may be a common theme on Tammy Wynette records, but it was virgin territory for Iron Maiden.

It's clear from the first song, "Sign of the Cross," that this band was using *The X Factor* to chart an entirely new course. That song and the ten that follow all reject such familiar group trademarks as harmonized guitars and soaring vocals. Bayley sounds utterly unlike Dickinson, and you can almost imagine fans tapping out after his first handful of words for that reason alone.

There had been other changes, too. Album cover designer Hugh Syme, who had created sleeves for bands like Megadeth and Fate's Warning, created a photorealistic three-dimensional sculpture of band mascot Eddie for the new album cover. He said the reception to his cover was similar to the reception Bayley was getting. People wanted what they were used to, and not everyone was thrilled about changing things.

"Some people were very intense that the more animated sort of graphic novel approach to their covers from the past was eclipsed by this new approach," he said. "Some people loved it, some people didn't like it, and some people didn't even like the fact that there was a new singer in the band."

The X Factor is for sure a less accessible album than others in the Maiden catalog, in part because it's such a left turn from where the band left off on *Fear of the Dark*. The album rewards patience, though, and if you listen to it a few times, there's quite a bit here to like.

Both "Lord of the Flies" and "Man on the Edge" are engrossing and up-tempo, and "Judgment of Heaven" is damn near upbeat. But once you start digging into the album, you realize that "Fortunes of War," "The Edge of Darkness," and "The Unbeliever"—all the album's most miserable songs—are the best ones.

Even the B-sides were worth hearing. "Justice of the Peace" is an energetic Harris/Murray composition that should have been on the album, and the same can be said for the Bayley/Gers effort "Judgement Day." Fortunately, those B-sides got a wider airing on the *Best of the 'B' Sides* compilation, along with versions of "Blood on the World's Hands" and "The Aftermath," recorded on November 1, 1995, in Gothenburg, Sweden. Bayley's vocals on both those live versions are even better than on their studio counterparts.

JANICK GERS, STEVE HARRIS, BLAZE BAYLEY, NICKO MCBRAIN, AND DAVE MURRAY IN 1996, PROUDLY CARRYING THE MAIDEN FLAG AT A TIME WHEN METAL WAS THE LEAST HIP MUSIC ON EARTH.

The X Factor is a solid, focused effort for those who can accept the changes. Unfortunately, many people just couldn't get with the program. Stephen Erlewine of AllMusic gave it two stars out of five, calling it "lackluster" and saying "there's a noticeable lack of energy to the performances."

The album went on to win the ignominious award of selling the smallest number of copies of any Maiden album up to that time. However, it has since gotten some much-overdue love from a segment of the fan base. In 2022, Dom Lawson wrote in *Classic Rock* that the much-maligned album was ripe for reappraisal.

"*The X Factor* stands up far better than the naysayers would have us believe," he wrote. "Brooding bookends 'Sign of the Cross' and 'The Unbeliever' are two magnificent epics, 'Man on the Edge' and 'Lord of the Flies' are rampaging crowd pleasers and the pitch-black 'Blood on the World's Hands' is one of Maiden's great unsung gems."

One man who always knew this to be the case was Steve Harris. Despite the conventional wisdom that *The X Factor* marks a low point in Iron Maiden's catalog, the bassist always believed in the record, and in a 2018 appearance on the *Talk Is Jericho* podcast, he said that he knew people would come around someday.

"I remember saying at the time that those albums that we did with Blaze, that people would in the future come to appreciate them a lot more later on," the bassist said. "And they are—they are starting to do that now."

THREE: MEN ON THE EDGE | 103

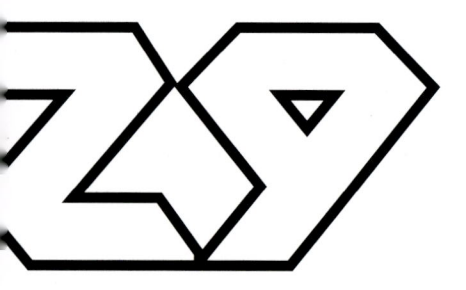

29
PUT YOUR MASK ON
BEST OF THE BEAST COMPILATION

The X Factour (ha ha) started on September 28, 1995, with three dates in Israel, followed by South Africa, the Czech Republic, and Slovenia, before the final show in Monterrey, Mexico, on September 7, 1996. Like many metal bands at the time, Maiden's popularity had declined, and the band was reduced to playing in small venues like nightclubs. Bayley told *Rolling Stone* in 2022 that while he was fine with that, it had been a difficult transition for the rest of the group, who had long ago paid their dues.

"I think it was very tough for the guys," he said. "Everything seemed against us."

Between that and the unspectacular sales of *The X Factor*, it was clear that the band was in a tough spot, along with heavy metal in general. Bayley recalled seeing one of his all-time heroes open for Maiden when he was a member, and it demonstrated to him what dire straits the genre was in.

"The toughest part was when Ronnie James Dio was supporting Iron Maiden," he said. "I'm the lead singer of Iron Maiden, and Ronnie James Dio is literally God of heavy-metal singing. I've loved him. He's my inspiration to be a heavy-metal singer. I've got everything he's done on vinyl. I've seen him in concert four or five times, and he's supporting me? God is supporting me?"

As the tour ended, the *Best of the Beast* compilation album was released. It contained a new song called "Virus," whose songwriting was credited to the entire band, minus McBrain. It has a two-and-a-half-minute introduction with soft-loud-soft dynamics consistent with the more dynamic direction of *The X Factor*.

After two-plus minutes of introductory foreplay, "Virus" turns into a stomping, aggressive song bearing all the traditional Iron Maiden trademarks. It's worth mentioning that Bayley sounds excellent on this, in a way that makes you understand what the band saw in him in the first place.

Best of the Beast sold respectably for an album mainly consisting of music the fans already owned, but if it was meant to reinforce or solidify Bayley's standing within the group among the hardcore fans, it didn't do that. Nonetheless, the singer took it in stride and felt that better days lay ahead. He was, after all, the new guy, and fans sometimes need to give the new guy some time before accepting him as part of the group. He understood that, and he knew Maiden was creating dense music with a lot of substance. Once the fans accepted him, they would recognize it, too.

"I was thinking, 'I'm in this unique situation—it's like I'm in the rebirth of Iron Maiden,'" he said. "'We'll get through this. Things will start changing because people will see that this music,

IRON MAIDEN PERFORMS FOR A HOMETOWN CROWD AT LONDON'S BRIXTON ACADEMY ON NOVEMBER 10, 1995. (L–R) DAVE MURRAY, STEVE HARRIS, BLAZE BAYLEY, AND JANICK GERS. NICKO MCBRAIN IS SOMEWHERE IN THE DARKNESS, HITTING THINGS.

this tough, hard, melodic music, is so much deeper, and has so much more to give you than other things around at this time.'"

With that, the band set about making their eleventh album, their second with Bayley. Hopefully, it would help reinforce his standing in the group and give fans who weren't sold on him a second look.

Hugh Syme said bands that replace a singer will have their work cut out for them in getting diehard fans to accept it. It can be done, and Brian Johnson of AC/DC is proof of that, but generally speaking, the odds weren't great.

"I didn't know until later that [Bayley] was challenging the loyalties of fans and their preferences," he said. "Everybody's good at what they do, but it's just a question of, 'Can you accept change?'"

BLAZE BAYLEY AND STEVE HARRIS AT LONDON'S BRIXTON ACADEMY ON NOVEMBER 10, 1995. THIS WAS DURING THEIR TOUR FOR THEIR TENTH ALBUM, THE X FACTOR WHICH THEY CLEVERLY CALLED THE X FACTOUR, HA HA.

IRON MAIDEN
T·H·E
95 X 96
FACTOUR
CREW AFTERSHOW GUEST PRESS PHOTO
PHOTO

30
COMO ESTAIS, AMIGOS

"THERE WAS SOME KIND OF FUNNY VIBE"

The eleventh Iron Maiden album, *Virtual XI*, was released on March 3, 1998. If the intention was to make a shorter and snappier record than *The X Factor*, it certainly did the job. It featured just eight songs, starting with "Futureal," a three-minute rager that instantly sounds like classic Maiden. In fact, the band continued to perform it live even after this lineup ended.

Despite starting so well, the record is almost fatally wounded by the second song, "The Angel and the Gambler." It's frankly amazing the record survives it. The song is, hands down, unquestionably, indubitably the absolute worst song in the entire Iron Maiden catalog. Since Steve Harris is widely acknowledged as the band leader, it's a good thing he wrote this song entirely by himself—only he has to take responsibility for it.

It goes on for an interminable ten minutes, and it's impossible to understand Harris's motivation for any of it. While "Bring Your Daughter. . . to the Slaughter" is also a bafflingly terrible song that never should have been written or recorded, it at least comes in at under five minutes in length, thank God. "The Angel and the Gambler" shows no such mercy.

The good news is that *Virtual XI* is redeemed by quite a few good songs. Like its predecessor, *Virtual XI* is a grower, and all the songs don't hit right away in the same way that "Futureal" does. But if you're patient with it, there's a lot there.

If there's any song on the album that you could say is the real showstopper, it's "The Clansman," which was inspired by the Mel Gibson epic movie *Braveheart*. It's nine minutes long, but you don't feel the length at all, and it's one of those very immediate songs you can listen to repeatedly without ever getting your fill. The structure is pretty simple, and there are no abrupt tempo or key changes, making it a song that wisely grabs hold of its glorious, mighty riff and rides it off into the sunset.

The song is too good to deny and has stayed in the band's set lists over the years. It also surprised the hell out of everybody by being sampled by R&B singer Brandy for the song "I Tried" on her 2004 album *Afrodisiac*. Sadly, she does not paint her face blue or yell "freedom" in any portion of the song.

The album closer, "Como Estais Amigos," is a heartfelt ballad about the loss of life on both sides of the 1982 Falklands War. You can tell that this Bayley/Gers cowriting exercise meant a lot to them when they wrote it, and the genuine nature of their feelings comes through loud and clear.

The album received the same dismissive reception from critics as *The X Factor*, with Steve Erlewine of *AllMusic* giving it a thrashing that was no improvement on his review of their previous album.

"It sounds lifeless to all but the most devoted fan," he said. "And even those fans, pleased as they may be to have a new Maiden album, will admit that the group sounds tired."

The band went on tour to support the record, and at first, it seemed their fortunes had improved slightly. Grunge music was finally over, and the tour was received well as it wound through Europe and Scandinavia.

Blaze Bayley puts up his dukes for the cause of all things metal on March 22, 1998, in Stockholm.

IRON MAIDEN AT ROSELAND IN NEW YORK CITY ON JULY 7, 1998. SINGER BLAZE BAYLEY SAID THAT WHILE HE LOVED PLAYING CLUBS, IT WAS HARD FOR THE REST OF THE BAND TO ACCEPT THE STADIUM-TO-NIGHTCLUB DOWNGRADE THEY GOT IN THE UNITED STATES DURING THE 1990S.

110 | IRON MAIDEN AT 50

"Things were really looking up," Bayley said. "We sold out this huge ice-rink in Stockholm, and the promoter told us we'd sold more for our concert than when Prince had played the last time. It felt like things were really going in a positive direction."

While the band received a hero's welcome in most markets where they performed, audiences in the UK and the United States weren't budging. They remained standoffish to this iteration of Iron Maiden and showed no signs of warming up to the new frontman. He had a great attitude, loads of energy, and boundless enthusiasm, but for whatever reason, audiences in those territories would have none of it.

Bayley began to feel that something was off when the band played a barnstorming set in Rio De Janeiro a few days before the tour's end. Despite being well-received by an audience of thousands, the band didn't do an encore, which he said seemed strange at the time.

December 12, 1998, was the final night of the tour. They played another set the singer thought was great, this time in Buenos Aires, but you don't have to take his word for it. The video of his final concert with Maiden is on YouTube, and he completely kills it from the very first song. Still, he felt some weirdness in the air that he couldn't ignore.

"I had a sense there was some kind of funny vibe," he said in *Run to the Hills*. "At the time, I put it down to an end-of-tour kind of vibe."

His gut had been right. Something was up, and he would find out what it was soon enough.

IT'S MAY 27, 1998, AT THE ZENITH IN MONTPELLIER, FRANCE, AND JANICK GERS TAKES TIME FROM HIS GYMNASTICS ROUTINE TO POINT HIS GUITAR AT A PHOTOGRAPHER.

THE GALLOP
MUSICAL MOTIF BECOMES A MAIDEN HALLMARK

COMPOSER GIOACHINO ROSSINI IN 1865. HE WROTE THE OPERA GUILLAUME TELL, WHOSE OVERTURE CONTAINED THE "GALLOP," ALSO KNOWN AS THE MOST METAL (AND MOST MAIDEN) MUSICAL MOTIF OF ALL TIME.

Iron Maiden has always had many trademark attributes in its sound: harmonizing twin guitars, operatic vocals, and an aggressively up-front bass sound. But perhaps more than any other, the band's most recognizable trait is the ever-familiar "gallop" rhythm that has appeared in the band's songs for years. It's nothing more than a repeating figure containing two sixteenth notes followed by one eighth note, but it has been known to create an enthusiastic frenzy in all who hear it.

It made its flagship appearance on the song "Killers" in 1981. It turned up again on "The Trooper," which had a video depicting galloping horses, and "Run to the Hills" not only had that but even contained the lyric "galloping hard on the plains," in case anyone missed the point. It's appeared on many other songs throughout the band's career, and it's something that every aspiring heavy metal guitarist aspires to perfect from the day of their first lesson.

Though Maiden gets a lot of credit for this musical motif, they did not invent it. Not by a long shot. Numerous examples exist in other hard rock and heavy metal songs from the 1970s, such as "Barracuda" by Heart and Led Zeppelin's "Achilles Last Stand." Well before that, it turned up in the *William Tell* Overture by nineteenth-century Italian composer Gioachino Rossini. That composition was popularized when it was used as the theme for *The Lone Ranger* radio show in 1933, and it was also used as the theme for the television show of the same name that aired during the 1950s.

The *William Tell* Overture became so associated with the masked man that some people refer to it as "the *Lone Ranger* song," in the same tragically misinformed way that many refer to Richard Strauss's "Thus Spake Zarathustra" as "the *2001* song" or "Ride of the Valkyries" as "the *Apocalypse Now* song." But while some people may get the name wrong, there's no disputing that the motif itself has always been effective at getting across the feeling of holding on for dear life while riding one's mount at high speed across rocky terrain.

The figure is so frequently associated with Iron Maiden that other artists who use it stand a good chance of being accused of stealing it. They did it anyway. Many heavy metal bands took it for themselves and used it in their songs. It's turned up on "Battery" and "Disposable Heroes" by Metallica, "Holy Diver" by Dio, and "Raining Blood" by Slayer. Even the American indie-rock band Hüsker Dü took a crack at it in their 1984 song "Turn on the News."

The reason it gets used so often—apart from the fact that it's very cool—is that it's one of the most metal guitar motifs in existence. It does not appear in punk, dubstep, reggaeton, or any other form of popular music. If you're playing that figure, you are permanently committing to an identity as a heavy metal musician.

Artists who used the motif strengthened their heavy metal credentials by playing it. Slayer, for example, wanted their music to be as metal as possible, and the riff immediately put them in that camp. It set them apart from lighter fare like Bon Jovi and won them loyal fans in the heavy metal underground, which was trying to distinguish itself as a separate phenomenon at the time. Poison might have been called "heavy metal" by the mainstream media, but they didn't gallop. That was the secret knock that let you into the underground metal clubhouse, and pop metal just didn't go there.

Harris was asked about the motif in a 1992 interview with writer Tony Bacon. While he acknowledged that it featured prominently in some of the band's most famous songs, he was modest about its importance in the Maiden catalog and his role in popularizing it.

"There's been I suppose three or four songs like that along the way: 'The Trooper,' 'Evil That Men Do,' stuff like that," he said. "'The Trooper' was a big song, a lot of people really like that, but that's not just what we're about. There's a lot more to it than that. But the thing is, that type of song is very—you can play it up-tempo and it's quite an attacking style of song."

Iron Maiden had many attributes in their music that drew a line between what was metal and what wasn't. They may not have necessarily intended to do that. Indeed, they may have only been thinking about their own sound and playing what they thought was cool.

Still, Iron Maiden has always been unapologetically metal and unapologetically themselves. Whether they meant to or not, they inadvertently created norms that every metal band needed to live up to in order to be taken seriously by the fans. The gallop rhythm was one of them, and if you were an upstart metal band in the 1980s dreaming big in your garage rehearsal space, making sure you had a few of those riffs in the songs was the first order of business. Oh, and if you were a bass player who could do it with your fingers, you were usually offered a spot in the band right then and there.

STEVE HARRIS IN SOFIA, BULGARIA, ON JUNE 4, 2007, AT THE LOKOMOTIV STADIUM ON THE *A MATTER OF LIFE AND DEATH* TOUR. THEY USED THIS TOUR AS AN OCCASION TO PERFORM THE WHOLE ALBUM IN ITS ENTIRETY, ELICITING THE OCCASIONAL BOO FROM THE PUNTERS WHO JUST WANTED TO HEAR "THE TROOPER."

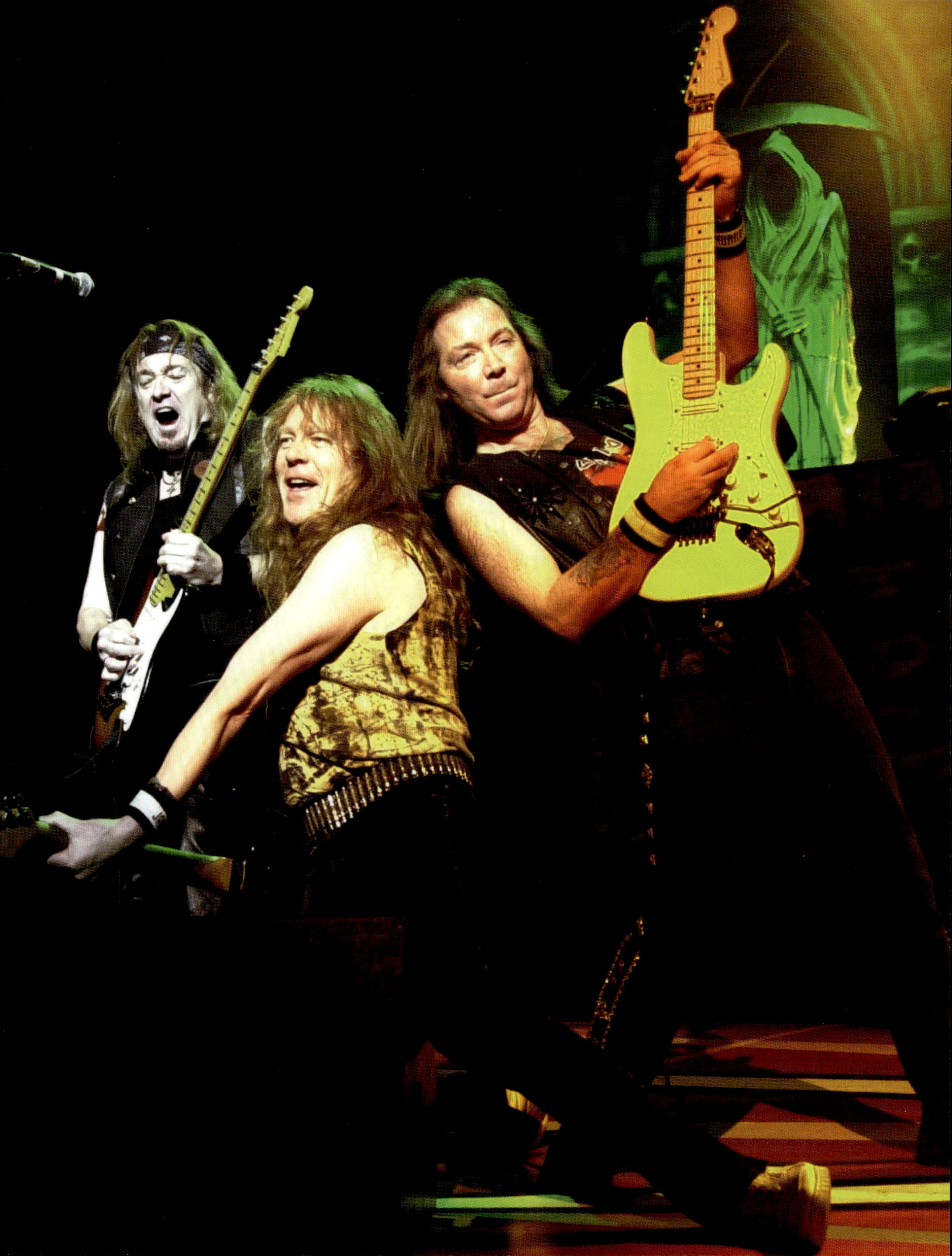

four
THE THREE AMIGOS

31

"THAT WAS IT FOR ME"

EMI PUTS ITS FOOT DOWN

While Iron Maiden had experienced a bit of a rough ride during the 1990s, Bayley felt the band was methodically working toward the goal of reestablishing itself after Dickinson's departure. They had released two albums with him, and while the reception had been mixed, he thought his potential third album with the band would clinch it.

"I really thought that the third record with Maiden with me would be the charm," he told *Rolling Stone* in 2022. "I thought, 'When this third album comes out, that is going to change the hardcore fans and put them back with us. . .' I absolutely believed in my heart that would happen."

It did not. And while a pernicious myth has persisted that proposes Bayley was to blame for his ouster because of some subpar performances, that wasn't it. There was a much more plausible explanation, and that was money.

"At the end, it was the commercial pressure from EMI," Bayley said, citing successful reunions with lead singers by bands such as Black Sabbath, who reunited with original singer Ozzy Osbourne in 1997. "These were all big successes that bumped their numbers up. . . . That was it for me. It was a commercial thing. And there I was."

And that was it. Bayley was given his walking papers after just two albums. Between that, his booming baritone voice, and the decades it took for the fandom to appreciate him, he was truly the Timothy Dalton of Iron Maiden singers.

It hadn't been an easy decision for the band. Regardless of their commercial fortunes during the 1990s, they all got along with Bayley and enjoyed working with him. Harris said in *Run to the Hills* that giving him his notice was one of the hardest things he had ever done.

"He took it very well," the bassist said. "We'd had some discussions here and there already, so I don't think it was like it was totally out of the blue. But it was a very tough thing to do."

While it was not his happiest memory, the singer said he bore no ill will toward the band. He said they acquitted themselves well of giving him the bad news and conducted themselves honorably.

"They did the proper thing," he said. "We had a meeting with everyone around the table. 'With the greatest respect, everyone is doing this. It's a huge deal. We're sorry. We can't carry on.'"

Years later, Bayley continues to have a magnanimous attitude toward his former bandmates. He recalled the whole experience fondly and has had nothing but good things to say about the guys he toured the world with during the single crappiest era for heavy metal.

"I was very well treated by the guys, absolutely," he said. "I was disappointed, obviously, gutted, because I loved it. As difficult as it was to keep your voice at that level, and all of that, I still loved it."

Bayley eventually dusted himself off and embarked on a solo career, which, as of 2024, consists of eleven studio and five live albums. He also made a guest appearance on "The Clansman" on the 2013 Thomas Zwijsen album *Nylon Maiden*, which consists of eleven classical guitar covers of Iron Maiden songs.

BLAZE BAYLEY IN SÖLVESBORG, SWEDEN, AT THE SWEDEN ROCK FESTIVAL ON JUNE 7, 2024. THIS WAS A LITTLE OVER A YEAR AFTER THE SINGER SUFFERED A NEAR-FATAL HEART ATTACK.

When he's not making records, Bayley's touring the world and bringing the goods to very appreciative audiences in the sweaty and poorly ventilated clubs of the world. That may seem like a massive downgrade from the audiences of 75,000 that he sang to with Maiden, but he said that the up-close and personal experience that he has on tour every night as a solo artist feels natural and right to him. It's what he wants.

"I'm microscopic compared to Iron Maiden, but what I am is free," he said. "I am the record company... I'm a priority artist since I'm the only one."

Bayley has also had nothing but good things to say about Bruce Dickinson. He said they know each other, run into each other, and can understand each other. They had both lived the daunting task of fronting the most metal band in the world and bringing it to thousands of people worldwide. They each understood the job's demands in a way few others could.

"The pressure was this," he said. "You are playing soccer for England. It is the World Cup final. And you must win. That's the pressure of being the singer of Iron Maiden. And so when Bruce and I see each other, we don't really have to speak. We look at each other and go, 'I know, I know.' We know what it takes, but it's the best job. It's the best job in the world that somebody like me could have. It's tough, but it has joy."

The Bayley albums occupy a unique place in the history of Iron Maiden. They're not as well-known as *The Number of the Beast* or *Powerslave*, and some fans will never warm up to them under any circumstances. But decades after their release, they've held up, and if you've never heard them—or if you heard them decades ago and reflexively dismissed them—it's worth checking them out again with the benefit of hindsight.

32

"THE WORLD NEEDS IRON MAIDEN"

BUT WHAT ABOUT JANICK?

BRUCE DICKINSON VISITS BRITISH TROOPS STATIONED IN SARAJEVO IN 1998 ON BEHALF OF THE PRINCE'S TRUST.

With the unpleasant task behind them of asking Bayley to step aside, Iron Maiden could go about trying to change its fortunes after five challenging years. One of the first things to address was having Dickinson get his old job back.

"It was never going to be something Steve would decide on the spot," Rod Smallwood said in *Run to the Hills*. "There was a lot to take into consideration, and even then he wouldn't commit to anything either way until he'd actually sat down and talked to Bruce again."

For his part, Dickinson would be leaving behind a solo career that had been good for five well-received studio albums up to that point. It also saw him take his solo band to Sarajevo to perform in 1994, an active war zone. He told *Kerrang!* in 2020 that the band was brought in by helicopter and given UN protection, blue helmets, and flak jackets while they performed.

"When we flew out, it was like *Apocalypse Now*," he said. "There was a guy in the back with a belt-fed machine gun with the hatch open."

While much has been made over the years of Iron Maiden's commercial decline in the 1990s, it would be accurate to say that their former singer wasn't exactly selling records in *Thriller* quantities either. His records may not have received the sneering rebukes that the Bayley albums did, but none had been the type of breakout hit that would have transformed his career. As Joe DiVita put it so poetically in *Loudwire* in 2023, "They didn't light up the charts."

Smallwood had approached Dickinson before Bayley's ouster to gauge his interest in returning. Dickinson said he didn't want to come back if it was just in the name of nostalgia. If he was going to come back, he wanted the band to make challenging music that looked forward and exceeded what they had done before he left.

"If we were back together, then potentially Iron Maiden is looking at being nothing less than the best heavy metal band in the world again," he said. "I really wasn't prepared to compromise on that idea."

When Dickinson decided to return, there was still the matter of his solo career to think about. He told *Kerrang!* his band was very supportive and said something that gave him the perfect rationale for going back.

"They went . . . 'The world needs Iron Maiden,'" he said. "I never thought of it like that. But you're right—the world does need Maiden."

As long as Dickinson was coming back, Harris thought it would also make sense to invite Adrian

JANICK GERS AT ROSELAND IN NEW YORK CITY ON JULY 7, 1998. THE CROWD MAY HAVE BEEN SMALLER, BUT THE GUITARIST PUT ON HIS USUAL AEROBICS ROUTINE FOR THE AUDIENCE JUST THE SAME.

Smith to come back. The guitarist had already worked with Dickinson on the 1997 solo album *Accident of Birth*, and critics were only too happy to point out the similarities between their music and that of their former band.

"It couldn't help but have that sound," Smith said. "Of course it was gonna sound like Maiden."

Harris was happy to make the phone call to invite Smith back. He conceded that the guitarist had always been an asset, and not just for his fleet-fingered lead guitar prowess.

"I've always valued Adrian's writing," Harris said. "I think maybe Maiden lost something when Adrian left. '2 Minutes to Midnight' is a superb song. 'Stranger in a Strange Land' was different again, as well. He adds a different dimension to the band."

But what of the lithe and acrobatic Janick Gers? Would he need to slink aside to make room for Smith to return?

Not only did Harris not want to dismiss Gers, but it was now possible for Iron Maiden to become a three-guitar band, a concept that Harris had always been infatuated with. This was how they could see this change in lineup not as a reunion or a throwback, but as an evolution. This was a new lineup, and they would not play the nostalgia circuit. You were never going to see them perform on a cruise ship.

Smith said the new six-man configuration made nostalgia and feelings of stagnation impossible. It was its own animal, and while it may not sound like having a third guitarist would be a significant change, it was.

"If I had gone back and it had been the same five guys, there would have been a lot of baggage, but having Janick there seems to make it all fresh again," Smith said. "It's not the old band; it's a whole new thing, which makes it great."

While Gers was happy that his tenure with Iron Maiden would continue, it wasn't something he was necessarily banking on. But when asked to stay as part of the new Iron Maiden, as one of a triumvirate of guitars referred to as "The Three Amigos," he characterized it as consistent with the good fortune he'd always had as a professional musician. He said he had never even considered that he might be in Maiden one day, but here he was anyway.

"It never crossed my mind in the slightest to join Iron Maiden," he said. "They'd got Adrian and Dave. What would they want three guitarists for? That was my attitude, until they told me different."

FOUR: THE THREE AMIGOS | 119

33

"WE ARE ALL SONS OF MAIDEN"

THE BAND BECOMES THE MOTHERSHIP

In 1999, Iron Maiden released the compilation album *Ed Hunter*, which contained 20 tracks (and one hidden bonus track), all chosen by the fans on Iron Maiden's website. It also included a video game that the band had been working on even before *Virtual XI* was recorded but decided at the time that it just wasn't good enough to bear the band's name or seal of approval.

"It was crap," Bayley said of the game in 1997.

Two years later, it found a home on this new compilation, and the release gave the band a perfect opportunity to promote their new lineup. The set list consisted entirely of songs the fans had chosen for the compilation, and that included three songs from the Bayley era—"Man on the Edge," "Futureal," and "The Clansman." Those songs and others from the Bayley era stayed in the set off and on for years, and Bayley told *Rolling Stone* in 2022 that keeping his era of the band alive was consistent with Harris's view of the group.

"I think for Steve Harris, it very much is a band," he said. "He wanted it to stay a band and have the energy of a band and the camaraderie of a band. . . .I'm part of this journey of Iron Maiden."

Dickinson took the baton from Bayley and resumed his vocal duties on July 11, 1999, in Saint Johns, New Brunswick, Canada. While he had spent years fronting the band before, he said things felt different this time. Much of that was due to the pep talk his solo band had given him when he said he was returning.

"When I went onstage for that first show, it was in the back of my head: the world needs Iron Maiden, and here we are," he told *Kerrang!* in 2020. "I felt a lot more confident about who I was and how I was performing."

Furthermore, he said the break from the band had done him a lot of good. The passage of time had given everyone a little wisdom, something they didn't have in the 1980s.

"Back then we were in our twenties and jockeying for position, full of piss and vinegar and adrenaline," he said. "When we got back together again in '99, we kind of became family, on the basis that we could look at Maiden and go, 'Actually, that's the mothership. We are all sons of Maiden.'"

While the band could easily go onstage and cycle through their greatest hits, they still needed to make a new record with this lineup, and it needed to be a truly great one. A lot of suffering, wailing, and gnashing of teeth had taken place for the "Three Amigos" lineup to happen, and if their new record were a dud, it would have been a crushing disappointment to the fans and the band.

A SIX-MAN MAIDEN FOR THE NEW MILLENNIUM, BACKSTAGE AT CHICAGO'S UIC PAVILLION DURING THE *BRAVE NEW WORLD* TOUR ON OCTOBER 17, 2000. (L–R) STEVE HARRIS, NICKO MCBRAIN, BRUCE DICKINSON, DAVE MURRAY, JANICK GERS, AND ADRIAN SMITH.

ADRIAN SMITH AND STEVE HARRIS AT THE UIC PAVILLION IN CHICAGO DURING THE BRAVE NEW WORLD TOUR. WHATEVER THEY'RE SINGING, THEY'RE FEELING IT.

Luckily, 2000's *Brave New World* was a truly remarkable record. Released on May 29, 2000, and coproduced by Kevin Shirley and Steve Harris, it was recorded live in the studio and has a very energetic vibe. In 2003, Adrian Smith said it featured four songs that the band had been working on during the *Virtual XI* sessions—"Nomad," "Dream of Mirrors," "Mercenary," and a fourth one that Smith said he couldn't remember, although Steve Harris would say it was "Blood Brothers."

The album picks up where *The X Factor* and *Virtual XI* left off in the sense that, as Bayley said, the albums from his tenure were where the band started to stretch out and become more progressive. On *Brave New World*, much of its 67-minute running time is spent on crescendos and changes in dynamics. The longest song on the album, "Dream of Mirrors," reaches the 9:21 mark that way, to great effect.

"The Wicker Man" and "The Fallen Angel" are immediately accessible songs that seem designed for entire stadiums full of people to sing along to. "Blood Brothers" became a popular sing-along selection at concerts as well, and it's taken on a lot of importance in the setlist as a tribute to the fallen. The mighty Ronnie James Dio had the song dedicated to him from the stage when he passed away in 2010.

Iron Maiden needed to return to audiences in the twenty-first century in a bigger, badder, and louder configuration than ever before. *Brave New World* showed they were up to the challenge without relying on their past or disavowing it.

34

RETURN TO RIO
AN ABSOLUTELY ESSENTIAL LIVE ALBUM

BRUCE DICKINSON GETS SOME AIR DURING THE TWIN-GUITAR SHELLING OF DAVE MURRAY AND JANICK GERS. SURE, HE CAN BELT IT OUT LIKE AN OPERA SINGER WHILE RUNNING AROUND ONSTAGE FOR TWO HOURS AND THEN FLY THE BAND TO SOUTH AMERICA IN A 757, BUT WHAT SETS HIM APART?

When Iron Maiden came to South America to play at the Rock in Rio festival in 2001, it wasn't their first rodeo. They first played at the flagship festival in 1985 as part of the *World Slavery* tour, alongside other artists such as Queen, Rod Stewart, and Ozzy Osbourne. Even with all that high-caliber competition, their performance broke through to the crowd.

It was, as they say, the start of a beautiful friendship. They returned to the South American city several times after that, including to the Rock in Rio festival in 2001 during the *Brave New World* tour.

The Rio show was the last of a string of dates that had started seven months earlier. As it happened, it was recorded and released the following year on DVD and compact disc under the title *Rock in Rio*, and it captured a high-energy performance that defies its almost two-hour length. It just never lets up.

The eighteen-song set (nineteen if you include the "Arthur's Farewell" intro) is long enough to be comprehensive but savage enough that the momentum never flags. It features seven of the ten songs from 2000's *Brave New World*, all better than their studio counterparts. That's really saying something since this particular studio album was itself pretty damn good.

The set features numerous classics, like "2 Minutes to Midnight," "The Trooper," and "Run to the Hills," songs that any self-respecting Maiden fan would expect to hear at a concert. Even though they're songs the band has played a million times, all of them are performed with a rage and ferocity that's frankly still startling to hear.

It's all the more remarkable when you realize the band is at the end of an exhausting seven-month intercontinental slog. There's nothing routine about the performances, and they still communicate the same intensity as the band's club days. Decades later, they still sound like a band with something to prove.

The band plays two songs from the Bayley era, "Sign of the Cross" and "The Clansman." Dickinson introduces the latter as "a song about medieval Scotland," just to make sure people know it's "clansman" as in *Braveheart* and not "Klansman" as in *Birth of a Nation*.

Bayley was like Judas Priest's Tim "Ripper" Owens and Black Sabbath's Tony Martin in that he had replaced their band's most famous singers. In the cases of Owens and Martin, the music written during their eras disappeared from the sets once the singers they replaced returned to their bands in the new millennium, so no one got to hear Rob Halford sing any *Jugulator* songs, and Ozzy Osbourne never sang "When Death Calls." It was like the whole thing had never happened.

On the other hand, Maiden acknowledged Bayley's contributions and kept songs from his era in the set. While they were written without Dickinson, he sings them like they're fan favorites that the band has been performing since 1982. He never seems to have any attitude about the fact that these are songs the band wrote without him.

For many groups, live albums can be a formality, something the record company puts out to collect a few Benjamins while the band is sunning themselves on vacation, taking much too long in the studio, or convalescing in rehab. Iron Maiden is not one of those bands. Their live recordings indicate a group that wants to reach every last one of the 250,000 audience members in attendance and make them feel like whatever the ticket cost, it was money well spent.

IRON MAIDEN'S TRUSTY MASCOT, EDDIE THE HEAD, COMES TO LIFE TO TERRORIZE THE ROCK IN RIO AUDIENCE ON JANUARY 19, 2001.

35
CLIVE AID
"WE CALL IT THE CLIVEMOBILE"

Clive Burr either left or was fired from Iron Maiden in 1982, depending on whose version of the story you believe. Perhaps it was one of those situations so many of us have been in at various places of employment, where we left one Friday afternoon with all the personal effects from our desks in a cardboard box, unsure whether we had quit or been fired.

Either way, Burr went about playing for other bands, including Trust, which had been home to the guy who replaced him, Nicko McBrain. He also played in Gogmagog, a virtual who's who of people who had been fired from 1980s heavy metal bands, such as original Iron Maiden singer Paul Di'Anno and former Def Leppard guitarist Pete Willis.

Burr had resolved to stay positive and keep busy, but as the 1990s got underway, he started to experience strange physical sensations. It began with a tingling feeling in his hands, which he initially attributed to years of aggressive drumming. However, it persisted and intensified until he couldn't ignore it anymore. He told *Classic Rock* that in 1994, he noticed he was losing not just the ability to play drums but to participate in daily life.

"I kept dropping things," he said. "I couldn't grip properly. I could barely keep hold of my sticks."

He went to a doctor, and after several months of tests, the diagnosis came back. It was a bad one. Burr was living with multiple sclerosis. The illness compromises the nervous system's ability to transmit signals to the rest of the body, and while it can be managed, there's no cure.

The drummer continued deteriorating, and medical bills were piling up. At the same time, he was still in touch with his former bandmates, and while his tenure had ended on a not particularly great note, they wanted to help him nonetheless. They decided to play a string of charity concerts to benefit their old friend, referring to the effort as the Clive Burr MS Trust Fund.

Held at London's Brixton Academy on two March dates in 2002, these concerts were successful enough that there was now enough money to significantly upgrade the quality of life of their now wheelchair-bound former drummer.

"They bought me a vehicle," he said. "We call it the Clivemobile. It's a Volkswagen Caddy with blacked-out windows. It's like an American gangster's car. They've put concerts on to raise money, not just for me but for other people with MS. They put a stair-lift in our house. Sometimes I'll go up and down the stairs, looking at the gold and platinum records on the stairwell."

His partner, Mimi, who also suffered from MS, told *Classic Rock* that while her husband was grateful for all the improvements they were able to make with the money from the benefit concerts, the thing he was most moved by was being back in the fold with his old friends, even if he couldn't play drums for them anymore.

"They say if ever you need anything, just ring, just call," she said. "Whenever they play in London, Clive knows that he's only got to pick up the phone and he's got two of the best tickets in the house. It might not sound like much, but it is to Clive. Finally, to him, it's like his achievements—who he is and what he did—are being recognized."

CLIVE BURR, BRUCE DICKINSON, AND JANICK GERS AT A BENEFIT FOR THE CLIVE BURR MS TRUST IN 2005. WHEN HE WAS DIAGNOSED WITH MULTIPLE SCLEROSIS, HIS FORMER BANDMATES RAISED MONEY TO HELP WITH HIS MEDICAL EXPENSES.

THE GREAT AND MIGHTY CLIVE BURR, WHOSE DRUMMING ON THE FIRST THREE IRON MAIDEN RECORDS WAS PERFECT AND CAN NEVER BE IMPROVED UPON.

36

EDDIE'S ARCHIVE

HAMMERSMITH 1982 COMES OUT OF COLD STORAGE

In its fifty-year history, Iron Maiden never released a comprehensive, multi-disc retrospective box set spanning their entire career like artists such as Led Zeppelin or Jimi Hendrix did. There were single-disc and double-disc compilations, but no sprawling multi-disc set illustrating the band's development was ever made.

Maiden broke with this tradition (sort of) in 2002 when they released *Eddie's Archive*, a six-disc set boxed in an embossed metal package bearing the likeness of mascot Eddie's face and including a shot glass. It also included a poster showing the band's family tree, and if you think that one's messy, you should see Uriah Heep's.

The discs did not present a chronological best-of but three different packages—*BBC Archives*, *Beast over Hammersmith*, and *Best of the 'B' Sides*. While the B-side package has a few good nuggets on it, specifically the live 1981 recording of "Remember Tomorrow" and the live 1999 recording of "Futureal," the vast majority of the songs on the B-side compilation utterly deserve their afterthought status. Bluntly, most of them just aren't that good. The band members may have been fans of Montrose and Led Zeppelin, but they had no business covering their songs. Maiden simply play in too technical and studied a way to pull off the tight-but-loose quaalude rock of the 1970s.

BBC Archives is much better, although it must be said it's for hardcore fans. Of course, you could say that about any Iron Maiden release since they have nothing but hardcore fans. However, their 1979 appearance on *Radio 1 Rock Show* will only interest collectors who must have an early recording of "Sanctuary" somewhere on their media shelf.

All the performances are excellent, particularly the Reading Festival selections from 1980 and 1982. If you can pretend you don't know people were killed at the 1988 performance at Donington, you can enjoy eight songs from that set. It's all good stuff, but again, it's mostly for collectors.

Beast over Hammersmith is the jewel in the crown of this collection and makes whatever price you paid for the set worth paying. Recorded at London's Hammersmith Odeon on the eve of the release of *The Number of the Beast*, this is simply one of the best Iron Maiden live recordings ever released. It's funny to hear the band play "Run to the Hills" and "The Number of the Beast" when they were still new songs, and while new guy Bruce Dickinson was still proving himself to the fans.

These performances cannot be denied, and when you listen to them, it's easy to see why this lineup seemed to get everything right. The best performance on all of *Beast over Hammersmith* is "Hallowed Be Thy Name." No offense to Martin Birch or anyone else involved in making the band's 1982 studio album, but this is hands down the definitive version of the song, and there's no contest. It's almost unfair.

While some Maiden fans have never been sold on Dickinson's more refined approach to the Di'Anno material, he performs those songs with belligerence and abandon, especially "Phantom of the Opera," whose very rapidly paced lyrics are sung with perfect clarity and diction without sounding like a fussy conservatory exercise.

On the whole, *Eddie's Archive* mostly has more value as a collector's item than as something you would listen to, except in the case of the Hammersmith concert. Man, you can listen to that thing over and over and over again without ever getting enough of it. There's some excellent stuff on *BBC Archives*, too. But *Best of the 'B' Sides*? Ugh! What the hell did we do to deserve this? Anyway, if you see the now out-of-print *Eddie's Archive* and have available the hundreds of dollars that third-party sellers are asking for, treat it like a four-disc set by leaving *Best of the 'B' Sides* in the handsome metal container. You will never listen to it.

EDDIE THE HEAD, WHO CLEARLY FAILED TO ATTEND THE HUMAN RESOURCES DEPARTMENT'S SEXUAL HARASSMENT SEMINAR AT THE CORPORATE OFFICE.

IRON MAIDEN
EDDIE'S ARCHIVE

THE CASKET COLLECTION—
77 RARE RECORDINGS ON 6 DISCS
BBC ARCHIVES
BEAST OVER HAMMERSMITH
BEST OF THE B'SIDE
YOU CAN'T KEEP A GOOD CORPSE DOWN.

FOUR: THE THREE AMIGOS | 129

37
NO MORE LIES
IT WASN'T AN ACCIDENT

BRUCE DICKINSON, ADRIAN SMITH, STEVE HARRIS, DAVE MURRAY, AND JANICK GERS AT THE READING FESTIVAL ON AUGUST 28, 2005.

It would not be wrong to surmise that 2000's *Brave New World* was the album whose job was to reintroduce Iron Maiden to the fans who might have lost confidence in them during the 1990s. Some couldn't accept Bayley as the frontman, and others had even checked out after *No Prayer for the Dying*. *Brave New World* was designed to win back the fans they may have lost, and *Rock in Rio* was meant to cement that. In both cases, they succeeded in what they were intended to do.

The real test was the 2003 studio album *Dance of Death*. Anyone can make one good album and declare themselves comeback kids, but if the next one isn't any good, people will think it was a fluke. So, as vital as it was for *Brave New World* to herald the band's glorious twenty-first-century return, *Dance of Death* had to keep the rally going. Luckily, it did.

Dance of Death was made with the assistance of Kevin Shirley, who had worked with the band on *Brave New World*. It contained a first—the song "New Frontier" had been cowritten by drummer Nicko McBrain, who had never written a note of music for the band before. Dickinson and Smith also had a hand in writing it, and it's a solid, no-frills tune whose five-minute running time goes by very quickly. McBrain also instituted another Iron Maiden first on the song "Face in the Sand" by using a double bass pedal. Surprisingly, despite being the archetypal metal band, they had never used double bass, that staple of the genre's drumming.

The distribution of labor on the album's songwriting is pretty even. Harris has only one sole songwriting credit, "No More Lies," which is a real highlight of the album. It takes a couple of minutes to get going, which was quickly becoming a standard approach to the band's material. The songs increasingly used alternating dynamics and slow crescendos, which take time to build up properly.

Some listeners have complained that this iteration of Maiden risked becoming slaves to that formula and using the same approach to many songs. They were not wrong. Still, the album has too many good songs to pooh-pooh it. "Rainmaker" is compact and effective, and it almost—almost—flirts with pop melody.

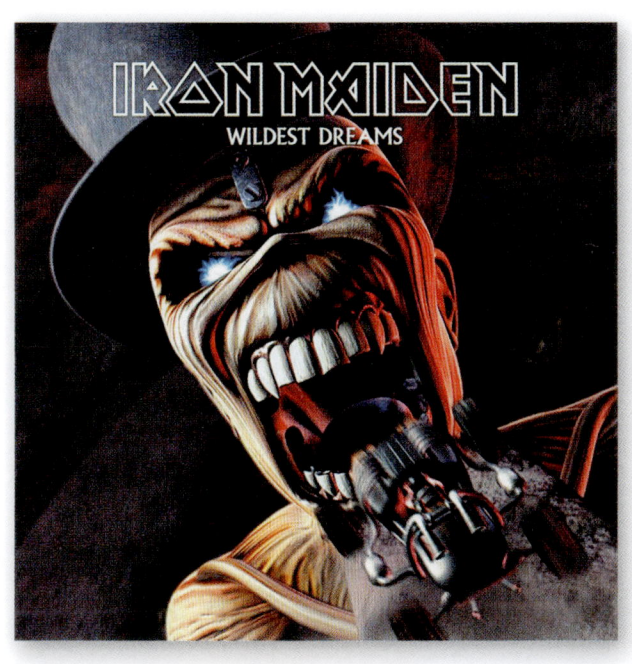

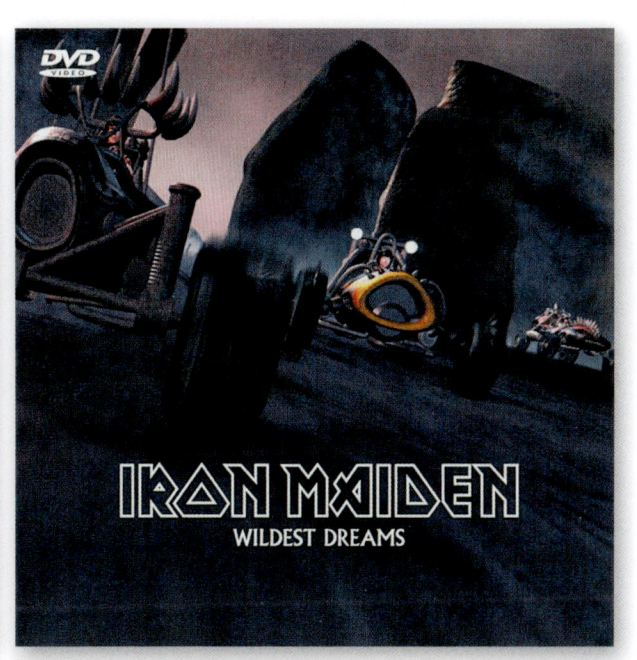

IRON MAIDEN LIVE AT OZZFEST IN DEVORE, CALIFORNIA, ON AUGUST 20, 2005. DURING THE CONCERT, AN ALLEGED CERTAIN SOMEONE WAS SAID TO THROW EGGS AT THEM WHILE THEY PERFORMED.

The anthemic "Gates of Tomorrow" is simply glorious. It's tempting to think that for this song, Harris took "The Angel and the Gambler" from *Virtual XI*, halved it from ten to five minutes, made the lyrics less repetitive, and turned it into something decent.

One song off this album that doesn't get nearly enough attention is "Montségur," which is based around a monstrously heavy riff that will make you bang your head involuntarily. This puts it in good company with other Iron Maiden songs, such as "Run to the Hills" or "Aces High," which make you react physically the second the music starts. It's one of those songs you can listen to all day, and while your family might tire of it, you won't.

The *Dance of Death* album caught a lot of flak for its cover, a cluttered affair that looked like someone had dropped five hits of acid and started playing with MS Paint, overlaying every prefabricated design element they could find. The website WhatCulture ranked it fifth in a feature called "10 Hilariously Terrible Album Covers and Why They Exist."

"The band asked artist David Patchett to provide the cover art," the article said. "The band randomly decided mid-way through the artist's drafting process to use a completely unfinished version of the artwork, which was still in need of substantial work."

While creating an album cover for a band of Iron Maiden's stature would seem like a plum gig for any visual artist, Patchett was so horrified that he asked to remove his name from the album credits. According to a Drowned in Sound article by James Lawrenson, Patchett probably made the right decision in turning it into an Alan Smithee album jacket.

"Heavy metal is known for its ridiculous cover designs, but this was just a bit shit," Lawrenson said.

Oh well, at least they got the music right. Critics generally were sold on the record, and Dom Lawson of *Kerrang!* gave it a rave review.

"*Dance of Death* is Iron Maiden's best album since 1988's *Seventh Son of a Seventh Son*," he wrote. "Heavier and darker than *Brave New World* and with none of that album's long-winded rambling, this is as passionate and fired-up as the band have EVER sounded."

Lawson took every opportunity to slag the Bayley albums in this review, a quite fashionable pastime of rock critics during the early 2000s. Meanwhile, the band went on tour, and their November 24, 2003, concert in Dortmund, Germany, was recorded and released in 2005 under the name *Death on the Road*. One of the songs is the Bayley era's "Lord of the Flies," and it joined "Sign of the Cross," "Man on the Edge," "Futureal," and "The Clansman" in the band's regular set lists. The band was proud of that era, and the naysayers could go pound sand.

38

THE LONGEST DAY
MAYBE THEY'LL STOP AFTER THE EIGHTH SONG?

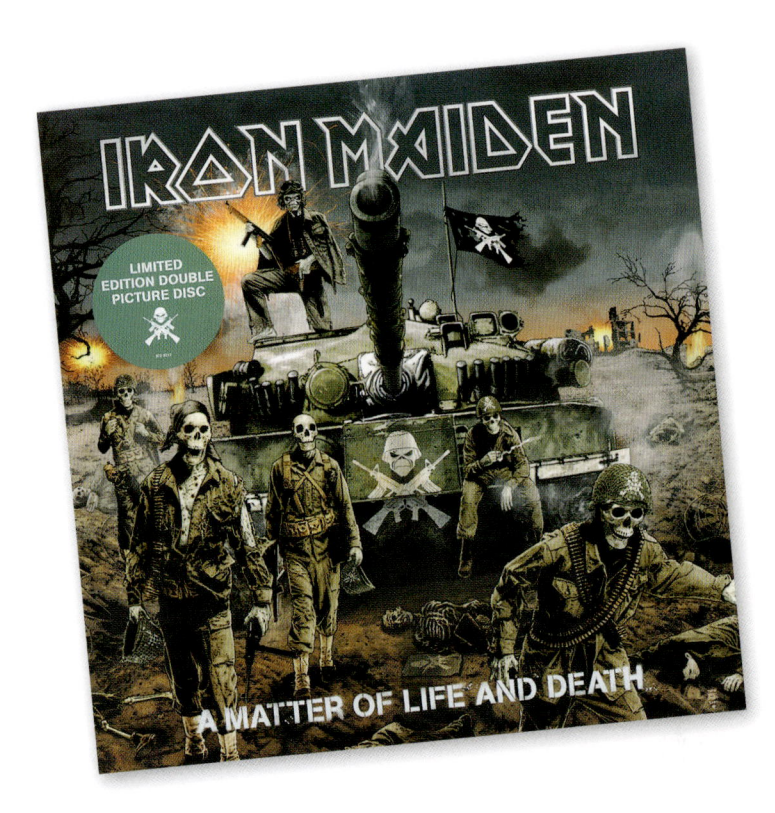

Iron Maiden's fourteenth studio album, *A Matter of Life and Death*, was released in 2006, and it marked a first for the band in any configuration—it debuted at number nine on the US *Billboard* chart, the first time any Maiden release had ever made the US top ten. It was a valuable lesson for aspiring musicians everywhere—if you believe in yourself and create compelling work, it will only take fourteen studio albums and twenty-six years to get in the US top ten.

The SoundScan system of tabulating album sales figured prominently in the band's improving fortunes. In the past, *Billboard* had done that by getting anecdotal information over the phone from record stores about what was selling, not exactly the most ironclad method of tabulation. SoundScan, introduced in 1991, was much more accurate, according to the *New York Times*.

"Three weeks ago, *Billboard*, the music industry's leading trade magazine, introduced a new and more accurate measurement system for compiling its pop album chart by using SoundScan, a computerized system that electronically counts records as they are being sold," the publication said.

This system changed overnight what many people thought were popular artists and records. As it turned out, a lot of music had been getting short shrift for years.

"It upended the conventional music business wisdom about what sold, as well as when and how," Michaelangelo Matos wrote in *Billboard* in 2021. "It revealed the popularity of several genres—alternative rock, country, hip-hop, harder metal—that had been seen as commercially marginal compared to bread-and-butter pop-rock bands."

While there are great bits all over *A Matter of Life and Death*, it's probably safe to assume that it sold as well as it did because of the band's relentless touring and recording schedule, which had kept them in the public eye since 1980. It is much less likely that it charted because of its hit sound since it didn't have one. The lead single, "The Reincarnation of Benjamin Breeg," was seven minutes long, and there was no single edit. While the song is good, nothing about it would send it up the charts like Cardi B's "WAP." The band had instead earned the right to do what they wanted, and the fans were right there with them.

It must be said, however, that at ten songs clocking in at seventy-two minutes, *A Matter of Life and Death* gets a bit trying to sit through. There are only so many hushed bass intros you can listen to before it starts to sound a bit repetitive. They didn't master the record either, so the sound is completely dry. Fans lapped it up anyway, and critics gave it very high marks. This included Andy Maclarty of the BBC.

STEVE HARRIS AT THE BELL CENTRE IN MONTREAL ON OCTOBER 10, 2006.

JANICK GERS IN QUEBEC CITY ON OCTOBER 9, 2006, AT COLISÉE PEPSI. SOME MORE CONSERVATIVE AND RISK-AVERSE IRON MAIDEN FANS HAVE EXPRESSED DISCOMFORT AT GERS'S FREQUENT BALLETIC LEAPING DURING CONCERTS BECAUSE IT'S NOT GRIM AND METAL.

"'For the Greater Good of God' and 'The Longest Day' are outstanding with the partnership of guitar, bass and drum (and now even keys) flowing and developing throughout," he said. "'Lord of Light' is one of those epic tracks destined to be listened to again and again—each time giving something new."

While more than one critic grumbled about the song lengths, James Christopher Monger wrote in *AllMusic* that long songs and extended instrumental passages are the whole point.

"On a record that positions beloved avatar [Eddie] on top of a tank with a machine gun leading a weary troop of skeletal soldiers to their doom, any act of brevity, no matter how expertly crafted, sticks out like a saxophone solo," he wrote.

Unfortunately for many people who saw that tour, the band did something unforgivable. They played their whole new record in its entirety, in order. This crime against humanity is worse than an unaccompanied thirty-minute drum solo or Fergie singing the national anthem. Gavin Allen of the *South Wales Echo* said as much in his review of the band's performance, calling the decision to play the whole album "selfish."

"When five tracks in, [Dickinson] confirmed they would play the whole album, there was a negative reaction; largely silence, even the odd boo," he wrote.

The band defended their decision, and to this day, they've made no apologies. Whether it came off well live is a matter of opinion, but Dickinson had said he only wanted to return to the band in 1999 if it was going to be a potent creative force that challenged its audience and didn't just trot out the oldies.

Amusingly, the very next thing they did was embark on the *Somewhere Back in Time* tour, which saw them spend most of 2008 and 2009 bringing their most popular 1980s songs to audiences. It may not have been an apology tour, but they were forgiven nonetheless.

ADRIAN SMITH IN QUEBEC CITY ON OCTOBER 9, 2006. STEVE HARRIS WAS HAPPY TO HAVE HIM REJOIN THE BAND FOR HIS TOP-NOTCH GUITAR PLAYING AND VERY VALUABLE SONGWRITING CONTRIBUTIONS.

39
"PLAY CLASSICS"
THE BAND FLIES AROUND ON ED FORCE ONE

The *A Matter of Life and Death* tour traveled the world in 2006 and 2007. Despite some complaints about playing their new album in its entirety, Dave Murray said in a 2006 interview with Christina Fuoco of *LiveDaily* that the band saw nothing wrong with it.

"We thought the songs were so strong it justifies playing them live," he said. "There's a lot of highs and kind of lows—there's a lot of moods with these songs. They're not just straight-ahead bang, bang, bang. There's quite a lot of quiet passages and where it changes tempos. The fans can stand there and listen to the music as opposed to going out there and bashing their head away for two hours."

The unsolicited feedback from audiences was hard to ignore. A clip made it to YouTube of Dickinson ripping up a sign thrown onstage by an audience member at Nassau Coliseum in Uniondale, New York. The sign said, "Play classics." In an interview with the *Friday Night Rocks* show conducted one day later, McBrain said the decision to play the entire album had been a calculated risk.

"We knew we were gonna get various amounts of flak for it," he said.

The band changed the set list for the 2007 leg of the tour. It was the twenty-fifth anniversary of *The Number of the Beast*, and there was no way of not acknowledging that from the concert stage.

That leg of the tour saw the band cut down the number of songs from *A Matter of Life and Death* to five and add four songs from the 1982 classic album. They also threw in "Wrathchild," "The Trooper," and other songs from the band's 1980s output. Iron Maiden may have set out in 2006 to promote their newest material unapologetically, but by the time 2007 rolled around, there had been a change in approach.

ED FORCE ONE, THE BOEING 757 PILOTED BY BRUCE DICKINSON AS THE BAND PLAYED VARIOUS CONTINENTS DURING THE SOMEWHERE BACK IN TIME WORLD TOUR.

IRON MAIDEN ON AUGUST 12, 2008, AT THE SZIGET FESTIVAL IN HUNGARY, WHICH BEGAN AFTER THE FALL OF COMMUNISM. IRON MAIDEN HAD PLAYED IN POLAND IN 1984, HELPING TO BUILD AN UNDERGROUND HEAVY METAL MOVEMENT BEHIND THE IRON CURTAIN. WHEN COMMUNISM FELL, MILLIONS OF HUNGRY EASTERN EUROPEAN HEAVY METAL FANS FINALLY GOT TO SEE THEM PERFORM.

The band fully embraced the new strategy in 2008 and 2009 when they embarked on their *Somewhere Back in Time* world tour. It coincided with the release of a compilation album by the same name, and in both cases, the set included only the band's classics from the 1980s. It even replicated elements from the *World Slavery* tour stage show.

It started in Mumbai, India, on February 1, 2008, and wound its way through Australia and Japan, North America, South America, and Europe. After hitting up the United Arab Emirates, it ended in Sunrise, Florida, on April 2, 2009. It was more than a year on the road, and the many far-flung cities in the itinerary were not ones you could drive the tour van into. That's why it was a boon to the "Three Amigos" lineup of the band that Dickinson had become a fully qualified commercial airline pilot, as he could take the band from one exotic destination to another in a Boeing 757, dubbed "Ed Force One" by the band.

The plane could carry the musicians, crew, and equipment to any country with a landing strip. In *Metal Storm*, the lead singer and trained aviator said this was the only practical way to tour many countries they wanted to visit.

"Looking at the list of places we would like to play we have always had problems joining up the dots," Dickinson said. "With sea containers in various places it slows down the whole touring process, which is fine if you want a holiday but not if you want to play. It's great to see places, but we don't want to sit around for a week waiting for gear to get from, say, Australia to South America, so this way we can get to more fans in more places en route in the same time period."

For his part, Harris was happy that Ed Force One would allow the band to bring back one of his favorite stage sets and take it to places the band had never visited before.

"I always loved the *Powerslave* show, which I think was arguably our most spectacular ever, so taking it out again is really going to be a lot of fun," he said. "Taking our own 757 really makes it a lot more flexible for us. . . taking us to some places we haven't been in a long while like Australia and some we have never been to like Columbia and Costa Rica. It's a lot of flying but will be well worth it."

LOVELY ENGLISH LAD AND HOMETOWN BOY NICKO MCBRAIN GRABS A CYMBAL IN LONDON IN 2008.

40

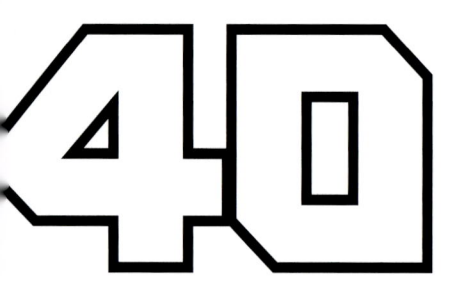

"AFTER 20,000 MILES, YOU RELAX A BIT"

BANGERFILMS GOES TO INDIA

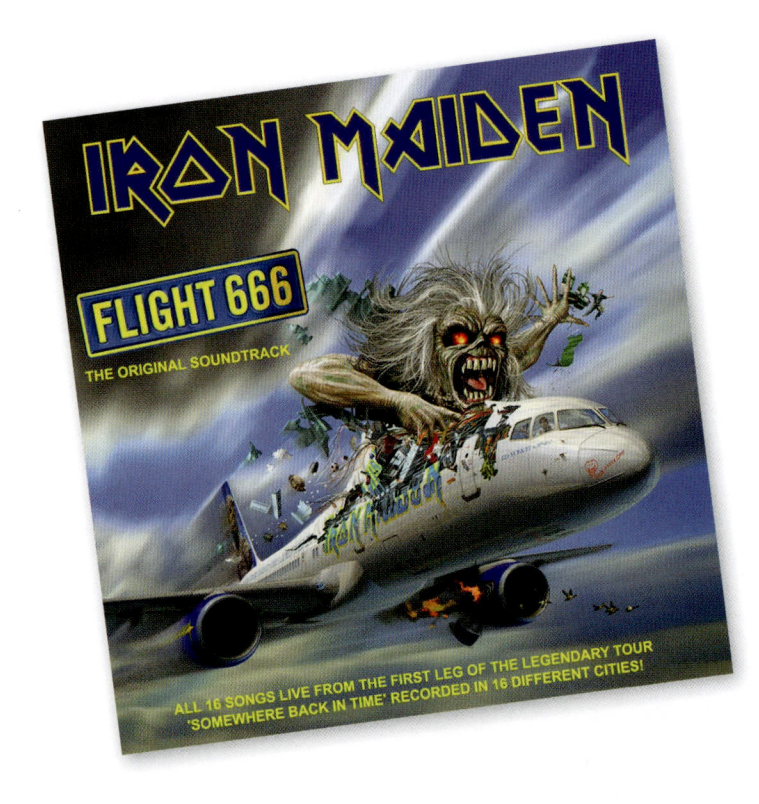

While Iron Maiden was filling the world's stadiums in 2008, the Canada-based Banger Films recorded the first couple of months of the tour. During February and March of that year, concerts from India to Japan and back to Toronto were filmed and used for the 2009 documentary *Iron Maiden: Flight 666*.

Banger Films had previously made the 2005 documentary *Metal: A Headbanger's Journey*, proving its metal credentials. They were the natural choice to create the documentary about the most metal band of all time.

Rather than spend a lot of its running time interviewing band members, the movie mainly stresses the performances and, most importantly, the fans. Dickinson told *Rolling Stone* in 2009 that was exactly the right approach.

"Two-thirds of the film is not about us," says Dickinson. "It's about the fans and the crew—which is the way it should be."

The filmmakers did have some understandable concerns about their pilot. Was he just some rookie who used his fame to finagle a pilot's license to boost his own ego, possibly leading to a horrific and deadly collision with a mountain? The short answer was "no."

"We were nervous the first day when he took off," said *Iron Maiden: Flight 666* codirector Scot McFadyen in Reuters. "After 20,000 miles, you relax a bit."

People who couldn't catch the movie theatrically were consoled by the home video and soundtrack album. In both cases, the performances crackle with the energy of a new band getting its first taste of playing in front of an enthusiastic audience. Despite pushing 30 years as a group, they play not just like their lives depend on it but like the lives of thousands of audience members depend on it.

They oblige in every case, with even "Aces High," the first song of the first concert, sounding equally aggressive and majestic. On *Live After Death*, Dickinson's tour-weathered voice showed some wear during that song. Here, he perfectly hits every operatic note and projects it so that even people in the nosebleed seats could feel like he was right next to them, hogging the armrest. Even the long ones, like "Rime of the Ancient Mariner," never show signs of flagging energy.

In the new millennium, Iron Maiden's live releases became more frequent, and it's tempting to look at each like they were just cash grabs, this one included. After all, there was already the home video, and almost all of these songs had already appeared on the band's previous live offerings. It was tempting to view the whole enterprise as a bunch of washed-up fifty-year-olds going through the motions for a paycheck.

Then, you listen to the thing and realize that the soundtrack to *Iron Maiden: Flight 666* is not only not a cash grab but contains some of the band's most outstanding live performances. It's an album you can keep going back to and enjoy, and every performance is solid and holds up.

It's also tempting to say that the band only sounds good because they're playing in new countries and are trying to showboat for new audiences. Well, the final performance on the Flight 666 soundtrack, "Hallowed Be Thy Name," was recorded in Toronto, where the band had made countless appearances since the *Killers* tour in 1981. In fact, according to the fan site Maiden Fans, they played in Toronto nineteen times as of 2017. So no, they weren't just excited to play somewhere for the first time.

The *Somewhere Back in Time* tour and the *Iron Maiden: Flight 666* documentary helped the band close the decade spectacularly. It had been rocky, starting with their decision to pink-slip Bayley and reorganize the band around three guitarists and the returning Dickinson. If the public hadn't accepted them, it would have been a lot of pain and suffering for nothing, but they were not only welcomed back but accepted by old fans, new fans, and people who were just curious what the fuss was all about.

A heavy metal flight attendant, Adrian Smith, Nicko McBrain, Bruce Dickinson, and Janick Gers at the Iron Maiden: Flight 666 premiere at the Kensington Odeon.

The DVD cover from Iron Maiden: Flight 666. While many bands release live products of dubious value, the performances in this film are all excellent and stand shoulder to shoulder with the band's best studio albums.

FOUR: THE THREE AMIGOS | 143

DOES IRON MAIDEN PLAY CLASSICAL MUSIC?

In 2009, Canadian rocker Neil Young was interviewed by *Guitar World*. While talking alternate tunings, interviewer Richard Bienstock asked him a question he probably didn't get very often.

"Were you aware of, say, Tony Iommi from Black Sabbath, another guy who tuned down his guitar?"

Young, to his credit, gamely answered the question and offered a nugget of wisdom to ponder.

"Not so much," he said of Iommi. "But I love that music. It's like classical rock and roll. The Scorpions, Iron Maiden. . . . That whole thing is quite strong."

Many heavy metal bands have been said to be "classically influenced," and Iron Maiden has been one of them with much frequency. But does the term apply? And if it does, which classical music are people talking about? The term describes a musical genre that spans hundreds of years and has taken many forms. So, do they mean something like Johann Sebastian Bach from the eighteenth-century Baroque period? Do they mean something like "The Rite of Spring" by Igor Stravinsky, composed two centuries later and said to have caused riots the first time it was performed?

Dr. R. Douglas Helvering, composer and host of the *Daily Doug* YouTube channel, said it's not just Iron Maiden who gets the "C" word flung at them willy-nilly. He said that the "classical influence" accusation is one that many heavy metal artists have had to deal with, partly because much guitar showboating in that genre consists of the rapid-fire playing of arpeggios, the three notes that make up a chord.

"People will say, 'Marty Friedman is neo-Baroque because he's doing a whole lot of arpeggios,'" he said. "Well, that's what any virtuoso player is going to do when they go to play their instrument. . . I don't hear functional tonality in the music of Iron Maiden. I hear modality, I hear power riffs, and I hear very good songwriting and storytelling, but not a ton of reliance on classical music."

Part of the issue is that the guitars and bass double each other's riffs and play them together in lockstep. It sounds glorious and is the building block of all heavy metal, but it's not a classical approach. Dr. Helvering said that would require more counterpoint and independent melodies juxtaposed against basslines. And while he was sure Steve Harris had a passing familiarity with classical music like everyone else, he didn't hear anything in the band's music that suggested he fancied himself a classical composer.

"He's not, in my opinion, saying, 'I know how to write like a classical composer does,' or 'I'm going to turn Bach into metal,'" he said.

He also noted that the band does things rarely—if ever—used in classical music, no matter the era. "The Rime of the Ancient Mariner" has a hushed middle section in which the bass plays a repeated augmented figure, and while it's exotic and not something you would hear on a Venom record, it still ain't classical music.

"That's something you don't hear in classical music," he said. "We don't use augmented chords very often."

He said that the chorus in "Aces High" functions in a way that nothing in classical music ever would. The chorus is in E minor, then goes up to the relative major key of G major, but the chord progression is actually in G minor. That means that the chorus behaves in a compositionally unique way that they don't teach you at music school.

Dr. Helvering explained that even though the song doesn't show any classical influence, that doesn't mean the music theory behind it isn't solid. When the chorus of "Aces High" plays and goes up to the higher key, he explained why it causes listeners to go into berserker mode, even after listening to it every day for forty years.

"Functionally, it gives the singer a quarter higher of a range," Dr. Helvering said. "So the intensity of the singer's voice is naturally going to just up the ante ever so slightly because they're singing everything a quarter of an octave higher. It gives just a little bit more intensity."

If Iron Maiden is not influenced by classical music, where do they get the inclination to play things that sound like it to the average heavy metal listener? He said that prog rock, the genre that gave us Yes and King Crimson, was hugely influential to how the band wrote music, and any classical music DNA that may have crept in can be attributed to that. Prog rock bands generally consist of elite musicians, such as Rick Wakeman of Yes, who can play anything. He received classical training before donning his sequined cape and putting on ice shows telling the story of King Arthur, so if you hear any classical music connection in the music of Iron Maiden, prog rock is likely where it comes from.

"Progressive rock music owes much of its pull to classical training," Dr. Helvering said.

While Iron Maiden may not be influenced by classical music, their music nonetheless sounds terrific when classical musicians play it. YouTube is chock-full of performances of classic Maiden tunes being played by classically trained musicians on harps, harpsichords, and violins, and they sound uniformly excellent. Natural, even.

In 2022, Ulf Wadenbrandt, conductor of the Sweden Symphony Orchestra, took the song "Fear of the Dark" and transformed it into a full orchestral piece performed by 160 musicians. Many performed over the teleconferencing platform Zoom, but it sounded great anyway. And even if it isn't influenced by classical music, Wadenbrandt didn't seem to think it mattered.

"Iron Maiden have quite simply written a great song that works perfectly for symphony orchestras," he told *Louder Sound*. "It's a magical arrangement that releases the orchestra's energy and fantastic sound."

BRUCE DICKINSON GETS HIS
SHERLOCK HOLMES ON AND
SOMEHOW MAKES IT METAL,
SOMETHING ONLY HE CAN DO. BUT
WHICH ONE'S WATSON?

FOUR: THE THREE AMIGOS | 145

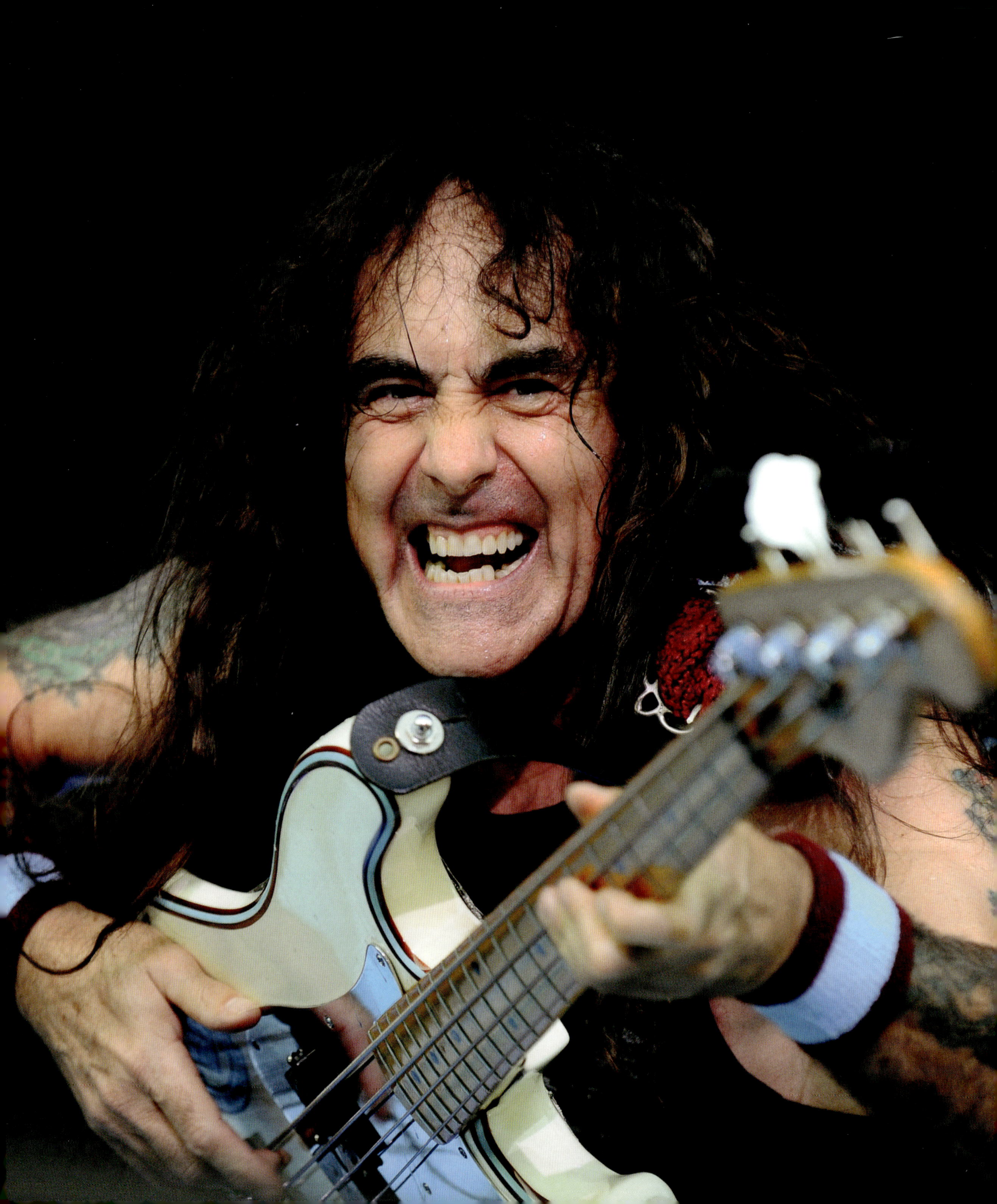

five

"WE'LL ALL PROBABLY DROP DEAD ONSTAGE"

41

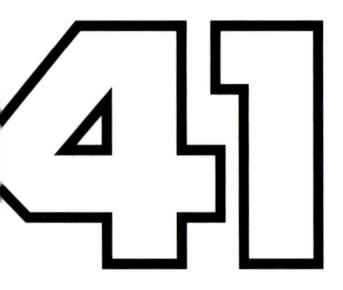

NO, IT'S NOT THE FINAL ALBUM

MAIDEN SHARES THE CHARTS WITH TAY TAY

The Final Frontier is Iron Maiden's fifteenth studio album. It was released in August 2010 and had a running time of almost seventy-seven minutes over the course of ten songs. The band had committed to a more progressive direction during the Bayley era, and by gum, they would keep exploring what they could do with a bunch of nine-minute and eleven-minute songs for as long as they could.

Upon its release, it reached the number four spot on the US charts, their highest yet. If the length of the songs made it difficult for radio stations to accommodate them, it didn't matter. They were selling out arenas, and record buyers picked up the album without even hearing it first—it was an automatic buy. According to *Billboard*, the band was now charting right alongside Eminem, Taylor Swift, and Lil Wayne, and it was all thanks to doing it the hard way with relentless touring.

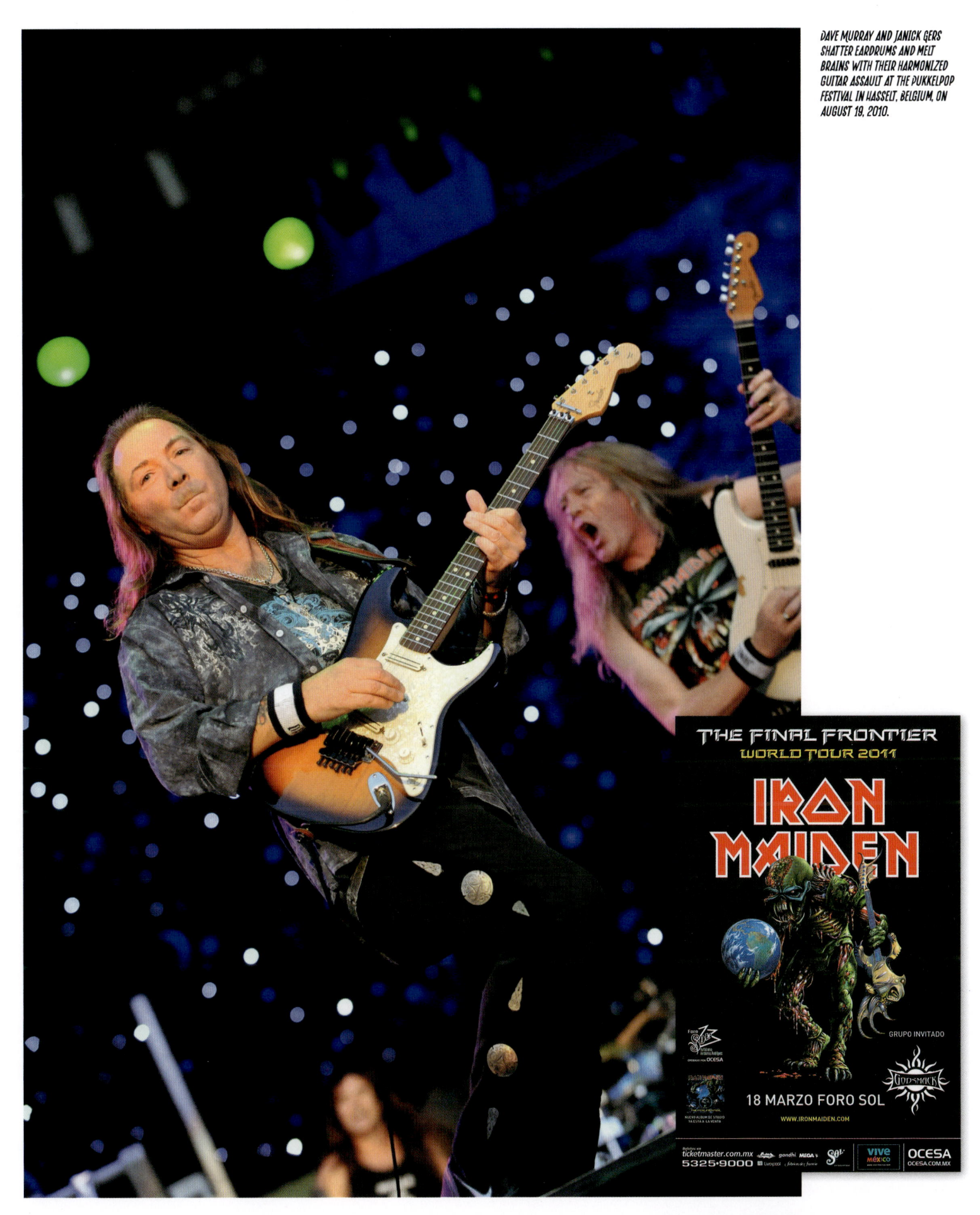

DAVE MURRAY AND JANICK GERS SHATTER EARDRUMS AND MELT BRAINS WITH THEIR HARMONIZED GUITAR ASSAULT AT THE PUKKELPOP FESTIVAL IN HASSELT, BELGIUM, ON AUGUST 19, 2010.

FIVE: "WE'LL ALL PROBABLY DROP DEAD ONSTAGE | 149

INSANE SKINSMAN, RESTAURANTEUR, AND WRISTBAND ENTHUSIAST NICKO MCBRAIN AT THE PUKKELPOP FESTIVAL IN HASSELT, BELGIUM, ON AUGUST 19, 2010.

150 | IRON MAIDEN AT 50

FLORIDA MEN DAVE MURRAY, BRUCE DICKINSON, AND ADRIAN SMITH PERFORMING ON APRIL 17, 2011, IN TAMPA.

Naturally, giving the album a title like *The Final Frontier* led to speculation that this was the band's last album. While they wouldn't confirm or deny that, Murray said that this six-piece version of the band would be the last one ever, and there would be no further changes. They had remained in the same iteration for eleven years now, their longest period without a lineup change, and Murray told *Rock News Desk* that this was the one that got it right.

"It's the strongest and most creative lineup Maiden has ever had," he said. "Also, it's my favorite lineup, and it's the same for most of the other guys. . . . We won't be changing anymore."

As far as the quality of *The Final Frontier*, it sure doesn't sound like a band that has quitting on their minds. As they had been doing for the past decade-plus, they explored progressive textures in the music, and much of it fared well. Interestingly, the best songs are the protracted epics, while the shorter and more radio-friendly ones are the least remarkable.

The album opens with "Satellite 15...The Final Frontier," which is really two songs sewn together. The first half is all buildup and crescendo, and it's a mechanical-sounding, dissonant section that recalls Voivod. After that bit, the song's second half starts, and it's a surprisingly "classic rock" FM radio type of tune based around a very simple riff and melody. It works, and both sections offset each other very well, but if you're in a hurry and want to get to the song part of the song, skip ahead to the 4:35 mark.

It's followed by four songs that are short by twenty-first-century Iron Maiden standards: "El Dorado," "Mother of Mercy," "Coming Home," and "The Alchemist." Strangely, that grouping creates a lull in the album simply because the songs aren't as good as the others. They sound like afterthoughts in comparison to the epics.

The last five songs on the album are all extended pieces, and they all work. One gets the sense that the band is getting much more satisfaction from writing sprawling compositions than compact ones.

Of all the epics that round out the album, "The Talisman" is the best. It starts in the same "quiet buildup" way that had become compulsory for the band as of 1995. Still, it never seems formulaic or like the band is trying to artificially manufacture an epic by sticking on long, slow introductory sections. Dickinson also pours a lot of genuine emotion into his performance, particularly in the section that starts with, "No there's no one going back, no there's not a second chance." He sounds like he means it.

"When the Wild Wind Blows" wraps up the album in all its eleven-minute glory. At this point, the band was doing what they wanted and had earned the right to craft material that might take a few listens to fully digest. The only real issue is that the length of this anthemic and inspiring song prevented it from being played live on any tours after 2011. They had other very long songs to perform!

42
TECH FINDS THE FANS...
...ALLEGEDLY

In 2012, Iron Maiden released *En Vivo!*, a live souvenir of their performance in Santiago, Chile, on April 10, 2011. Perhaps as an act of kindness for more impatient fans, the CD indexes "Satellite 15" and "The Final Frontier" as two separate tracks, so you don't have to listen to four-and-half minutes of buildup before you get to the actual song.

Half of the songs on *The Final Frontier* appear on *En Vivo!*, and they appear alongside tracks from *Brave New World* and *Dance of Death*, as well as 1980s classics like "The Trooper" and "Hallowed Be Thy Name." Maybe they had taken to heart some of the criticism of their decision to play all of *A Matter of Life and Death* live, and maybe they hadn't, but either way, *En Vivo!* is an excellent document of their performance in front of a rabid crowd.

As with *Rock in Rio*, the South American audience seems to fuel the band with their infectious enthusiasm, and you can hear Bruce et al. playing well off of them. This is not to say that *Death on the Road*, recorded in Dortmund, Germany, is a snooze. However, the band had visited Germany many times since its founding and had started visiting South America regularly only in the new millennium. They had played Rock in Rio in 1985, but an attempt to play in Chile in 1992 was met with resistance when local religious authorities said the band was Satanic, leading venues there to refuse to book them.

They played numerous South American dates during the Bayley era, but the continent became a regular tour stop in the new millennium. Kory Grow wrote in *Rolling Stone* that the band chose to visit South America due to certain data points and scientific findings.

Allegedly—*allegedly*—the band tracked BitTorrent traffic, which showed that many people in South America and Central America were illegally downloading the band's music. Rather than sue them all, the band took this rumored bit of information and extrapolated from it that they should be touring in that part of the world because that was where fans craved their music so badly they were willing to break the law to hear it. Allegedly.

While that bit of information has been disputed, what hasn't been is that the UK music analytics service Musicmetric found that Brazil, Chile, Colombia, Mexico, and Venezuela were among the top ten countries where people followed Iron Maiden on the platform formerly known as Twitter. The band saw a lot of increased activity from that part of the world on all its social media pages, welcoming over 3 million new people between 2011 and 2012.

According to *Blabbermouth*, 2012 was a triumphant year for Iron Maiden for another reason. Rock n Roll Ribs, a Florida barbecue restaurant co-owned by drummer Nicko McBrain, won the honor of "Best Ribs 2012" from the *New Times Broward-Palm Beach*.

While the band had always been about bringing it to the fans and exploring every nook and cranny of the globe where even a single new listener might exist, it must be said that it was in Maiden's interest to play these shows—according to *Rolling Stone*, the band's March 2, 2008 concert in Sao Paulo, Brazil, grossed over $2.5 million.

Obrigado, indeed.

ED FORCE ONE PILOT AND IRON MAIDEN SINGER BRUCE DICKINSON IN SANTIAGO, CHILE, ON OCTOBER 10, 2013, STILL ABSOLUTELY KILLING IT.

43

"A SUBTLE HINT OF LEMON"
MAIDEN CHECKS THE NATION-STATUS BOXES

TROOPER BEER, THE OFFICIAL IRON MAIDEN–BRANDED BEVERAGE MADE FROM BRUCE DICKINSON'S OWN RECIPE. WHILE THEY PROBABLY COULD HAVE GOTTEN AWAY WITH SLAPPING A BAND LOGO ON A MEDIOCRE PRODUCT, THEY MADE SURE THE BEER TASTED GOOD.

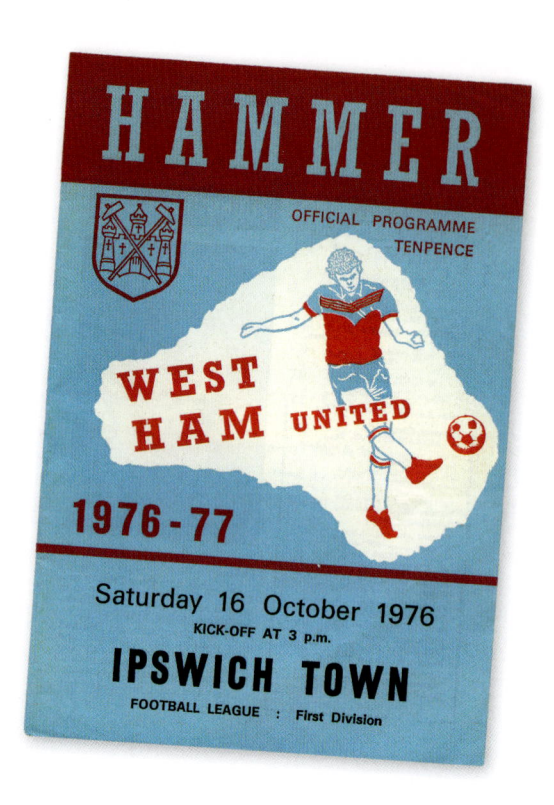

> "YOU CAN'T BE A REAL COUNTRY UNLESS YOU HAVE A BEER AND AN AIRLINE. IT HELPS IF YOU HAVE SOME KIND OF A FOOTBALL TEAM, OR SOME NUCLEAR WEAPONS, BUT AT THE VERY LEAST YOU NEED A BEER."
> —FRANK ZAPPA, *THE REAL FRANK ZAPPA BOOK*, 1989

Iron Maiden's members may not have realized it when Frank Zappa laid out the ideal conditions for a real country, but they were already on their way to fulfilling the criteria. While the late guitarist undoubtedly meant "football" in the American sense, to the rest of the world, football means "football," which Americans have decided they have to refer to as "soccer" because the former British colony is special.

In any event, the band founded its own football club in the 1980s, the better to emulate Harris's cherished West Ham United. They even put on games with journalists and professional athletes in 1998 to promote the *Virtual XI* album. According to *Metal Hammer*, this was more apparent when you opened the CD booklet than when you looked at the cover.

"They included a picture of the band all kitted up alongside some of the biggest footballers of the era," wrote Stephen Hill. "Clown prince of 90s football Paul Gascoigne, England hardman Stuart Pearce, French midfielder Patrick Vieira, flying Dutch winger Marc Overmars, Columbian forward Faustino Asprilla and arch poacher Ian Wright. Quite the team."

In whatever sense Zappa meant "football," it didn't change the fact that the band had checked that box. Additionally, they had their own airline, which consisted of a single 757 flown by their singer. And while they sadly never managed to secure their own nuclear weapons, they did check the third box of four in 2013 when they launched their own beer, called "Trooper."

The drink is made by Robinsons Brewery, a small, family-run brewery founded in 1849 in the British county of Cheshire. It was announced in March 2013 and described on its website as having "malt flavors and citric notes from a unique blend of Bobec, Goldings, and Cascade hops" with a "subtle hint of lemon." The recipe came from Dickinson, although Robinsons approached the band rather than vice versa.

"I'm a lifelong fan of traditional English ale," the singer said. "I thought I'd died and gone to heaven when we were asked to create our own beer."

The singer joked that he was on edge when sharing the recipe with the brewery. He may have sung before stadiums packed with thousands of crazed heavy metal lunatics, but creating a beer that tasted good and wasn't a novelty item was entirely different.

"I have to say that I was very nervous," the singer said. "Robinsons are the only people I have had to audition for in thirty years."

The label on the beer depicted the mascot Eddie as he appeared on the sleeve for the single release of "The Trooper," an easy choice. They had to change the label so the beer could be sold in Sweden, where "elements of war, weapons or aggression" are verboten on products being sold there. That little snag aside, the beer was quickly accepted by the ale enthusiasts of the world. In 2014, just one year after its rollout, it had sold 3.5 million pints. By 2018, it had sold 20 million pints.

The effort was so successful that the company rolled out other Maiden-branded beers. These include 666, which was Trooper with more alcohol; Red 'N' Black, which the official Trooper Beer site said has "a blend of chocolate and crystal malt [that] gives this full-bodied beer a roasted malt and caramel backbone," and even a nonalcoholic variant called "Running Free."

While it's tempting to dismiss Trooper beer as a stupid vanity product designed to fleece gullible fans, it wouldn't have sold in the quantities it did if people didn't like it. It certainly wouldn't have been expanded to a line of multiple iterations, including nonalcoholic, if people weren't buying it. Like everything else Maiden, the band refused to put their name on a product they weren't confident in.

When he's not playing bass for the most metal band of all time, Steve Harris enjoys being captain of the Iron Maiden football team, pictured on June 9, 2000, in Monza, Italy.

FIVE: "WE'LL ALL PROBABLY DROP DEAD ONSTAGE | 155

44

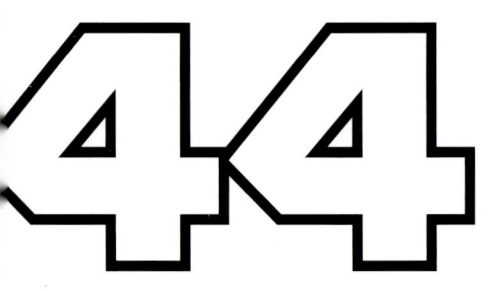

RIP CLIVE BURR
TRIBUTES POUR IN FROM MAIDEN NATION

While 2013 had been a good year for Iron Maiden, it also dealt the band its first major blow. On March 12 of that year, original drummer Clive Burr passed away from complications related to multiple sclerosis, just days after his fifty-sixth birthday. The next day, the band posted a tribute to him on its official website.

"We are deeply saddened to report that Clive Burr passed away last night," the message began. "He had suffered poor health for many years after being diagnosed with Multiple Sclerosis and died peacefully in his sleep at home."

It was a terrible knock for the band, who were on a break from their massive *Maiden England* tour. That jaunt began on June 21, 2012, in Charlotte, North Carolina, and, a few breaks in the itinerary notwithstanding, it continued until the final tour date, July 5, 2014, in Knebworth.

It coincided with the release of *Maiden England '88*, a document of the band's appearance at Birmingham's National Exhibition Centre in November 1988 during the *Seventh Son of a Seventh Son* tour. It was previously released as *Maiden England* on VHS and as a single disc in 1994, but this 2013 version contained the entire set list throughout two discs.

Almost half the songs derive from Burr's tenure with the band, and songs he played on have figured prominently in the band's set lists to the present day. He may have been out after *The Number of the Beast*, but Maiden never stopped playing the songs he performed on. He was still a big part of it thirty years later.

"Clive was a very old friend of all of us," Harris said. "He was a wonderful person and an amazing drummer who made a valuable contribution to Maiden in the early days when we were starting out. This is a sad day for everyone in the band and those around him and our thoughts and condolences are with his partner Mimi and family at this time."

Dickinson also weighed in, even though he and Burr had only made one album together in the group.

"He was a great guy and a man who really lived his life to the full," the singer said. "Even during the darkest days of his MS, Clive never lost his sense of humor or irreverence."

Tributes came in from all over the heavy metal world. The names and pedigrees of the musicians who made statements show just how influential Burr had been, even in the handful of years he was with the band. The three albums he played on were almost instruction manuals for anyone wishing to play heavy metal drums correctly.

"His style was inspiring and the albums he recorded with Iron Maiden are touchstones of my music education," said Dave Lombardo of Slayer. Paul Bostaph, the man who replaced Lombardo in Slayer twice and also pounded the skins for Exodus, Forbidden, and Testament, also gave a tribute to his fallen hero.

"His drumming has had and still has a strong influence on my playing style," he said. "Godspeed, Clive!"

People who didn't play the drums still recognized Burr's monumental influence. Slash of Guns N' Roses, David Ellefson of Megadeth, and Richie Faulkner of Judas Priest all gave tributes, as did Tom Morello of Rage Against the Machine.

"RIP Clive Burr, original Iron Maiden drummer, who rocked those first 3 records HARD," Morello said.

Greg Prato of *Rolling Stone* also gave big ups to Burr. The publication may have been ambivalent toward heavy metal over the years, but Prato understood what the drummer had brought to the band and said so in his obituary.

"It was Burr's drumming that proved a major ingredient on such early Maiden classics as 1980's self-titled debut, 1981's *Killers* and 1982's *The Number of the Beast*, and such headbanging anthems as 'Running Free,' 'Wrathchild,' and 'Run to the Hills.'"

While Burr's illness stopped him from playing drums and compromised his quality of life, his presence on the first three Maiden albums has stood the test of time and will continue to do so forever. If the only thing he had ever done was playing the cymbals during the chorus of "Run to the Hills," he would still be legendary. So rest in power, Clive Burr—you may be gone, but your playing on those albums is being copied by kids today who are just learning how to play the drums, and those records will still be classics a thousand years from now.

THE GREAT CLIVE BURR, WHO LEFT US MUCH TOO SOON IN 2013 AT THE AGE OF 56. EVERY ASPIRING DRUMMER SHOULD STUDY HIS PLAYING ON THE FIRST THREE IRON MAIDEN ALBUMS.

FIVE: "WE'LL ALL PROBABLY DROP DEAD ONSTAGE | 157

45
THE BOOK OF SOULS

DICKINSON TANGLES WITH THE BIG C

After finishing the *Maiden England* tour in 2014, the band went quiet. This was understandable, as they had been on the road for three years, and even the heartiest and most energetic person on earth might want a little break.

While Bruce Dickinson can credibly be described as the heartiest and most energetic person on earth, he went quiet for a different reason, and it was a big one. As the year was winding down, the singer had gone to the doctor, who found something you never want to hear that they found.

"Just before Christmas, Maiden vocalist Bruce Dickinson visited his doctor for a routine check-up," a statement on the band's official website read. "This led to tests and biopsies, which revealed a small cancerous tumor at the back of his tongue."

The statement was posted a couple of months after the discovery. Fans were shocked at the diagnosis, but the good news was that it had been caught early, and he had already received treatment for it.

"A seven-week course of chemotherapy and radiology treatment was completed yesterday," the statement continued. "As the tumor was caught in the early stages, the prognosis, thankfully, is extremely good. Bruce's medical team fully expect him to make a complete recovery with the all-clear envisaged by late May."

The statement said that Dickinson needed a few months to recuperate, and everyone was optimistic about his recovery. What they may not have expected was a new album that same year. It was recorded from September through December 2014, just before the discovery of the tumor.

It was released in the fall of 2015 under the title *The Book of Souls*, and when you listen to it, you would never guess the singer is ailing in any way. Dickinson sings like a man in perfect health who not only drinks wheatgrass juice but can bench-press 300 pounds. There's nothing to indicate that anything was wrong.

If you didn't enjoy the band's tendency to write long songs, you would have had a few issues with *The Book of Souls*. It's over 92 minutes long, a record in the annals of the band's albums. For the most part, the songs don't seem overlong, and similar to their previous studio album, *The Final Frontier*, the short songs are the least interesting. The absolute shortest song, "Tears of a Clown," is, shall we say, not great, and "Speed of Light," which was released as a single, is also subpar.

The good news is that two of the sprawling epics that exceed ten minutes—the title track and "The Red and the Black"—are glorious and earn every second of their running time. They may be long on the clock, but when you listen to them, you don't feel the length, "The Red and the Black" in particular.

The third and final epic on the album is the Dickinson-penned "Empire of the Clouds." At eighteen minutes, it's the album's centerpiece, and it's a significant achievement for the group, who at this point could have probably gotten away with calling themselves a progressive rock band. The days of short bursts of aggression had given way to a more thoughtful period in which the songs had more depth than the band generally got credit for. Maybe people groaned at the prospect of sitting through a song almost as long as "Close to the Edge" by Yes, but even at eighteen minutes, it was masterful.

The band spent most of the next two years on the road promoting the album. Rather than do a scaled-back tour to avoid placing too many burdens on the just-recovered frontman, they played in thirty-five countries, including such new territories as China, El Salvador, and Lithuania. They were flown there by their recovering singer, who clearly didn't give a toss about taking it easy at that point.

According to *Louder Sound*, the only change was that Ed Force One was no longer a 757. That had been swapped out in favor of a 747-400, a much bigger plane that required Dickinson to get additional training to pilot.

A document of the tour, *The Book of Souls: Live Chapter*, was released in November 2017. The performances are uniformly strong, and the band plays with their usual conviction. Everything on the record is worth hearing, again making it impossible to write this band off, even if every part of you wants to say, "What? *Another* live album?"

DOUBLE, DOUBLE, TOIL AND TROUBLE. BRUCE DICKINSON PERFORMS BESIDE HIS CAULDRON ON THE BOOK OF SOULS TOUR IN FORT LAUDERDALE, FLORIDA, ON FEBRUARY 24, 2016.

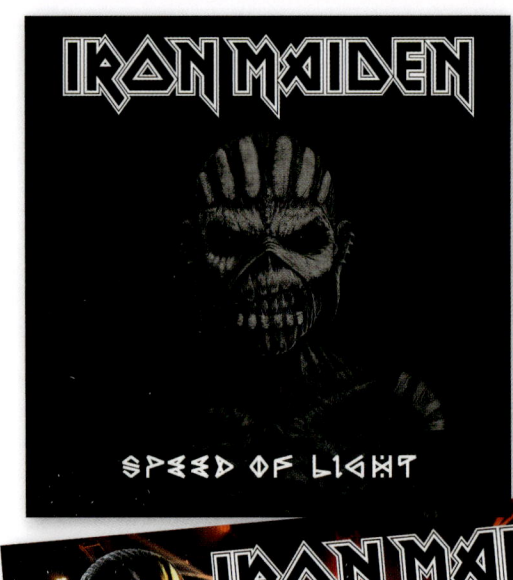

Janick Gers during the Book of Souls tour in 2017. The band chose not to play "Run to the Hills" on this jaunt, causing many furrowed brows and much consternation among the fans.

Nicko McBrain sits atop the drum throne in Shanghai, China, on April 26, 2016. By this point, performing in countries never visited by Western artists was old hat to the Maiden guys.

Honestly, it's hard to believe the singer on this album had only just dodged the Big C, particularly in a part of his body that he needed to sing. The fact that his performance is as strong as it is—"Children of the Damned" on this thing is a beauty—and shows no signs of physical compromise means he damn well should be proud, and everyone should hear him sing every chance they get.

One person especially inspired by Dickinson's recovery was his friend and bandmate McBrain. He said that the singer's recovery had inspired him so much that it had led him to stop drinking.

"When he got the all-clear, I looked at Bruce and thought, 'Here's my mate, he's been through hell, beaten cancer, and none of it was his fault,'" McBrain said in a 2016 interview with *The Drummer's Journal*. "And there I was, putting myself through hell, too, except I was doing it to myself with drink . . . I knew my drinking was getting bad when I saw footage of an interview I'd done when I was pissed . . . I was slurring words and not making any sense. I don't remember doing the interview at all."

He admitted that it was a struggle sometimes to avoid alcohol when everyone around him was drinking. However, ultimately, he knew his priorities and what mattered.

"I'm just glad Bruce is alright," he said.

JANICK GERS, STEVE HARRIS, AND DAVE MURRAY TEAM UP TO DESTROY ANOTHER CITY WITH RAPID-FIRE HEAVY METAL ARTILLERY ON THEIR BOOK OF SOULS TOUR IN 2017.

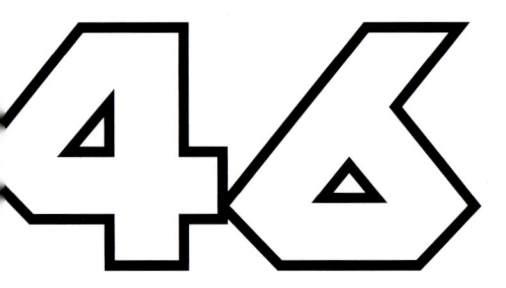

46
LEGACY OF THE LOCKDOWN
COVID-19 THROWS A CURVEBALL

Iron Maiden shared some great news on their official website in 2018. They were hitting the road again for the *Legacy of the Beast* tour. This would be another intercontinental trek that would take them to every corner of the globe.

The tour was intended to coincide with the band's new mobile game and comic book of the same name, and a chunk of material from the 1980s was to feature prominently in the set list. Manager Rod Smallwood said on the band's website that this followed a carefully laid plan.

"We've been following a particular touring cycle ever since Bruce and Adrian rejoined Maiden at the start of the millennium, alternating new album tours with 'History/Hits' tours," he said. "For this History/Hits tour we decided to base the theme around the *Legacy of the Beast* name."

The tour began on May 26, 2018, in Tallinn, Estonia, and it was a rousing success, being extended beyond its original ending date twice, in 2019 and again in 2020. That last excursion was intended to see the band perform dates in Australia, New Zealand, and Asia, where they would play in the Philippines for the first time in their history.

Unfortunately, there were problems—specifically, COVID-19 problems. In March 2020, public events worldwide began to be postponed or canceled entirely due to the pandemic. Maiden postponed their remaining concert dates until 2021, but when the world didn't automatically go back to normal with a snap of the fingers, they pushed it to 2022.

They made the best of a crappy situation by taking recordings culled from their four-night stint in Mexico City in September 2019 and releasing them on a double-disc set with the very long title *Nights of the Dead, Legacy of the Beast: Live in Mexico City* in 2020. It was a welcome distraction for people living in their pajamas, attending Zoom meetings, and wondering if it was the apocalypse.

Recorded in front of a very enthusiastic crowd at Palacio de los Deportes, the band makes good on its promise to play selections from its 1980s era, opening with "Aces High" and going on to play "The Trooper," "Flight of Icarus," and "The Evil That Men Do." They also threw in a few surprises, such as "The Clansman" and "Sign of the Cross" from the Bayley era. They even perform "For the Greater Good of God," their runaway hit single from the *A Matter of Life and Death* album.

The album was likely to emerge whether the pandemic happened or not since it was now customary for the band to record its concerts and release a tour souvenir every time. This tour would have been no different, and the fans would have bought it. However, the pandemic happened, and this album became essential listening. It was an artifact from the Before Time and suggested the tantalizing possibility that this all might blow over one day. There was precious little else to get excited about then, but this album indicated that there might be something to look forward to in the future. At the time, it meant a lot.

Unfortunately, in 2020, the sad news came that the band's longtime producer, Martin Birch, had passed away. Tributes poured in from all over the hard rock and metal world, with artists such as Black Sabbath's Tony Iommi and Whitesnake's David Coverdale praising him. People from the Maiden family also gave tributes.

"He was just absolutely brilliant," Harris said on the band's official website. "He wasn't just a producer; he was a hands-on engineer, too, so he knew how to get a great sound. He was also fantastic at motivating people; he just had a knack of getting the best out of you."

Dickinson credited Birch with helping him take his vocals to the next level.

"Martin was a mentor who completely transformed my singing," he said. "He was not a puppeteer; he did not manipulate the sound of the band. He just reflected it in the best possible way."

BRUCE DICKINSON IN COPENHAGEN, DENMARK, ON JUNE 5, 2018. YOU GET THE FEELING THE GUY LIKES PLANES.

FIVE: "WE'LL ALL PROBABLY DROP DEAD ONSTAGE | 163

STEVE HARRIS IN OSLO, NORWAY, ON JUNE 23, 2022. WHILE NORWAY IS THE WORLD CAPITAL OF BLACK METAL, THE MAIDEN GUYS FAILED TO BURN DOWN ANY STAVE CHURCHES WHILE VISITING.

47

THE WRITING ON THE WALL

SECRET UNRAVELED BY ATTENTIVE FANS

In 2019, Dickinson's past returned to haunt him in the best possible way. He was made an honorary citizen of the city of Sarajevo. He had performed there in 1994 during his time away from Iron Maiden, doing so at a time when he and the members of his band could have been killed just for being there. The city's mayor, Abdulah Skaka, presented him with the award.

"The arrival of Mr. Dickinson in Sarajevo in 1994 was one of those moments that made us in Sarajevo realize that we will survive, that the city of Sarajevo will survive, that Bosnia-Herzegovina will survive," he said in the Associated Press.

That same year, something else happened in Maiden World that was very cool. The band recorded an entire new album without telling anybody, then kept it a secret for two years. It emerged in 2021.

According to *Blabbermouth*, the Italian fan site Maiden Concerts conjectured that the band was recording something when they learned all the band members, their wives, and coproducer Kevin Shirley were in Paris, better known as the home of the Guillaume Tell recording studio. Furthermore, Dickinson made veiled comments about new music coming "sooner than you think."

Other than that, the whole enterprise had been successfully kept under wraps. In 2021, four days after the album's release, McBrain told radio station WGRD how this could happen in this day and age without news leaking, to say nothing of the album itself leaking. Basically, Harris had the only copy.

"There were no copies sent to anyone," the drummer said. "We were all sworn to absolute secrecy with it. We couldn't even tell our friends about it."

News of the album's release came in July 2021, just two months before its September release date. The first single, "The Writing on the Wall," was released at that time along with an animated video, and the album would have the very commercial title of *Senjutsu*. This Japanese word means "tactics and strategy."

The album artwork featured a Samurai Eddie, and the running time was 82 minutes. Since a single compact disc can't hold more than 80 minutes of audio, it was a two-disc set to accommodate those two extra minutes.

"They certainly know how to make an entrance," Paul Travers wrote in *Kerrang!* "The title track is easily their finest opener since "The Wicker Man" from 2000's *Brave New World*, and one of the heaviest tracks they've ever cut, opening on dramatic war drums and one of their chunkiest ever riffs. . . . 'Stratego' giddies things up to a familiar gallop and is as compact as modern Maiden gets, driven by simple refrains and clean melodic leads. Then 'The

Writing on the Wall' throws a wonderful curveball, with heavy blues-rock guitars and a blazing solo. This one is credited to Bruce and Adrian and could easily have slotted into Bruce's late-'90s solo album, *The Chemical Wedding*—which is very much a compliment."

If you don't like the band's longer songs, then you really, really won't like the last three songs on *Senjutsu*. "Death of the Celts," "The Parchment," and "Hell on Earth" together add up to over 34 minutes of music, also known as the entire running time of Black Sabbath's *Master of Reality* album from 1971. But let's not fixate on such trivial concerns. The album was a soaring and inspiring collection that showed the band continuing to break new ground, and yet again, the three longest songs at the end of the album are the best ones, especially "The Parchment."

Once again, the band had chosen to exercise their right to do whatever the hell they wanted, commercial considerations be damned. One must also commend them on doing whatever they had to do to keep the album a secret for two years—a secret from the media, a secret from the music industry, and a secret from all but the most dedicated fans willing to put in the sleuthing.

FIVE: "WE'LL ALL PROBABLY DROP DEAD ONSTAGE | 165

48

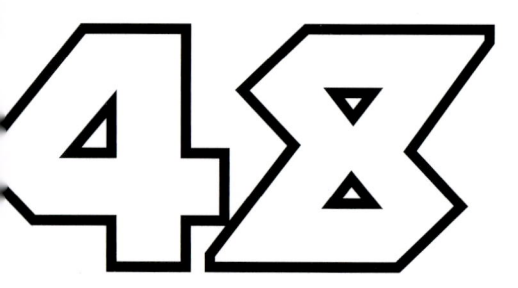

"I'LL BE FOREVER GRATEFUL"

THE BAND HELPS AN OLD FRIEND

Iron Maiden parted ways with their original singer, Paul Di'Anno, in 1981, but he never stopped playing music. He played in various bands, including Killers and later Praying Mantis, with former Iron Maiden guitarist and Steely Dan enthusiast Dennis Stratton in tow. None of those bands would climb to the same dizzying heights as Maiden, but he seemed to be enjoying himself.

Di'Anno had an unfortunate run-in with the authorities in 2011 when he was jailed for fraud. According to the *Guardian*, he claimed he was too disabled to work after an injury, but unfortunately for the singer, videos were posted to YouTube showing him performing, and they were seen by the Department for Work and Pensions. Prosecutor James Newton-Price showed no mercy when detailing the singer's actions.

"His touring took him to Europe, India, Brazil, Canada, Russia, and Mexico," Newton-Price said. "There is footage on YouTube of over 50 live performances between 2004 and 2007. He admitted in an interview at one of his concerts in 2005 that he was living in Brazil for a time and that he played to crowds of 10,000 people."

Di'Anno's health had suffered numerous setbacks. According to *Blabbermouth*, he had surgery in 2016 to remove an abscess on his lungs that was "rugby ball–sized." He also required knee replacement surgeries after being in numerous motorcycle accidents. Di'Anno was ultimately forced to perform while sitting down to give his legs a break.

In December 2019, he spoke with the Spanish website MariskalRock.com and gave the details of surviving a deadly infection four years prior.

"I had sepsis in Argentina," he said. "I just about made it home to England and then straight to hospital. I've been in and out of the hospital for four years now. I had operations done on both legs. I [haven't been able to] walk for four years. It's been very, very tough for me at the moment. Because of the sepsis, I keep getting infections, so they can't do the operations on my legs and stuff like that when they want to do them. . . . I haven't stopped playing music, and I've got no plans to retire—I wanna keep playing—but I need to get well."

He revealed that he had caught another infection two weeks earlier. His health had taken a bad turn on a flight home to England from Argentina, but he didn't understand how bad it was until he was home.

"I didn't realize I was actually dying," he said. "When I actually got home and I collapsed on the floor, I had my cell phone with me. I was on my own, 'cause my wife and kids were over in America. I got the ambulance people. They came down and they kicked my door in and took me to the hospital. I spent eight months in that hospital. . . . And you've got 45 minutes to pump you full of antibiotics or you'll die. I just about made that. Eight months recovery there, then into a care home for another three months, and then I moved into this new house of mine, which is adapted for wheelchair users at the moment . . . now I've got this other thing called MRSA, which you get from being in hospital, which is unfortunate. But, anyway, at the moment, I'm clearing out very well, so I'm waiting for the next call I get, which will be for surgery, and get things done."

In 2021, a crowdfunding campaign was launched to help Di'Anno raise money for knee surgery, which the JustGiving page said he had put off "for the past 5–6 years" but now wished to get done quickly by going the private route. He finally had the surgery in September 2022. The following year, he revealed that his former bandmates had pitched in to help pay for it after he ran out of money.

"The last bit of the treatment, the band was really cool," he told Mexico's *MB Live*. "They paid for the last couple of months' worth of treatments, which was good. I'll be forever grateful for that."

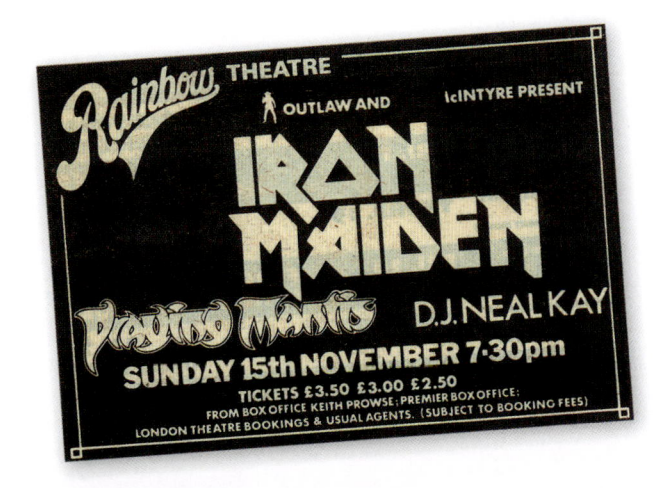

PAUL DI'ANNO PERFORMS AT HARD ROCK HELL ON DECEMBER 4, 2010. HE EXPERIENCED HEALTH PROBLEMS THAT PLAGUED HIM HIS ENTIRE LIFE, AND HIS FORMER IRON MAIDEN BANDMATES STEPPED UP TO HELP PAY HIS MEDICAL EXPENSES, JUST AS THEY HAD DONE FOR FORMER DRUMMER CLIVE BURR.

RAINBOW THEATRE
FINSBURY PARK
IRON MAIDEN
JUNE 20th
£3   7·30
STALLS
Incl. VAT
N 49
TO BE RETAINED   For conditions of sale see over

49

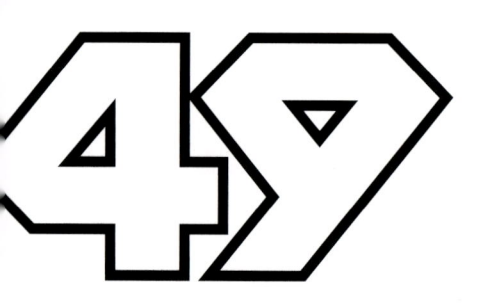

A MESSAGE FROM NICKO
"I CAN'T GET IT"

On August 3, 2023, Nicko McBrain released a video to the band's YouTube channel with a very bland and innocent title, "A Message from Nicko." What could it be? Had he gotten a new endorsement deal with Paiste?

It turned out to be an announcement of something with the potential to end his career. He revealed that he had suffered a stroke in January 2023, which had paralyzed the entire right side of his body from the shoulder down.

For a drummer, that could have been the end of the story right there. But just as Def Leppard gave their friend and drummer Rick Allen a chance to prove he could still play after losing his left arm in a car accident, Iron Maiden did the same for their drummer.

He underwent ten weeks of physical therapy before joining the band for rehearsals in May. Rod Smallwood wrote in the video's comment section on behalf of himself and the entire band, expressing admiration for the drummer.

"We honestly did not know if he would be able to play a whole show until band rehearsals started in May, and there was just so much support for him from the band and then genuine relief for all when we saw he was going to be able to do it," the manager said.

In 2024, McBrain conceded that he had not been able to recover 100 percent of his drumming skills after the transient ischemic attack. He told the *Washington Tattoo* podcast some of the more rapid-fire fills that were trademark parts of certain Iron Maiden songs were not possible for him anymore, no matter how much true grit he put into recovering his abilities. If the song he was playing wasn't very fast, he could play everything he used to play, but if it was one of the band's high-tempo ragers, he couldn't do it.

"I can't do a 16-note [sic] roll going into 32nd-note rolls anymore," he said. "So I've had to adjust my fills now. I mean, I don't play 'The Trooper' fill anymore because I can't get it."

McBrain's perseverance in the face of a potentially career-ending medical event is truly impressive. At the same time, it's not that surprising. He's always been defiant in the face of setbacks, as he related to *The Drummer's Journal* in an anecdote about his uniquely shaped nose, which he got courtesy of a fistfight with an old friend.

"I had a fight at school with one of my best mates, Peter Beecham," the drummer said. "He broke my nose . . . it started off with a duffle bag fight, then he clobbered me. We started a slapping fight and I clapped him one. He hated it, 'You fucking bastard!' And the fists came out. It was after school, everybody came in the circle, 'Fight! Fight! Fight!' He clobbered me good, the bastard."

McBrain summed up the situation in his incomparable way, giving his former school chum a remote update on his condition now that he was an adult. The other kid may have broken his nose, but the drummer took the long view.

"Look what you did," he said. "Look where I am now, though—fuck you!"

McBrain announced that December 7, 2024, would mark the end of his touring career with Iron Maiden, although he did not leave the band. Simon Dawson of Steve Harris's side project British Lion was announced as the group's new touring drummer.

NICKO MCBRAIN AT HIS ROCK N ROLL RIBS RESTAURANT IN CORAL SPRINGS, FLORIDA, ON NOVEMBER 25, 2019. THE DRUMMER SUFFERED A STROKE IN JANUARY 2023 AND RETIRED FROM TOURING ON DECEMBER 7, 2024. HE DID NOT LEAVE THE BAND AND STILL INTENDS TO CONTRIBUTE IN THE STUDIO, BUT HIS RETIREMENT FROM TOURING IS WELL DESERVED.

50
RIP PAUL DI'ANNO
"END OF STORY"

THE GREAT PAUL DI'ANNO, IRON MAIDEN'S ORIGINAL SINGER, WHO GAVE THE BAND MUCH OF ITS INITIAL STREET CREDIBILITY. THIS GIANT OF A MAN LEFT US IN 2024 AT THE AGE OF 66.

On July 13, 2024, something happened that had never happened before, and it was strange that was the case. Longtime Iron Maiden singer Bruce Dickinson met Paul Di'Anno, the singer he had replaced.

The meeting took place in Zagreb, Croatia, where Dickinson was promoting his new solo album, *The Mandrake Project*, with his band. He had joined Maiden forty-three years earlier, and you'd think the two would have run into each other at least once in all that time. But be that as it may, the two men had never met face-to-face until then.

In the intervening years since leaving the band, Di'Anno had many opportunities to be bitter. While he always spoke his mind and never shied away from criticizing things he felt were worth criticizing, such as Harris and Smallwood's control over the group, he was gracious and complimentary toward the band and its camp most of the time.

In a 2022 interview with the Greek *Rock Hard* publication, he was asked whether the band had treated him well when it came to money. He had no qualms about setting the record straight on that score. Just as the band had helped Clive Burr with medical expenses in the 2010s, they had helped their original singer as well. For all the ups and downs and lineup changes, the band was a unit, if not a family, and they were not going to leave a man on the field of battle, no matter what had been said in the press decades earlier.

"I got paid very well," he said. "They looked after me. End of story."

Sadly, on October 21, 2024, just three months after meeting Dickinson, Di'Anno passed away at the age of sixty-six. The cause of death was not released until the following month on his official Facebook page.

"His sisters Cheryl and Michelle confirmed the following," the post said. "He had a tear in the sac around the heart and blood filled inside it from the main aorta artery and that caused the heart to stop. . . . Paul's death was instantaneous and hopefully painless. May he rest in peace."

On October 22, the day after Di'Anno's passing, Dickinson was tasked with paying tribute to his predecessor during their performance in St. Paul, Minnesota, during their *Future Past* world tour. After calling the late singer a "groundbreaking" figure, he led a moment of silence, followed by a familiar refrain.

"Paul, if you're listening, this is a little message from Minneapolis to wherever you are, upstairs or downstairs," Dickinson said. "Minneapolis, for Paul Di'Anno, scream for me!"

Despite losing the man who fronted the group when they presented more like a gang of toughs than virtuoso musicians with eighteen-minute songs about blimps, Maiden kept on, just as they did when Dickinson had cancer, and McBrain had a stroke.

The members of the band have suffered their share of physical health problems, emotional problems, popularity problems, you name it. In the face of that, it's natural that some might think those guys have had enough. Maybe they should hang it up. Maybe they should retire. Dickinson responded to the R slur—retirement—as only he could.

"We're not planning to retire at all, really," he said on the podcast *Full Metal Jackie*. "I think we'll probably drop dead onstage."

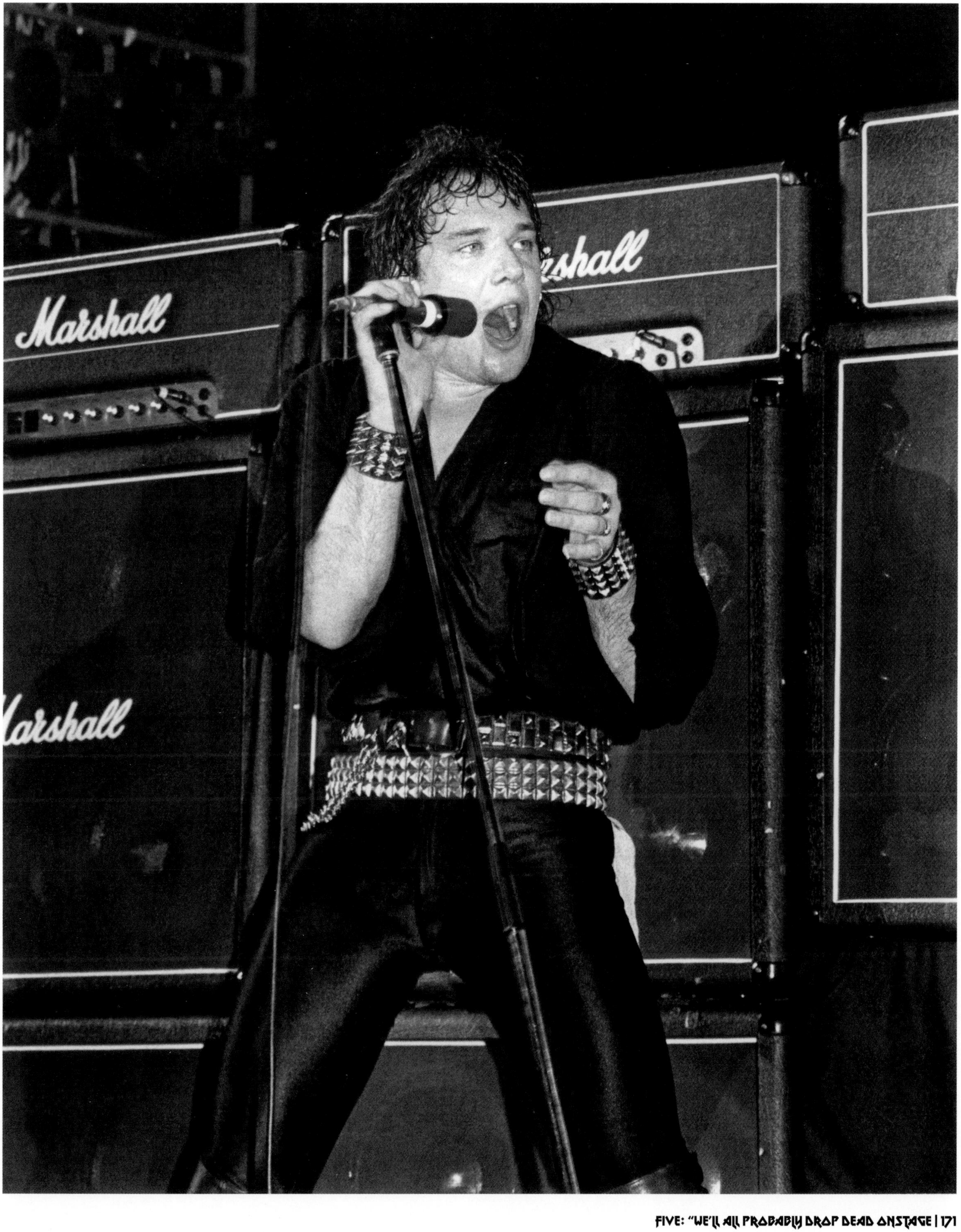
Marshall
Marshall
Marshall

THE MAN WHO WOULD NOT DIE
"A LOT OF LUCK, A LOT OF HELP"

After being shown the exit by Iron Maiden in 1999, Blaze Bayley admitted that he initially took the news pretty hard. He had fronted one of the biggest bands in the world for five years and guided them through a period in which the entire heavy metal genre was facing a downturn, and now he was being asked to step aside.

Eventually, he formed his own band called Blaze and released the album *Silicon Messiah* in 2000, one year after his exit from Maiden. Due to legal and financial matters too murky to sum up neatly, he renamed the effort Blaze Bayley, releasing the extremely heavy album *The Man Who Would Not Die* in 2008.

Mostly, he spent his time grinding out albums and touring. For a man who had played in front of thousands of people at one point, he seemed much more comfortable playing clubs and small theaters in parts of the world that many bands didn't visit.

If he could have spent every day of his life playing for rabid audiences who were so close he could smell them, that would have been his ideal version of the Bill Murray movie *Groundhog Day*. He even toured Russia in 2012 and 2013 with Paul Di'Anno, which was either a wonderful gesture for longtime Maiden fans or an expert troll.

It had taken a long time and a lot of hard work, but Bayley eventually established himself as a solo artist in his own right. While he remained forever grateful for the experience of fronting Maiden, he didn't want to be "Blaze Bayley of Iron Maiden." He just wanted to be himself, and he was.

He had been dealt a massive blow in 2008 when his wife, Debbie Hartland, suffered a fatal stroke, but he kept touring, taking to his official website to tell his fans how much their support was keeping him going.

"Through these darkest of days you have stood with me," he wrote. "You have held me up. . . The knowing of this unusual and yet certain bond you have given me has held me together."

Getting ousted from an internationally beloved band and losing one's spouse would probably be enough tragedy to break anybody, but he had pulled through. Then, on March 26, 2023, Bayley's management announced some *really* bad news.

"We sincerely regret to announce that Blaze had a heart attack at home yesterday evening," the announcement said. "He is in good spirits in the circumstances but utterly disappointed to have to postpone our imminent shows."

He eventually had to undergo quadruple bypass surgery. That's a lot of coronary arteries, and it demonstrates how severe the heart attack was—Bayley could easily have dropped dead right there. But he got through the surgery, and on April 19, 2023, less than a month after the heart attack, he was discharged from the hospital.

Less than two months later, Bayley took to YouTube to thank the fans for their support and concern while he recuperated. He thanked them from behind a stack of preordered live CDs that he was in the process of autographing one by one. Clearly, it was going to take a hell of a lot more than a mere life-threatening medical emergency to stop him.

"I have survived," he said. "Thank you so much for your good wishes, thank you for your concern . . . I hope that I will see you back in action at the end of the year. I will be onstage."

As promised, he returned to the stage and resumed his activities. It's remarkable that he did it as quickly as he did, but he wanted to get back to the life he loved, so it's understandable.

Not to take anything away from him as an individual, but perseverance in the face of terrible odds is a very Maiden quality, as Dickinson showed post-tumor and McBrain showed post-stroke. The band has always been about doing whatever it took to make things happen, and despite being a solo musician for twenty-five years, it's possible that some scintilla of his determination in the face of long odds may have had something to do with his time in Maiden.

Furthermore, while many musicians who part ways with famous groups make a whole second career out of feuding with their former bandmates—cough cough Roger Waters cough cough—Bayley never engaged in that for a minute. He has remained gracious, never uttering a bad word about his former bandmates. He was even insightful about the chilly reception he got from some fans in the 1990s and said he understood why some were slow to accept him, if they did at all.

"When your girlfriend or boyfriend leaves you for someone, and they are perhaps slimmer with more hair, more interesting and better looking, it doesn't feel good," he told *Metal Planet Music* in 2023. "You lose your favorite singer from your favorite band. . . I think that's awkward as well."

Still, Bayley had no illusions about the fact that some fans will continue to grumble about him and the albums he made with the group.

"I'm very lucky to have actually had the top job in my field," he said. "I wanted to be a heavy metal singer, and by some quirk of faith, a lot of luck and a lot of help, then I managed to become the lead singer of Iron Maiden . . . it's nice that people are still interested in that brief part of the Maiden history that contains me. And a lot of people think very nicely of me. But there are still a lot of people that absolutely hate me."

BLAZE BAYLEY PERFORMS IN ATHENS, GREECE, ON AUGUST 11, 2024. HE HAD A HEART ATTACK IN 2023, BUT HE REFUSED TO DIE. HE HAD CONCERT VENUES TO CONQUER AND FANS TO SING TO, AFTER ALL.

DISCOGRAPHY

The Iron Maiden discography comprises seventeen studio and thirteen live albums. Only those original, official albums appear here—no bootlegs, box sets, home videos, or singles.

To reduce redundancy, many corners have been cut. The songwriting credit that appears most frequently on Iron Maiden records is "Harris," per the band's official website. As we all know, it got much more complicated than that, but for this exercise, assume Steve Harris wrote all the lyrics and music unless otherwise specified in "Notes."

During the 1980s, Iron Maiden's most frequent lineup was the "classic" lineup, which consisted of Bruce Dickinson (vocals), Steve Harris (bass), Nicko McBrain (drums), Dave Murray (guitar), and Adrian Smith (guitar).

In the 1990s, the lineups were evenly split between two singers throughout four studio albums, but because Dickinson appears on the live albums from this era and Blaze Bayley does not, Dickinson is the most frequent vocalist on the band's 1990s output. So, the lineup on that decade's albums is Bruce Dickinson (vocals), Janick Gers (guitar), Steve Harris (bass), Nicko McBrain (drums), and Dave Murray (guitar).

Finally, every album the band released from 2000 on was made by the "Three Amigos" lineup, which was the "classic" 1980s lineup, plus Janick Gers. Yes, that's a handful, but believe it or not, it's the most straightforward and least redundant way of showing who did what and when. So, in all three cases, assume all the aforementioned unless something in "Notes" says otherwise.

Regarding songwriting, performing, and production credits, the official Iron Maiden website shows that the band didn't list those things in alphabetical order, and sometimes songwriters would be listed in terms of the importance of their contributions to the songs. For the sake of clarity, all of that will be listed alphabetically.

Albums have their tracks enumerated in a single list, like on a compact disc, digital download, or streaming platform. For live albums recorded in multiple cities, we've included the names of the cities and recording dates where available. Also, assume that anything recorded in the 1980s has the "classic" lineup unless otherwise specified in "Notes," and assume that anything recorded from 2000 on was performed by the "Three Amigos" lineup.

Since the default information comes from the band's official website, we've used the 2013 reissue of *Maiden England* (otherwise known as *Maiden England '88*) because that's the one they're using.

Also, their site lists *BBC Archives* and *Beast over Hammersmith* as two individual releases (even though they're part of *Eddie's Archive*, which we're not including because it's a compilation), so we're including them. Also, the band's website uses the 1998 set *A Real Live Dead One*, which was originally two separate 1993 releases, *A Real Live One* and *A Real Dead One*.

All performance, release, and songwriting information comes from the official Iron Maiden website. The catalog numbers come from Discogs.com and designate the original UK pressing because there's no more British heavy metal band out there than Iron Maiden. That said, drink in the Iron Maiden discography and do so greedily!

STUDIO ALBUMS

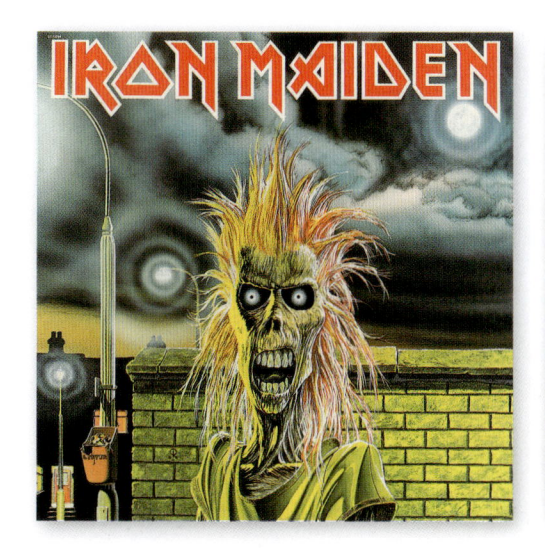

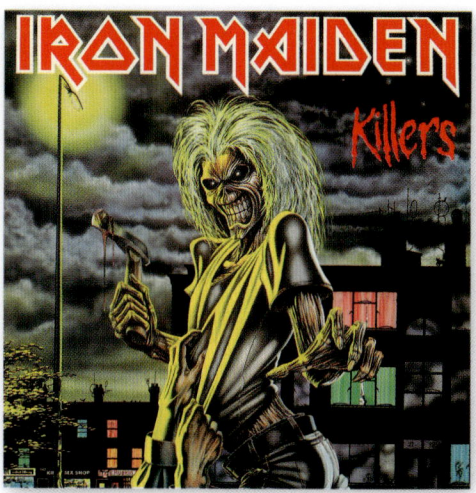

IRON MAIDEN

Released April 14, 1980, EMI (EMC 3330)

Recorded December 1979 at Kingsway Studios, London, England

Produced by Wil Malone

1. Prowler (3:55)
2. Remember Tomorrow (5:29)
3. Running Free (3:18)
4. Phantom of the Opera (7:21)
5. Transylvania (4:05)
6. Strange World (5:47)
7. Charlotte the Harlot (4:13)
8. Iron Maiden (3:34)

Notes: All music and lyrics by Steve Harris, except "Remember Tomorrow," "Running Free" by Paul Di'Anno, Steve Harris; "Charlotte the Harlot" by Dave Murray. Drums: Clive Burr; Vocals, Di'Anno; Guitar, Dennis Stratton.

KILLERS

Released February 2, 1981, EMI (EMC 3357)

Recorded November 1980–January 1981 at Battery Studios, London, England

Produced by Martin Birch

1. The Ides of March (1:45)
2. Wrathchild (2:55)
3. Murders in the Rue Morgue (4:19)
4. Another Life (3:24)
5. Genghis Khan (3:08)
6. Innocent Exile (3:53)
7. Killers (5:02)
8. Prodigal Son (6:13)
9. Purgatory (3:21)
10. Drifter (4:49)

Notes: "Killers" by Di'Anno, Harris. Drums, Burr; Vocals, Di'Anno.

THE NUMBER OF THE BEAST

Released March 22, 1982, EMI (EMC 3400)

Recorded January–February 1982 at Battery Studios, London, England

Produced by Martin Birch

1. Invaders (3:23)
2. Children of the Damned (4:35)
3. The Prisoner (6:03)
4. 22 Acacia Avenue (6:37)
5. The Number of the Beast (4:51)
6. Run to the Hills (3:53)
7. Gangland (3:49)
8. Hallowed Be Thy Name (7:11)

Notes: "The Prisoner," "22 Acacia Avenue" by Harris, Smith; "Gangland" by Burr, Smith. Drums, Burr.

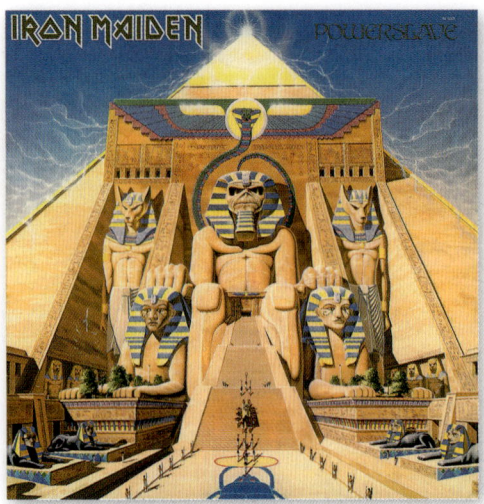

PIECE OF MIND

Released May 16, 1983, EMI (EMA 800)

Recorded January–March 1983 at Compass Point Studios, Nassau, Bahamas

Produced by Martin Birch

1. Where Eagles Dare (6:13)
2. Revelations (6:50)
3. Flight of Icarus (3:51)
4. Die with Your Boots On (5:27)
5. The Trooper (4:13)
6. Still Life (4:57)
7. Quest for Fire (3:43)
8. Sun and Steel (3:28)
9. To Tame a Land (7:29)

Notes: "Revelations" by Dickinson; "Flight of Icarus," "Sun and Steel" by Dickinson, Smith; "Die with Your Boots On" by Dickinson, Harris, Smith; "Still Life" by Harris, Murray.

POWERSLAVE

Released September 3, 1984, EMI (EJ 2402001)

Recorded February–June 1984 at Compass Point Studios, Nassau, Bahamas

Produced by Martin Birch

1. Aces High (4:32)
2. 2 Minutes to Midnight (6:04)
3. Losfer Words (Big 'Orra) (4:15)
4. Flash of the Blade (4:06)
5. The Duellists (6:08)
6. Back in the Village (5:03)
7. Powerslave (7:12)
8. Rime of the Ancient Mariner (13:39)

Notes: "2 Minutes to Midnight," "Back in the Village" by Dickinson, Smith; "Flash of the Blade," "Powerslave" by Dickinson.

SOMEWHERE IN TIME

Released September 29, 1986, EMI (EMC 3521)

Recorded January–June 1986 at Compass Point Studios, Nassau, Bahamas; Wisseloord Studio, Hilversum, Netherlands

Produced by Martin Birch

1. Caught Somewhere in Time (7:27)
2. Wasted Years (5:10)
3. Sea of Madness (5:44)
4. Heaven Can Wait (7:24)
5. The Loneliness of the Long Distance Runner (6:33)
6. Stranger in a Strange Land (5:47)
7. Deja-Vu (4:59)
8. Alexander the Great (356–323 B.C.) (8:37)

Notes: "Wasted Years," "Sea of Madness," "Stranger in a Strange Land" by Smith; "Deja-Vu" by Harris, Murray. Bass synthesizer, Harris; Guitar synthesizer, Murray, Smith; Backing vocals, Smith.

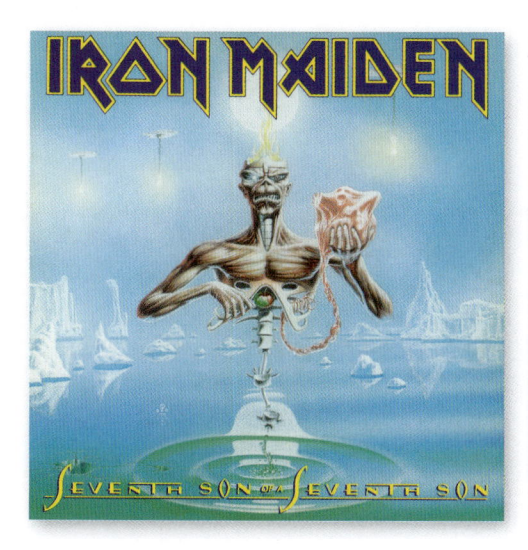

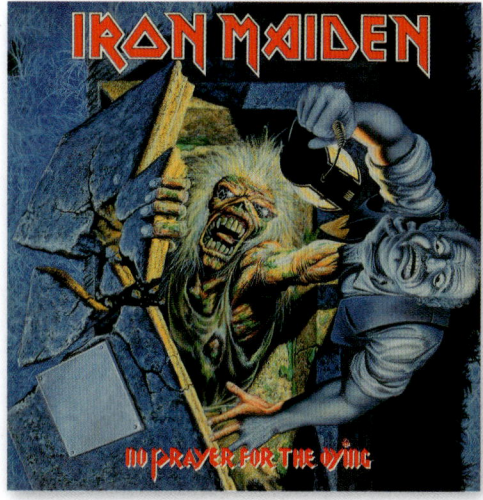

SEVENTH SON OF A SEVENTH SON

Released April 11, 1988, EMI (EDM 2006)

Recorded February–March 1988 at Musicland Studios, Munich, Germany

Produced by Martin Birch

1. Moonchild (5:41)
2. Infinite Dreams (6:09)
3. Can I Play with Madness (3:32)
4. The Evil That Men Do (4:34)
5. Seventh Son of a Seventh Son (9:54)
6. The Prophecy (5:06)
7. The Clairvoyant (4:27)
8. Only the Good Die Young (4:43)

Notes: "Moonchild" by Dickinson, Smith; "Can I Play with Madness," "The Evil That Men Do" by Dickinson, Harris, Smith; "The Prophecy" by Harris, Murray; "Only the Good Die Young" by Dickinson, Harris. String synthesizer by Harris; synthesizer by Smith.

NO PRAYER FOR THE DYING

Released October 1, 1990, EMI (EMD 1071)

Recorded June–September 1990 at Barnyard Studios, Essex, England

Produced by Martin Birch

1. Tailgunner (4:14)
2. Holy Smoke (3:49)
3. No Prayer for the Dying (4:23)
4. Public Enema Number One (4:14)
5. Fates Warning (4:11)
6. The Assassin (4:18)
7. Run Silent Run Deep (4:35)
8. Hooks in You (4:07)
9. Bring Your Daughter…to the Slaughter (4:44)
10. Mother Russia (5:32)

Notes: "Tailgunner," "Holy Smoke," "Run Silent Run Deep" by Dickinson, Harris; "Public Enema Number One" by Dickinson, Murray; "Fates Warning" by Harris, Murray; "Hooks in You" by Dickinson, Smith; "Bring Your Daughter…to the Slaughter" by Dickinson. Keyboards by Michael Kenney.

FEAR OF THE DARK

Released May 11, 1992, EMI (EMD 1032)

Recorded 1991–April 1992 at Barnyard Studios, Essex, England

Produced by Martin Birch

1. Be Quick or Be Dead (3:24)
2. From Here to Eternity (3:38)
3. Afraid to Shoot Strangers (6:57)
4. Fear Is the Key (5:35)
5. Childhood's End (4:41)
6. Wasting Love (5:51)
7. The Fugitive (4:54)
8. Chains of Misery (3:37)
9. The Apparition (3:55)
10. Judas Be My Guide (3:09)
11. Weekend Warrior (5:40)
12. Fear of the Dark (7:18)

Notes: "Be Quick or Be Dead," "Fear Is the Key," "Wasting Love" by Dickinson, Gers; "Chains of Misery," "Judas Be My Guide" by Dickinson, Murray; "The Apparition," "Weekend Warrior" by Harris, Gers. Keyboards by Kenney.

THE X FACTOR

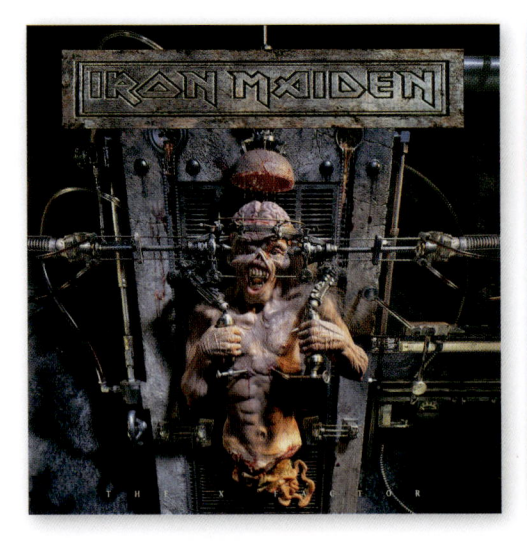

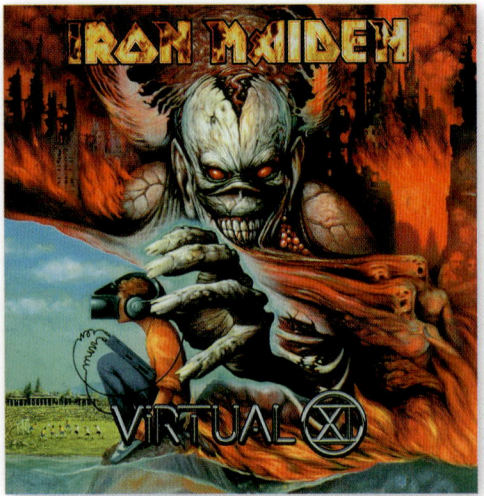

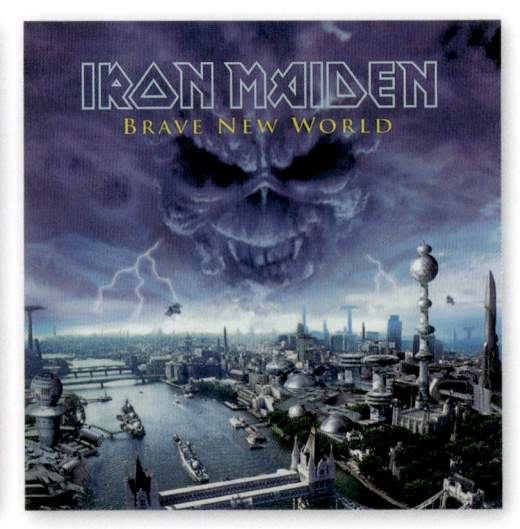

Released October 2, 1995, EMI (EMD 1087)

Recorded 1994–August 1995 at Barnyard Studios, Essex, England

Produced by Nigel Green, Steve Harris

1. Sign of the Cross (11:17)
2. Lord of the Flies (5:04)
3. Man on the Edge (4:14)
4. Fortunes of War (7:24)
5. Look for the Truth (5:10)
6. The Aftermath (6:21)
7. Judgement of Heaven (5:12)
8. Blood on the World's Hands (5:57)
9. The Edge of Darkness (6:39)
10. 2 A.M. (5:38)
11. The Unbeliever (8:10)

Notes: "Lord of the Flies," "The Unbeliever" by Gers, Harris; "Man on the Edge" by Bayley, Gers; "Look for the Truth," "The Aftermath," "The Edge of Darkness," "2 A.M." by Bayley, Gers, Harris. Vocals by Blaze Bayley. Keyboards by Kenney.

VIRTUAL XI

Released March 23, 1998, EMI United Kingdom (7243 8 35819 2 4)

Recorded 1997–February 1998 at Barnyard Studios, Essex, England

Produced by Nigel Green, Steve Harris

1. Futureal (2:55)
2. The Angel and the Gambler (9:53)
3. Lightning Strikes Twice (4:50)
4. The Clansman (9:00)
5. When Two Worlds Collide (6:17)
6. The Educated Fool (6:45)
7. Don't Look to the Eyes of a Stranger (8:04)
8. Como Estais Amigos (5:30)

Notes: "Futureal" by Bayley, Harris; "Lightning Strikes Twice" by Harris, Murray; "When Two Worlds Collide" by Bayley, Gers, Murray; "Como Estais Amigos" by Bayley, Gers. Vocals by Bayley. Keyboards by Harris, Kenney.

BRAVE NEW WORLD

Released May 29, 2000, EMI (7243 5 26605 2 0)

Recorded 1999–April 2000 at Guillaume Tell Studios, Paris, France

Produced by Steve Harris, Kevin Shirley

1. The Wicker Man (4:35)
2. Ghost of the Navigator (6:50)
3. Brave New World (6:19)
4. Blood Brothers (7:14)
5. The Mercenary (4:43)
6. Dream of Mirrors (9:21)
7. The Fallen Angel (4:01)
8. The Nomad (9:06)
9. Out of the Silent Planet (6:26)
10. The Thin Line Between Love and Hate (8:27)

Notes: "The Wicker Man" by Dickinson, Harris, Smith; "Ghost of the Navigator" by Dickinson, Gers; "Brave New World" by Dickinson, Harris, Murray; "The Mercenary," "Dream of Mirrors" by Gers, Harris; "The Fallen Angel" by Harris, Smith; "The Nomad," "The Thin Line Between Love and Hate" by Harris, Murray; "Out of the Silent Planet" by Dickinson, Gers, Harris. Keyboards by Harris.

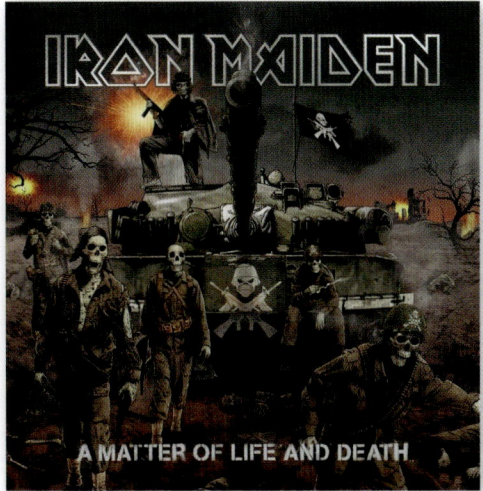

DANCE OF DEATH

Released September 8, 2003, EMI (592 3402)

Recorded January–February 2003 at Sarm West Studios, London, England

Produced by Steve Harris, Kevin Shirley

1. Wildest Dreams (3:52)
2. Rainmaker (3:48)
3. No More Lies (7:22)
4. Montségur (5:50)
5. Dance of Death (8:36)
6. Gates of Tomorrow (5:12)
7. New Frontier (5:04)
8. Paschendale (8:28)
9. Face in the Sand (6:31)
10. Age of Innocence (6:11)
11. Journeyman (7:06)

Notes: "Wildest Dreams," "Paschendale" by Harris, Smith; "Rainmaker" by Dickinson, Harris, Murray; "Montségur," "Gates of Tomorrow" by Dickinson, Gers, Harris; "Dance of Death" by Gers, Harris; "New Frontier" by Dickinson, McBrain, Smith; "Face in the Sand," "Journeyman" by Dickinson, Harris, Smith; "Age of Innocence" by Harris, Murray. Keyboards by Harris.

A MATTER OF LIFE AND DEATH

Released August 25, 2006, EMI (0946 372324 2 2)

Recorded March 1–May 4, 2006 at Sarm West Studios, London, England

Produced by Steve Harris, Kevin Shirley

1. Different World (4:18)
2. These Colours Don't Run (6:52)
3. Brighter Than a Thousand Suns (8:46)
4. The Pilgrim (5:08)
5. The Longest Day (7:48)
6. Out of the Shadows (5:37)
7. The Reincarnation of Benjamin Breeg (7:22)
8. For the Greater Good of God (9:25)
9. Lord of Light (7:25)
10. The Legacy (9:23)

Notes: "Different World" by Harris, Smith; "These Colours Don't Run," "Brighter Than a Thousand Suns," "The Longest Day," "Lord of Light" by Dickinson, Harris, Smith; "The Pilgrim," "The Legacy" by Gers, Harris; "Out of the Shadows" by Dickinson, Harris; "The Reincarnation of Benjamin Breeg" by Harris, Murray. Keyboards by Harris; guitar synthesizer by Smith.

THE FINAL FRONTIER

Released August 13, 2010, EMI (6477701)

Recorded January 11–March 1, 2010, at Compass Point Studios, Nassau, Bahamas; The Cave Studios, Malibu, California, United States

Produced by Steve Harris, Kevin Shirley

1. Satellite 15. . .The Final Frontier (8:40)
2. El Dorado (6:49)
3. Mother of Mercy (5:20)
4. Coming Home (5:52)
5. The Alchemist (4:29)
6. Isle of Avalon (9:06)
7. Starblind (7:48)
8. The Talisman (9:03)
9. The Man Who Would Be King (8:28)
10. When the Wild Wind Blows (11:01)

Notes: "Satellite 15. . .The Final Frontier," "Mother of Mercy," "Isle of Avalon" by Harris, Smith; "El Dorado," "Coming Home," "Starblind" by Dickinson, Harris, Smith; "The Alchemist" by Dickinson, Gers, Harris; "The Talisman" by Gers, Harris; "The Man Who Would Be King" by Harris, Murray. Keyboards by Harris.

THE BOOK OF SOULS

Released September 4, 2015, Parlophone (0825646089246)

Recorded September–December 2014 at Guillaume Tell Studios, Paris, France

Produced by Steve Harris, Kevin Shirley

1. If Eternity Should Fail (8:28)
2. Speed of Light (5:02)
3. The Great Unknown (6:38)
4. The Red and the Black (13:34)
5. When the River Runs Deep (5:53)
6. The Book of Souls (10:28)
7. Death or Glory (5:13)
8. Shadows of the Valley (7:32)
9. Tears of a Clown (4:59)
10. The Man of Sorrows (6:28)
11. Empire of the Clouds (18:01)

Notes: "If Eternity Should Fail," "Empire of the Clouds" by Dickinson; "Speed of Light," "Death or Glory" by Dickinson, Smith; "The Great Unknown," "When the River Runs Deep," "Tears of a Clown" by Harris, Smith; "The Book of Souls," "Shadows of the Valley" by Gers, Harris; "The Man of Sorrows" by Harris, Murray. Keyboards by Harris, Kenney.

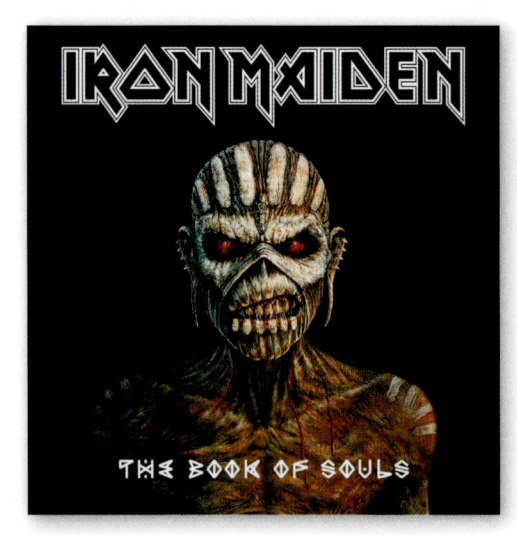

SENJUTSU

Released September 3, 2021, Parlophone (0190295015947)

Recorded 2019 at Guillaume Tell Studios, Paris, France

Produced by Steve Harris, Kevin Shirley

1. Senjutsu (8:20)
2. Stratego (5:00)
3. The Writing on the Wall (6:14)
4. Lost in a Lost World (9:32)
5. Days of Future Past (4:04)
6. The Time Machine (7:09)
7. Darkest Hour (7:20)
8. Death of the Celts (10:20)
9. The Parchment (12:39)
10. Hell on Earth (11:19)

Notes: "Senjutsu" by Harris, Smith; "Stratego," "The Time Machine" by Gers, Harris; "The Writing on the Wall," "Days of Future Past," "Darkest Hour" by Dickinson, Smith. Keyboards by Harris.

LIVE ALBUMS

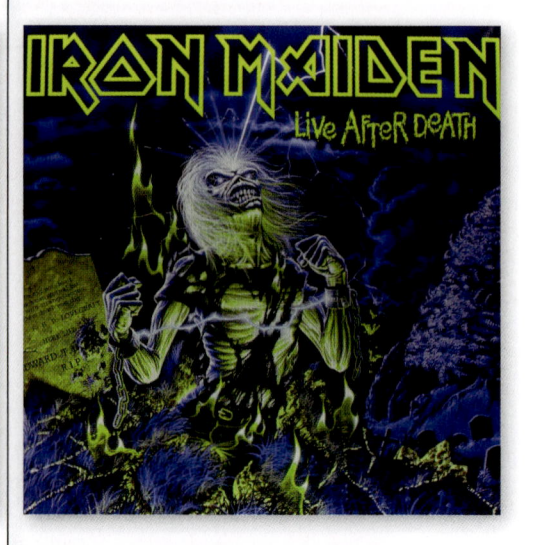

LIVE AFTER DEATH

Released October 14, 1985, 1985, EMI (ES 24 0426 3)

Recorded March 14–17, 1985, at Long Beach Arena, California, United States; October 8–12, 1984, at Hammersmith Odeon, London

Produced by Martin Birch

1. Intro: Churchill's Speech (0:49)
2. Aces High (4:37)
3. 2 Minutes to Midnight (6:03)
4. The Trooper (4:14)
5. Revelations (6:01)
6. Flight of Icarus (3:28)
7. Rime of the Ancient Mariner (13:19)
8. Powerslave (7:13)
9. The Number of the Beast (4:53)
10. Hallowed Be Thy Name (7:13)
11. Iron Maiden (4:20)
12. Run to the Hills (3:54)
13. Running Free (8:43)
14. Wrathchild (3:06)
15. 22 Acacia Avenue (6:18)
16. Children of the Damned (4:36)
17. Die with Your Boots On (5:12)
18. Phantom of the Opera (7:22)

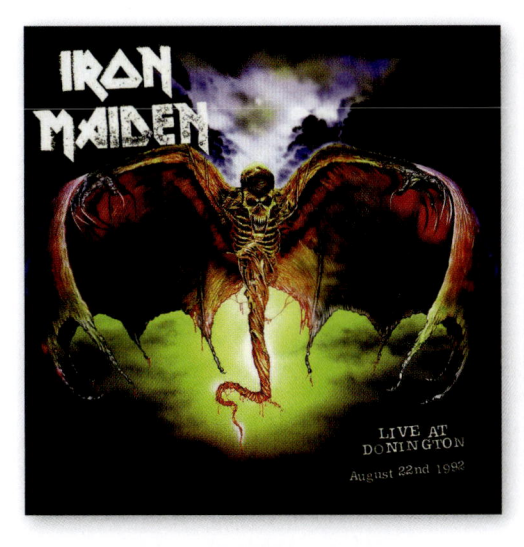

LIVE AT DONINGTON

Released November 8, 1993, EMI United Kingdom (7243 8 27511 2 0)

Recorded August 2, 1992, at Monsters of Rock festival, Donington Park, England

Produced by Martin Birch

1. Be Quick or Be Dead (3:53)
2. The Number of the Beast (4:54)
3. Wrathchild (2:54)
4. From Here to Eternity (4:44)
5. Can I Play with Madness (3:33)
6. Wasting Love (5:37)
7. Tailgunner (4:08)
8. The Evil That Men Do (7:51)
9. Afraid to Shoot Strangers (6:59)
10. Fear of the Dark (7:08)
11. Bring Your Daughter...to the Slaughter (6:12)
12. The Clairvoyant (4:22)
13. Heaven Can Wait (7:21)
14. Run to the Hills (4:16)
15. 2 Minutes to Midnight (5:43)
16. Iron Maiden (8:15)
17. Hallowed Be Thy Name (7:28)
18. The Trooper (3:53)
19. Sanctuary (5:18)
20. Running Free (7:54)

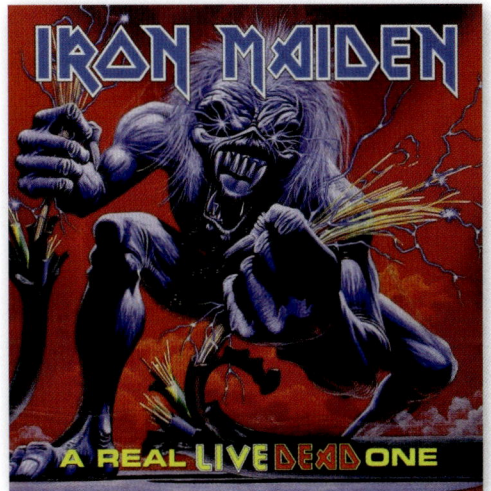

A REAL LIVE DEAD ONE!

Released September 22, 1998, EMI (496 9272)

Recorded August 15, 1992, at Super Rock festival, Mannheim, Germany; August 17, 1992, at Forest National, Brussels, Belgium; August 25, 1992, at Valby-Hallen, Copenhagen, Denmark; August 27, 1992, at Ice Hall, Helsinki, Finland; August 29, 1992, at Globe Arena, Stockholm, Sweden; September 2, 1992, at Brabanthallen, Den Bosch, Netherlands; September 4, 1992, at Patinoire de Malley, Lausanne, Switzerland; September 5, 1992, at Grande halle de la Villette, Paris, France; September 12, 1992, at Monsters of Rock festival, Reggio Nell Emilia, Italy; April 5, 1993, at Ostravar Aréna, Ostrava, Czech Republic; April 9, 1993, at Rijnhal, Arnhem, Netherlands; April 10, 1993, at Élysée Montmartre, Paris, France; April 17, 1993, at Grugahalle, Essen, Germany; April 30, 1993, at Palaghiaccio di Marino, Marino, Italy; May 27, 1993, at Patinoire du Littoral, Neuchâtel, Switzerland; June 4, 1993, at Olympic Stadium, Moscow, Russia.

Produced by Steve Harris

1. The Number of the Beast (4:55)
2. The Trooper (3:55)
3. Prowler (4:16)
4. Transylvania (4:26)
5. Remember Tomorrow (5:53)
6. Where Eagles Dare (4:49)
7. Sanctuary (4:53)
8. Running Free (3:49)
9. Run to the Hills (3:58)
10. 2 Minutes to Midnight (5:37)
11. Iron Maiden (5:25)
12. Hallowed Be Thy Name (7:52)
13. Be Quick or Be Dead (3:17)
14. From Here to Eternity (4:20)
15. Can I Play with Madness (4:42)
16. Wasting Love (5:48)
17. Tailgunner (4:10)
18. The Evil That Men Do (5:26)
19. Afraid to Shoot Strangers (6:48)
20. Bring Your Daughter...to the Slaughter (5:18)
21. Heaven Can Wait (7:29)
22. The Clairvoyant (4:30)
23. Fear of the Dark (7:11)

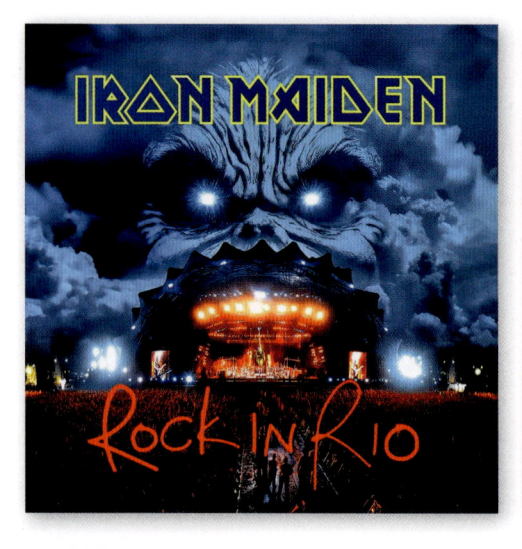

ROCK IN RIO

Released March 25, 2002, EMI (538 6430)

Recorded January 19, 2001, at Rock in Rio festival, Rio de Janeiro, Brazil

Produced by Kevin Shirley

1. Intro (1:56)
2. The Wicker Man (4:42)
3. Ghost of the Navigator (6:48)
4. Brave New World (6:07)
5. Wrathchild (3:06)
6. 2 Minutes to Midnight (7:08)
7. Blood Brothers (7:14)
8. Sign of the Cross (10:50)
9. The Mercenary (4:43)
10. The Trooper (4:24)
11. Dream of Mirrors (9:37)
12. The Clansman (9:19)
13. The Evil That Men Do (4:41)
14. Fear of the Dark (7:41)
15. Iron Maiden (5:56)
16. The Number of the Beast (5:01)
17. Hallowed Be Thy Name (7:24)
18. Sanctuary (5:22)
19. Run to the Hills (5:38)

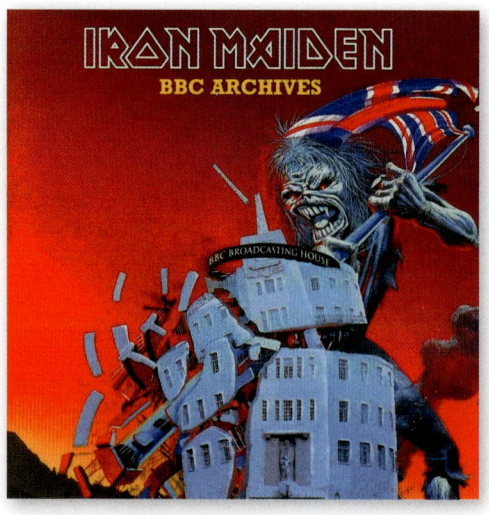

BBC ARCHIVES

Released November 4, 2002, EMI (7243 5 41277 2 4)

Recorded November 14, 1979, at Maida Vale Studios, London, England; August 23, 1980 & August 28, 1982, at Little John's Farm, Reading; August 20, 1988, at Monsters of Rock festival, Donington Park

Produced by Tony Wilson

1. Iron Maiden (3:46)
2. Running Free (3:10)
3. Transylvania (4:03)
4. Sanctuary (3:45)
5. Wrathchild (3:32)
6. Run to the Hills (5:36)
7. Children of the Damned (4:48)
8. The Number of the Beast (5:29)
9. 22 Acacia Avenue (6:36)
10. Transylvania (6:20)
11. The Prisoner (5:50)
12. Hallowed Be Thy Name (7:37)
13. Phantom of the Opera (7:02)
14. Iron Maiden (4:58)
15. Prowler (4:27)
16. Remember Tomorrow (5:59)
17. Killers (4:43)
18. Running Free (3:53)
19. Transylvania (4:49)
20. Iron Maiden (4:56)
21. Moonchild (5:43)
22. Wrathchild (3:00)
23. Infinite Dreams (5:51)
24. The Trooper (4:05)
25. Seventh Son of a Seventh Son (10:27)
26. The Number of the Beast (4:43)
27. Hallowed Be Thy Name (7:10)
28. Iron Maiden (6:01)

Notes: Drums on tracks 1–20 by Burr; Vocals on tracks 1–4 & 15–20 by Di'Anno.

BEAST OVER HAMMERSMITH

Released November 4, 2002, EMI (7243-541277-2-4)

Recorded March 20, 1982, at Hammersmith Odeon, London

Produced by Steve Harris

1. Murders in the Rue Morgue (4:32)
2. Wrathchild (3:31)
3. Run to the Hills (4:20)
4. Children of the Damned (4:38)
5. The Number of the Beast (5:08)
6. Another Life (3:45)
7. Killers (5:47)
8. 22 Acacia Avenue (6:56)
9. Total Eclipse (4:14)
10. Transylvania (5:51)
11. The Prisoner (5:49)
12. Hallowed Be Thy Name (7:31)
13. Phantom of the Opera (6:53)
14. Iron Maiden (4:20)
15. Sanctuary (4:13)
16. Drifter (9:19)
17. Running Free (3:44)
18. Prowler (5:00)

Notes: Drums by Burr.

DEATH ON THE ROAD

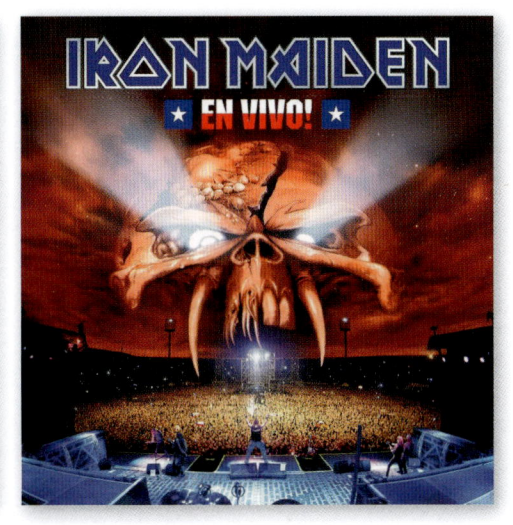

Released August 29, 2005, EMI (0946 336 4372 7)

Recorded November 24, 2003, at Westfalenhallen, Dortmund, Germany

Produced by Kevin Shirley

1. Wildest Dreams (4:52)
2. Wrathchild (2:49)
3. Can I Play with Madness (3:30)
4. The Trooper (4:12)
5. Dance of Death (9:23)
6. Rainmaker (4:01)
7. Brave New World (6:10)
8. Paschendale (10:17)
9. Lord of the Flies (5:04)
10. No More Lies (7:50)
11. Hallowed Be Thy Name (7:32)
12. Fear of the Dark (7:28)
13. Iron Maiden (4:50)
14. Journeyman (7:03)
15. The Number of the Beast (4:58)
16. Run to the Hills (4:24)

FLIGHT 666: THE ORIGINAL SOUNDTRACK

Released May 22, 2009, EMI (50999 6977572 7)

Recorded February 1, 2008, Mumbai, India; February 7, 2008, Melbourne, Australia; February 9, 2008, Sydney, Australia; February 16, 2008, Chiba, Japan; February 19, 2008, Inglewood, United States; February 22, 2008, Monterrey, Mexico; February 24, 2008, Mexico City, Mexico; February 26, 2008, San José, Costa Rica; February 28, 2008, Bogotá, Colombia; March 2, 2008, São Paulo, Brazil; March 4, 2008, Curitiba, Brazil; March 7, 2008, Buenos Aires, Argentina; March 9, 2008, Santiago, Chile; March 12, 2008, San Juan, Puerto Rico; March 14, 2008, East Rutherford, United States; March 16, 2008, Toronto, Canada

Produced by Kevin Shirley

1. Churchill's Speech (0:44)
2. Aces High (4:50)
3. 2 Minutes to Midnight (5:58)
4. Revelations (6:29)
5. The Trooper (4:02)
6. Wasted Years (5:07)
7. The Number of the Beast (5:07)
8. Can I Play with Madness (3:37)
9. Rime of the Ancient Mariner (13:42)
10. Powerslave (7:28)
11. Heaven Can Wait (7:36)
12. Run to the Hills (3:59)
13. Fear of the Dark (7:32)
14. Iron Maiden (5:26)
15. Moonchild (7:30)
16. The Clairvoyant (4:39)
17. Hallowed Be Thy Name (7:53)

EN VIVO!

Released March 23, 2012, EMI (50999 301590 2 0)

Recorded April 10, 2011, at Estadio Nacional, Santiago, Chile

Produced by Kevin Shirley

1. Satellite 15 (4:36)
2. The Final Frontier (4:10)
3. El Dorado (5:53)
4. 2 Minutes to Midnight (5:51)
5. The Talisman (8:46)
6. Coming Home (5:57)
7. Dance of Death (9:03)
8. The Trooper (3:59)
9. The Wicker Man (5:07)
10. Blood Brothers (7:04)
11. When the Wild Wind Blows (10:37)
12. The Evil That Men Do (4:17)
13. Fear of the Dark (7:30)
14. Iron Maiden (5:08)
15. The Number of the Beast (4:58)
16. Hallowed Be Thy Name (7:29)
17. Running Free (7:58)

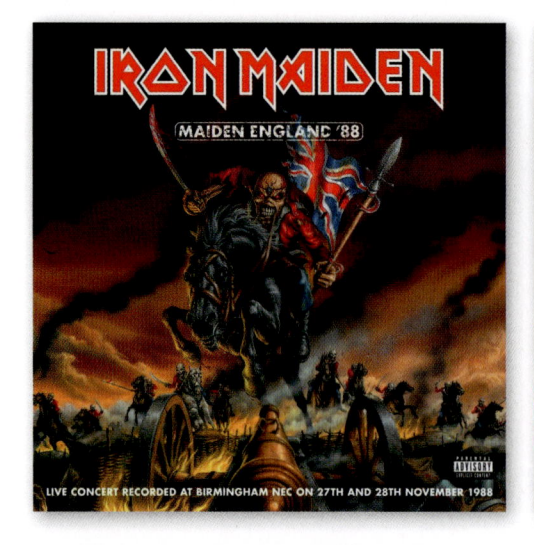

MAIDEN ENGLAND '88

Released March 25, 2013, EMI (50999 973 615 2 7)

Recorded November 27–28, 1988, at National Exhibition Centre, Birmingham, England

Produced by Martin Birch

1. Moonchild (6:23)
2. The Evil That Men Do (4:18)
3. The Prisoner (6:00)
4. Still Life (4:32)
5. Die with Your Boots On (5:19)
6. Infinite Dreams (5:53)
7. Killers (4:57)
8. Can I Play with Madness (3:25)
9. Heaven Can Wait (7:43)
10. Wasted Years (5:06)
11. The Clairvoyant (4:30)
12. Seventh Son of a Seventh Son (10:08)
13. The Number of the Beast (4:47)
14. Hallowed Be Thy Name (7:22)
15. Iron Maiden (5:12)
16. Run to the Hills (4:02)
17. Running Free (5:34)
18. Sanctuary (5:25)

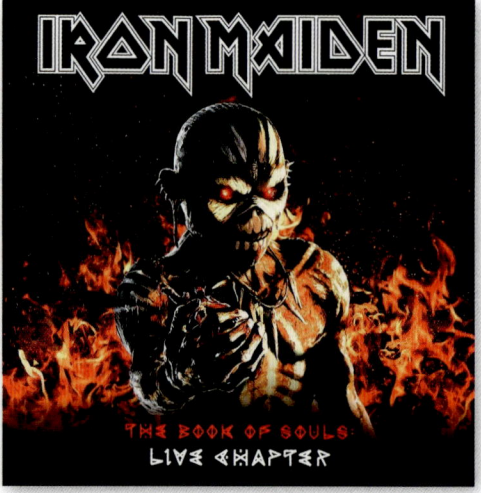

THE BOOK OF SOULS: LIVE CHAPTER

Released November 17, 2017, Parlophone (0190295760885)

Recorded March 6, 2016, at Estadio Jorge "Mágico" González, San Salvador, El Salvador; March 15, 2016, at José Amalfitani Stadium, Buenos Aires, Argentina; March 17, 2016, at HSBC Arena, Rio de Janeiro, Brazil; March 24, 2016, at Arena Castelão, Fortaleza, Brazil; April 1, 2016, at Bell Centre, Montreal, Canada; April 21, 2016, at Ryogoku Kokugikan, Tokyo, Japan; May 6, 2016, at Qudos Bank Arena, Sydney, Australia; May 18, 2016, at Grand Arena, Cape Town, South Africa; June 12, 2016, at Donington Park, Leicestershire, England; July 3, 2016, at Wroclaw Stadium, Wroclaw, Poland; July 26, 2016, at Piazza Unità d'Italia, Trieste, Italy; August 4, 2016, at Wacken Open Air, Wacken, Germany; May 6, 2017, at 3Arena, Dublin, Ireland; May 14, 2017, at Metro Radio Arena, Newcastle, England

Produced by Steve Harris

1. If Eternity Should Fail (7:47)
2. Speed of Light (5:09)
3. Wrathchild (3:00)
4. Children of the Damned (5:15)
5. Death or Glory (5:16)
6. The Red and the Black (13:17)
7. The Trooper (4:05)
8. Powerslave (7:32)
9. The Great Unknown (6:50)
10. The Book of Souls (10:50)
11. Fear of the Dark (7:34)
12. Iron Maiden (6:05)
13. The Number of the Beast (5:06)
14. Blood Brothers (7:35)
15. Wasted Years (5:39)

NIGHTS OF THE DEAD, LEGACY OF THE BEAST: LIVE IN MEXICO CITY

Released November 20, 2020, EMI (0190295204723)

Recorded September 27–30, 2019, at Palacio de los Deportes, Mexico City, Mexico

Produced by Tony Newton

1. Churchill's Speech (0:39)
2. Aces High (4:59)
3. Where Eagles Dare (5:13)
4. 2 Minutes to Midnight (5:54)
5. The Clansman (9:17)
6. The Trooper (4:02)
7. Revelations (6:32)
8. For the Greater Good of God (9:23)
9. The Wicker Man (4:44)
10. Sign of the Cross (11:01)
11. Flight of Icarus (3:43)
12. Fear of the Dark (7:47)
13. The Number of the Beast (5:00)
14. Iron Maiden (5:31)
15. The Evil That Men Do (4:26)
16. Hallowed Be Thy Name (7:38)
17. Run to the Hills (5:07)

BIBLIOGRAPHY

BOOKS

Bushell, Garry; Halfin, Ross. *Iron Maiden: Running Free. The Official Story of Iron Maiden.* Cherry Lane Books, 1984.

Ingham, Chris; Wall, Mick. *Run to the Hills: Iron Maiden, the Authorized Biography, 3rd edition.* Sanctuary Pub Ltd., 2004.

Occhiogrosso, Peter; Zappa, Frank. *The Real Frank Zappa Book.* Poseidon, 1989.

ARTICLES

Alderslade, Merlin, "Iron Maiden helped pay for former singer Paul Di'Anno's recent surgery and treatment: 'I only had 45 minutes to live,'" *Metal Hammer*, March 29, 2023.

Allen, Gavin, "Review: Iron Maiden's selfish decision was bound to disappoint sold-out crowd," *South Wales Echo*, December 12, 2006.

Andresen, Christer Bakke, "Review: Iron Maiden (1980)," maidenrevelations.com, October 13, 2012.

Bacon, Tony, "Interview: Steve Harris on Iron Maiden's foundation," reverb.com, July 23, 2020.

Barton, Geoff, "Geoff Barton's Buyers Guide to the new wave of British heavy metal," *Classic Rock*, December 27, 2013.

Barton, Geoff, "In 1980, Iron Maiden hit the road supporting Kiss. We were there," *Classic Rock*, September 20, 2022.

Bayley, Blaze, "The Road to Z7...," planetblaze.com, October 22, 2008.

Bienstock, Richard, "Neil Young: Gold Rush," *Guitar World*, September 29, 2009.

Billboard Staff, "Eminem Won't Budge from no. 1 on Billboard 200; Lil Wayne tops digital songs," *Billboard*, August 25, 2010.

"Blaze Bayley on joining Iron Maiden: 'I was very, very surprised that they chose me,'" Rockfiend Publications Scotland, April 15, 2019.

Brassneck, "Hello my name is... Steve Harris from Iron Maiden and British Lion," *Illinois Entertainer*, February 9, 2020.

"Chilean magazine slams Iron Maiden Why Music Matters animated film as 'Full of lies,'" bravewords.com, June 14, 2011.

DeRiso, Nick, "Iron Maiden's 'Trooper' beer has sold 3.5 million pints," ultimateclassicrock.com, March 5, 2014.

DiVita, Joe, "Why did Bruce Dickinson leave Iron Maiden in the '90s?" *Loudwire*, August 9, 2023.

Doran, John, "Iron lion scion: Steve Harris interviewed," *Quietus*, October 15, 2012.

Erlewine, Stephen, "*Virtual XI* review," allmusic.com.

Erlewine, Stephen, "*X Factor* review," allmusic.com.

"Ex-Iron Maiden singer Blaze Bayley discharged from hospital after undergoing quadruple heart bypass surgery," blabbermouth.net, April 19, 2023.

"Ex-Iron Maiden singer Paul Di'Anno: Crowdfunding campaign launched for long-overdue knee surgery," blabbermouth.net, January 15, 2021.

"Former Iron Maiden singer Blaze Bayley suffers heart attack, postpones live shows," blabbermouth.net, March 26, 2023.

"Former Iron Maiden singer Blaze Bayley to undergo triple heart bypass surgery," blabbermouth.net, March 29, 2023.

"Former Iron Maiden singer Paul Di'Anno: 'I nearly died four years ago,'" blabbermouth.net, December 5, 2019.

Giles, Jeff, "The history of Iron Maiden's 'Trooper' beer: 5 years, 20 million pints," ultimateclassicrock.com, May 9, 2018.

Greene, Andy, "Blaze Bayley on fronting Iron Maiden: 'It was like playing soccer for England in the World Cup,'" *Rolling Stone*, August 12, 2022.

Greene, Andy, "Iron Maiden's 'Flight 666': Bruce Dickinson on airborne adventure," *Rolling Stone*, June 25, 2009.

Grow, Kory, "Iron Maiden using BitTorrent analytics to plot tours," *Rolling Stone*, December 26, 2013.

Hill, Stephen, "'To promote an album and play some football, it's the ultimate for me': The bizarre story of the time Iron Maiden became a football team," *Metal Hammer*, May 2, 2024.

Hoare, Tom, "Brass tacks: Iron Maiden's Nicko McBrain," *Drummer's Journal*, March 28, 2016.

Holden, Stephen, "The pop life," *New York Times*, June 5, 1991.

Huey, Steve, "*Somewhere in Time* review," allmusic.com.

"Iron Maiden drummer defends band's decision to play entire new album live," blabbermouth.net, October 14, 2006.

"Iron Maiden drummer's restaurant honored for 'best ribs,'" blabbermouth.net, June 18, 2012.

"Iron Maiden flying to cinemas with 'Flight 666,'" reuters.com, April 15, 2009.

"Iron Maiden guitarist admits band used leftover ideas," blabbermouth.net, September 13, 2004.

"Iron Maiden guitarist on current tour: 'It's just a lot of great fun playing these songs,'" blabbermouth.net, October 20, 2006.

"Iron Maiden members were 'sworn to absolute secrecy' for more than two years about 'Senjutsu' album," blabbermouth.net, September 7, 2021.

"Iron Maiden singer Bruce Dickinson made honorary citizen of Bosnia's capital," Associated Press, April 7, 2019.

"Iron Maiden singers Bruce Dickinson and Paul Di'Anno meet for the first time," blabbermouth.net, July 13, 2024.

Johnson, Howard, "I went behind the Iron Curtain with Iron Maiden," *Louder*, September 20, 2022.

Kaufman, Spencer, "Iron Maiden's Bruce Dickinson undergoes treatment for cancerous tumor," loudwire.com, February 19, 2015.

Kennelty, Greg, "Iron Maiden's Bruce Dickinson on retirement: 'We'll probably drop dead onstage,'" metalinjection.net, March 12, 2022.

Kennelty, Greg, "Iron Maiden's Nicko McBrain discusses drumming after having a stroke," metalinjection.net, August 12, 2024.

Kielty, Martin, "Bruce Dickinson hater gave Iron Maiden singer his nickname," ultimateclassicrock.com, November 9, 2017.

Kielty, Martin, "Nicko McBrain's message to school friend who broke his nose," *Classic Rock*, September 20, 2022.

Lach, Stef, "Maiden to tour world in new Ed Force One," *Louder*, August 25, 2015.

Lach, Stef, "Paul Di'Anno was only joking when he compared Steve Harris to Adolf Hitler," *Metal Hammer*, November 13, 2022.

Lageat, Philippe, "Interview with Paul Di'Anno," *Rock Hard*, November 15, 2004.

Lawrenson, James, "When artwork goes wrong: The 10 worst album covers of the 00's," drownedinsound.com, November 4th, 2010.

Lawson, Dom, "Iron Maiden – four reissues of *The Beast*, reviewed," *Classic Rock*, September 20, 2022.

Lawson, Dom, "Kerrang 'Dance of Death' Review," *Kerrang!*, September 12, 2003.

"Legendary Iron Maiden and Deep Purple producer Martin Birch dead at 71," blabbermouth.net, August 9, 2020.

Maclarty, Andy, "*A Matter of Life and Death* review," bbc.co.uk.

"Maiden album's a 'maybe,'" rocknewsdesk.com, April 12, 2011.

Mier, Tomás, "Former Iron Maiden frontman Paul Di'Anno's cause of death revealed," *Rolling Stone*, November 11, 2024.

Miller, Nick, "Iron Maiden's football team: PL winner Colin Hendry, celebrity ringers and 'proper' matches," *New York Times*, November 24, 2023.

Monger, James Christopher, "*A Matter of Life and Death* review," allmusic.com.

Morris, Steven, "Former Iron Maiden singer jailed for benefit fraud," *Guardian*, March 11, 2011.

Neilstein, Vince, "In defense of Janick Gers, the [second] most badass dude in Iron Maiden," metalsucks.net, July 25, 2017.

O'Neill, Eamon, "Paul Di'Anno eonmusic interview December 2019," eonmusic.co.uk, December 2019.

Page, Theo, "Opinion: Why you should love 'Bring Your Daughter...' even though it's crap," *Metal Hammer*, September 20, 2022.

Prato, Greg, "Clive Burr, ex-Iron Maiden drummer, dead at 56," *Rolling Stone*, March 13, 2013.

Prato, Greg, "*Live After Death* review," allmusic.com.

Prato, Greg, "Why was Dennis Stratton sacked from Iron Maiden? 'Coming back from the Kiss tour, I knew there was a problem,'" ultimate-guitar.com, December 14, 2023.

"Raising Hell," ironmaiden-bg.com.

Ruskell, Nick, "Iron Maiden's Bruce Dickinson on the shows that made him who he is," *Kerrang!*, August 7, 2020.

Stagno, Mike, "*Live After Death*," sputnikmusic.com, October 5, 2006.

PHOTO CREDITS

"Steve Harris on Blaze Bayley's 'Bloody good' albums with Iron Maiden: 'It was an important part of our career,'" blabbermouth.net, December 8, 2018.

"This is what Iron Maiden's 'Fear of the Dark' sounds like played by a 160-piece orchestra," *Metal Hammer*, September 20, 2022.

Travers, Paul, "Metal legends Iron Maiden make a stunning surprise return with their 17th studio album, *Senjutsu*," *Kerrang!*, September 1, 2021.

"When drummer Clive Burr was ousted from Iron Maiden in 1982," *Classic Rock*, February 2011.

Wilson, Brian, "10 hilariously terrible album covers and why they exist," whatculture.com, March 17, 2016.

Wolfson, Perrin, "Guns n' Roses/Metallica Riot in Montreal 28 years ago Aug 8 1992, as remembered by Perrin Wolfson," themetalvoice.com, August 8, 2020.

WEBSITES

allmusic.com
billboard.com
blabbermouth.net
bravewords.co
classicrockmagazine.com
eonmusic.co.uk
foxnews.com
guitarworld.com
illinoisentertainer.com
ironmaiden.com
ironmaidenbeer.com
ironmaiden-bg.com
kerrang.com
loudersound.com
loudwire.com
maidenfans.com
maidenrevelations.com
melodicrock.com
metalinjection.net
metalsucks.net
nytimes.com
planetblaze.com
reuters.com
reverb.com
rocknewsdesk.com
rollingstone.com
sputnikmusic.com
thedrummersjournal.com
theguardian.com
thequietus.com
ultimate-guitar.com
ultimateclassicrock.com
ultimatemetal.com
whatculture.com
youtube.com

A = all, B = bottom, L = left, M = middle, R = right, T = top

Alamy Stock Photos: 13 (Vuk Valcic/ZUMA Press Wire), 23 (Goddard Archive Portraits), 31 (Trinity Mirror/Mirrorpix), 34-35 (Robert Landau), 40 (dpa picture alliance), 57L (dpa picture alliance), 58-59 (dpa picture alliance), 61T (dpa picture alliance), 65T (dpa picture alliance), 76-77 (dpa picture alliance), 84 (Fabio Diena), 85 (Fabio Diena), 86 (Fabio Diena), 95 (Trinity Mirror/Mirrorpix), 112 (Shawshots), 117L (Peo Möller/Alamy Live News), 130B (PA Images), 132-133 (© Kevin Estrada/MediaPunch, Inc.), 138 (Dinodia Photos), 139L (Avpics), 143L (Matt Crossick), 143R (Kemppainen), 146 (Vaclav Salek/CTK Photo/Alamy Live News), 151 (Storms Media Group/Alamy Live News), 155 (Fabio Diena), 159 (Hoo-Me/SMG), 160B (Imaginechina), 163L (Gonzales Photo - Lasse Lagoni), 165T (Gonzales Photo/Alamy Live News), 168-169 (Mpi04/Media Punch/Alamy Live News), 173 (NurPhoto SRL/Alamy Live New).

Avalon: 2 (Tony Mottram/Retna UK), 28-29 (Frank Griffin), 38B (Frank Griffin), 49B (dpa picture alliance), 99 (Ola Bergman), 109 (Ola Bergman), 127 (Simon Fowler), 129L (Simon Fowler).

Frank White Photo Agency: 7 (Frank White), 54-55 (Frank White), 62-63 (Frank White), 64 (Frank White), 69 (Frank White), 160TR (Steve Trager), 161T (Steve Trager).

Getty Images: 11L (Virginia Turbett/Redferns), 25 (Robert Ellis/Hulton Archive), 27 (Fin Costello/Redferns), 32 (Koh Hasebe/Shinko Music), 33T (Koh Hasebe/Shinko Music), 34-35 (Paul Natkin), 39 (Ebet Roberts/Redferns), 42L (Fin Costello/Redferns), 43T (Fin Costello/Redferns), 44 (Michael Putland/Hulton Archive), 47T (Paul Natkin), 51L (Pete Still/Redferns), 52TR (Paul Natkin), 53TL (Pete Still/Redferns), 67BL (Aaron Rapoport), 70-71 (Brian Rasic/Hulton Archive), 75 (Ebet Roberts/Redferns), 80 (Mick Hutson/Redferns), 83 (Ian Dickson/Redferns), 89 (Gie Knaeps/Hulton Archive), 90-91 (Stuart Mostyn/Redferns), 97T (Brian Rasic/Hulton Archive), 101 (Brian Rasic/Hulton Archive), 103T (Brian Rasic/Hulton Archive), 105T (Pete Still/Redferns), 106-107 (Brian Rasic/Hulton Archive), 110B (Mitchell Gerber/Corbis/VCG), 111T (STEPHANE/Gamma-Rapho), 113L (Mick Hutson/Redferns), 114 (Mike Guastella), 119 (Mitchell Gerber/Corbis Entertainment), 121 (Paul Natkin), 122R (Paul Natkin), 125T (Mick Hutson/Redferns), 126 (Leslie McGhie/WireImage), 135 (Annamaria DiSanto/WireImage), 136R (Annamaria DiSanto/WireImage), 137T (Annamaria DiSanto/WireImage), 140R (ATTILA KISBENEDEK/AFP), 141T (Richard Ecclestone/Redferns), 149L (Gie Knaeps/Hulton Archive), 150B (Gie Knaeps/Hulton Archive), 153 (FRANCESCO DEGASPERI/AFP), 157L (Virginia Turbett/Redferns), 167L (Metal Hammer Magazine), 171 (Ebet Roberts/Redferns).

IconicPix: 8 (George Bodnar Archive), 12 (George Bodnar Archive), 15 (George Bodnar Archive), 17 (George Bodnar Archive), 19 (George Bodnar Archive), 20 (Veuige/Dalle), 24TR (Jean Marc Birraux/Dalle), 72-73 (George Bodnar Archive), 79B (George Bodnar Archive), 118 (George Bodnar Archive), 124 (George Chin).

Robert Alford: 145.

ACKNOWLEDGMENTS

I am profoundly grateful to the following people who gave me their time, let me interview them, and made good-faith attempts to answer my strangest questions:

Dr. R. Douglas Helvering, composer and host of the *Daily Doug* YouTube channel.

Hugh Syme, *The X Factor* album cover designer.

Professor Deena Weinstein, PhD, sociologist and author of *Heavy Metal: The Music and Its Culture*.

Thank you to my parents, Albert and Joanna Bukszpan, my sister Claudia Rutherford, my mother-in-law Valborg Linn, and my ride-or-die lesbian work wife, Constance Brinkley-Badgett. Even if you don't think you did anything to help me, trust me—you did. You have supported me in every way throughout my career, and none of it could have happened without you.

Thank you to Dennis Pernu of Quarto/Motorbooks for letting me write this book and the two that came before it. Like everything we've done, writing a book about Iron Maiden has been on my bucket list for years. It is only because of you that I can now check that box, and I hope we get to do many more books in the future. Long may we reign.

Thanks to my son, Roman, for inspiring me every day of my life just by being a part of it. I'm proud of my accomplishments, but none of them make me as proud as you do just by being who you are. And thank you for letting Mom and I take you to Barclays Center in 2017 to see Iron Maiden as your first-ever rock concert. I'm sorry they didn't play "Run to the Hills" on that tour, but it was a blast anyway.

Finally, thank you to my wife, Asia, my companion at three Iron Maiden concerts and forever the love of my life. You have loved me as I am, you know me better than I do, and you have sustained and strengthened me through all the ups and downs, especially the latter, since there have been a lot of those. You even realized before I did that all of these books were already prewritten in my head—it was just a matter of typing them out and spell-checking them.

Most of all, thank you to Blaze Bayley, Clive Burr, Paul Di'Anno, Bruce Dickinson, Janick Gers, Steve Harris, Nicko McBrain, Dave Murray, Doug Sampson, Adrian Smith, and Dennis Stratton for making this timeless, unique, ferocious music, which has redeemed more atrocious, awful, appalling days of my life than I can count. Please keep it up.

INDEX

"Aces High," 6, 56, 142, 144, 162
"The Aftermath," 102
album covers, 39, 52, 88, 102, 133, 164
"Alexander the Great (356–323 B.C.)," 66
Allen, Gavin, 137

Bandwagon Heavy Metal Soundhouse, 12
Banger Films, 142
Barton, Geoff, 21–22
Bayley, Blaze
  on *Best of the Beast*, 104
  on Dickinson, 117
  entry into band and, 100
  ouster from band and, 116–117
  post–Iron Maiden career of, 172
  on songwriting, 100
  on tour for *X Factor*, 104
  on *Virtual VI* tour, 111
BBC Archives, 16, 22, 48, 73, 128
Beast over Hammersmith, 48, 128
Beazley, David, 38
"Be Quick or Be Dead," 88
Best of the Beast, 104
Best of the B-Sides, 18, 102, 128
Billboard magazine, 134, 148
Birch, Martin, 26, 46, 66, 82, 90, 162
BitTorrent traffic, 152
"Blood Brothers," 123
"Blood on the World's Hands," 102–103
The Book of Souls: Live Chapter, 159, 161
The Book of Souls, 159
Bostaph, Paul, 156
Brandy, 108
Braveheart, 108
Brave New World (album), 120, 123
"Bring Your Daughter . . . to the Slaughter," 74, 82, 84, 87, 108
Burr, Clive, 18, 46–49, 126, 156
Burton, Cliff, 21
Bushell, Gary, 12, 50, 59

Castle Donington, 72–73, 90
"Caught Somewhere in Time," 66
"Charlotte the Harlot," 21
The Chemical Wedding (Dickinson), 165

"Children of the Damned," 46
"The Clairvoyant," 68
"The Clansman," 108, 120, 125, 133, 162
classical music, 144
"Como Estais Amigos," 108
Cooke, Bayley Alexander. *See* Bayley, Blaze
COVID-19 pandemic, 162

Dance of Death, 131, 133
Darnley, John, 38
Death on the Road, 152
Def American Recordings, 100
"Deja Vu," 66
Di'Anno, Paul
  arrest at Hammersmith's Swan, 14
  death of, 170
  departure from band and, 33–34, 36
  Dickinson and, 45, 166
  Gogmagog and, 36, 49
  on Harris, 36
  on *Killers*, 33
  post–Iron Maiden career and, 166
  recruitment of, 11
  "Running Free" (song) and, 18
  "Women in Uniform" and, 26
Dickinson, Bruce
  on Birch, 162
  on Burr, 156
  cancer diagnosis and, 158
  departure from band and, 94, 96–98
  Ed Force One and, 141, 155, 159
  entry in band of, 42, 45–46
  flying and, 94
  The Number of the Beast and, 46
  Powerslave and, 56, 58
  on retirement, 170
  return to band, 118–119
  Sarajevo and, 118, 164
  Seventh Son of a Seventh Son and, 68
  solo career of, 118
  Somewhere in Time and, 66
  Trooper beer and, 152
  World Slavery tour and, 60, 66
Dio, Ronnie James, 123
DiVita, Joe, 118
Drake, Simon, 98
"Dream of Mirrors," 123

Eddie the Head (mascot), 6, 18, 38–39, 155
Eddie's Archive box set, 18, 128
"The Edge of Darkness," 102
Ed Hunter, 120
"El Dorado," 151
EMI, 14, 116
En Vivo!, 152
Erlewine, Stephen, 103, 108
"The Evil That Men Do," 68, 162

"The Fallen Angel," 123
"Fates Warning," 82
Fear of the Dark (album), 88, 90
"Fear of the Dark" (song), 144
The Final Frontier (album), 148, 151
"The Final Frontier" (song), 152
"Flash of the Blade," 56, 58
"Flight of Icarus," 50, 162
"For the Greater Good of God," 137, 162
Friday Rock Show, 16
"Futureal," 108, 120, 128, 133
Future Past tour, 6

"Gates of Tomorrow," 133
Gem, 42
Gers, Janick, 49, 74, 82, 87
Gillan, Ian, 74
Gogmagog, 36, 49
Grant, Melvyn, 88
Grow, Kory, 152
grunge, 82
guitar synthesizers, 66
Guns N' Roses, 72–73
Gypsy's Kiss, 18

"Hallowed Be Thy Name," 47–48, 128, 142, 152
Harris, Steve
  background of, 10
  on Bayley's ouster, 116
  on Birch, 162
  on Burr, 48, 156
  Di'Anno and, 34, 36
  on Dickinson's departure, 94, 96–97
  divorce of, 100
  on Ed Force One, 141
  formation of band and, 6, 11
  on the gallop, 112
  on Gers, 87

  influences of, 10
  on McBrain, 50
  Piece of Mind and, 52
  Polish shows and, 76
  Seventh Son of a Seventh Son and, 68, 70, 82
  on Smith, 25
  on *Somewhere in Time*, 66
  on *The X Factor*, 103
Hartland, Debbie, 172
Helvering, R. Douglas, 144
Herbert, Frank, 50, 52
Hill, Stephen, 154
Huey, Steve, 66

"Invasion," 12–13, 46
Iron Maiden: Behind the Iron Curtain, 77
Iron Maiden: Flight 666, 142
Iron Maiden: Run to the Hills (Wall), 10
Iron Maiden
  accusations of Satanism and, 53
  Ed Force One and, 141, 155, 159
  football club of, 154
  formation of, 6, 11
  gallop of, 30, 47, 53, 112
  influences on, 12, 144
  logo of, 11
  Polish shows and, 76–77
  Robinsons Brewery beer and, 155
  Spaceward Studios demo and, 12–14
  United States sales and, 68, 82
Iron Maiden (album), 21–22
"Iron Maiden" (song), 11–13, 21, 98

Jackson, John, 73
Johnson, Howard, 76
Judas Priest, 12, 66
"Judgement Day," 102

Kay, Neal, 12
Killers (album), 6, 26, 30, 33
"Killers" (song), 112
Kiss, 22, 72

Lawrenson, James, 133
Lawson, Dom, 103, 133
Legacy of the Beast tour, 162
Live After Death (album), 60, 62, 66, 142
Live After Death (DVD), 77
Live at Donington, 90, 96

London's Rainbow, 45
"The Longest Day," 137
"Lord of the Flies," 102–103, 133

McBrain, Nicko
   Dance of Death and, 131
   on Dickinson's cancer recovery, 161
   on Dickinson's departure, 97
   entry into band, 48
   flying and, 70
   on *A Matter of Life and Death* tour, 138
   on quitting drinking, 161
   Rock n Roll Ribs and, 152
   "Still Life" and, 53
   stroke and, 168
   World Slavery tour and, 60
McFadyen, Scot, 142
Maclarty, Andy, 134, 137
Maiden Concerts site, 164
Maiden England '88, 156
Maiden England tour, 156
Maiden England video, 74, 156
Malone, Wil, 21, 25
The Mandrake Project (Dickinson), 168
"Man on the Edge," 100, 102–103, 120, 133
The Man in the Iron Mask (film), 11
The Man Who Would Not Die (Blaze Bayley), 172
Matos, Michaelangelo, 134
A Matter of Life and Death, 134, 137–138
Metal Hammer, 154
Metal Sucks, 87
Millar, Robbi, 30
Monger, James Christopher, 137
Monsters of Rock festival (1988), 72–73
"Montségur," 133
Morello, Tom, 156
"Mother Russia," 82
Murray, Dave, 11, 18, 74, 96, 138, 151
Musicmetric, 152

Neilstein, Vince, 87
"New Frontier," 131
Newsted, Jason, 74
Newton-Price, James, 166
Nights of the Dead, Legacy of the Beast: Live in Mexico City, 162
"No More Lies," 131

No Prayer for the Dying (album), 6, 39, 82, 88, 90
"The Number of the Beast," 42, 46
The Number of the Beast (album), 46–47, 53
Nylon Maiden (Zwijsen), 116

Page, Theo, 84
Patchett, David, 133
"Phantom of the Opera," 21, 128
Piatt, Tony, 25–26
Piece of Mind (album), 50, 52–53
Powerslave (album), 6, 56, 58–59
"Powerslave" (song), 58
Prato, Greg, 60, 156
"The Prisoner," 46
prog rock, 10, 144
"Prowler" (song), 11–13, 21, 42
"Public Enema Number One," 82
punk rock, 12
"Purgatory," 30, 33

"Quest for Fire," 52

Radio 1 Rock Show, 128
"Rainmaker," 131
Raising Hell video, 98
Reading Festival (1980), 22
Reading Festival (1982), 48
A Real Dead One, 94, 96
A Real Live Dead One, 94
A Real Live One, 94, 96
"Remember Tomorrow," 21, 42, 45, 128
Richard, Cliff, 84
Riggs, Derek, 18, 38–39, 88
"Rime of the Ancient Mariner," 58–59, 142, 144
Robinsons Brewery, 155
Rock Hard Records, 14
Rock n Roll Ribs restaurant, 152
Rockpop in Concert appearance, 25
Rock in Rio, 124–125
Rock in Rio festival, 60, 124–125
Rossini, Gioachino, 112
Rubin, Rick, 100
Running Free (Bushell), 12, 14, 42
"Running Free" (song), 18, 42, 112
"Run to the Hills," 6, 47, 124
Run to the Hills (Wall), 25, 30, 34
Run for Your Lives tour (2025-2026), 6

Sampson, Doug, 11, 16, 18
Samson, 42
"Sanctuary," 21, 42, 128
"Satellite 15," 152
"Satellite 15 . . . The Final Frontier," 151
Senjutsu, 164–165
Seventh Son (Card), 68
Seventh Son of a Seventh Son (album), 68, 70
"Seventh Son of a Seventh Son" (song), 73
Shirley, Kevin, 131, 164
Shots, 42
"Sign of the Cross," 102–103, 125, 133, 162
Silicon Messiah (Blaze), 172
Skaka, Abdulah, 164
Smallwood, Rod
   Di'Anno and, 34
   Dickinson and, 42, 118
   Eddie mascot and, 38
   on Monsters of Rock festival (1988), 72
   on Smith side project, 74
   Soundhouse Tapes and, 14
   Stratton and, 22
   on touring strategy, 162
   World Slavery tour and, 60
Smiler, 10
Smith, Adrian
   "Adrian Smith and Project," 74
   on Burr, 48, 50
   departure from band and, 75
   on Dickinson, 46
   Donington (1992) show and, 90
   entry into band and, 25
   on Monsters of Rock festival (1988), 72–73
   Powerslave and, 56, 58
   return tom band and, 118–119
   World Slavery tour and, 60
Somewhere Back in Time tour, 137, 141–142
Somewhere in Time, 66
The Soundhouse Tapes, 12–14
SoundScan system, 134
Sounds magazine, 12, 30
speed metal, 68, 82
Spinal Tap, 59
Squire, Chris, 10
Stagno, Mike, 60
"Strange World," 12–13, 21

"Stratego," 164
Stratton, Dennis, 16, 22, 25, 166
Sweden Symphony Orchestra, 144
Syme, Hugh, 39, 102

"Tailgunner," 82
"The Talisman," 151
Tattooed Millionaire (Dickinson), 74, 94
"Tears of a Clown," 159
Travers, Paul, 164
"The Trooper," 6, 50, 52–53, 112, 124, 138, 152, 162
Trust, 126
"2 Minutes to Midnight," 56, 59, 124

Virtual XI (album), 100, 108, 111
"Virus," 104

Wadenbrandt, Ulf, 144
Wall, Mick, 10
"Wasted Years," 66
Weinstein, Deena, 12–13, 39, 50, 76–77
"The Wicker Man," 123
Wilcock, Dennis, 11
Wishbone Ash, 10, 26
Wiwczarek, Piotr, 77
Wolfsbane, 100
"Women in Uniform," 13, 26
World Slavery tour, 60, 66, 76
"Wrathchild," 30, 138
"The Writing on the Wall," 164–165

The X Factor (album), 39, 100, 102–104

Young, Neil, 144

Zomba, 26
Zwijsen, Thomas, 116

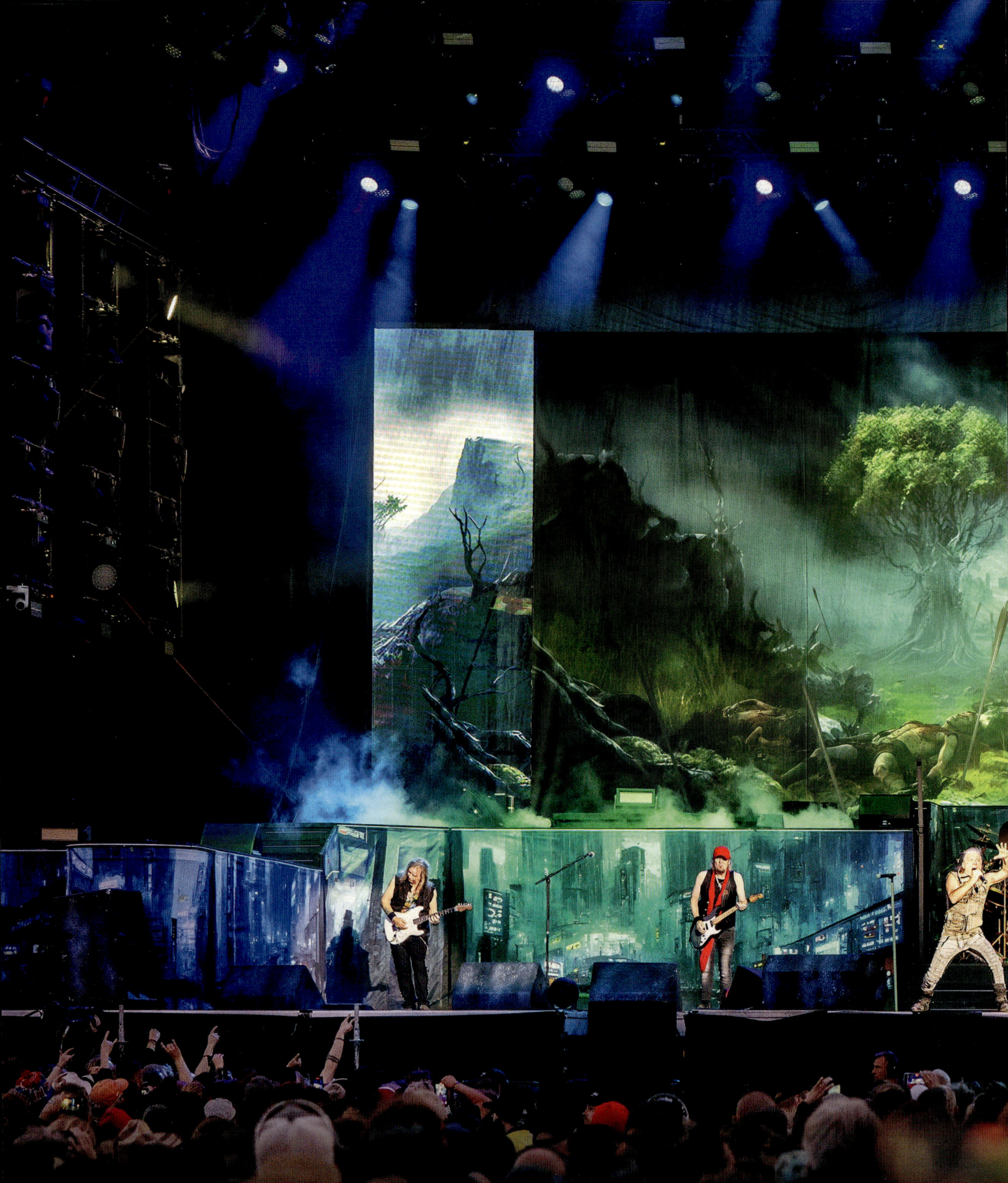

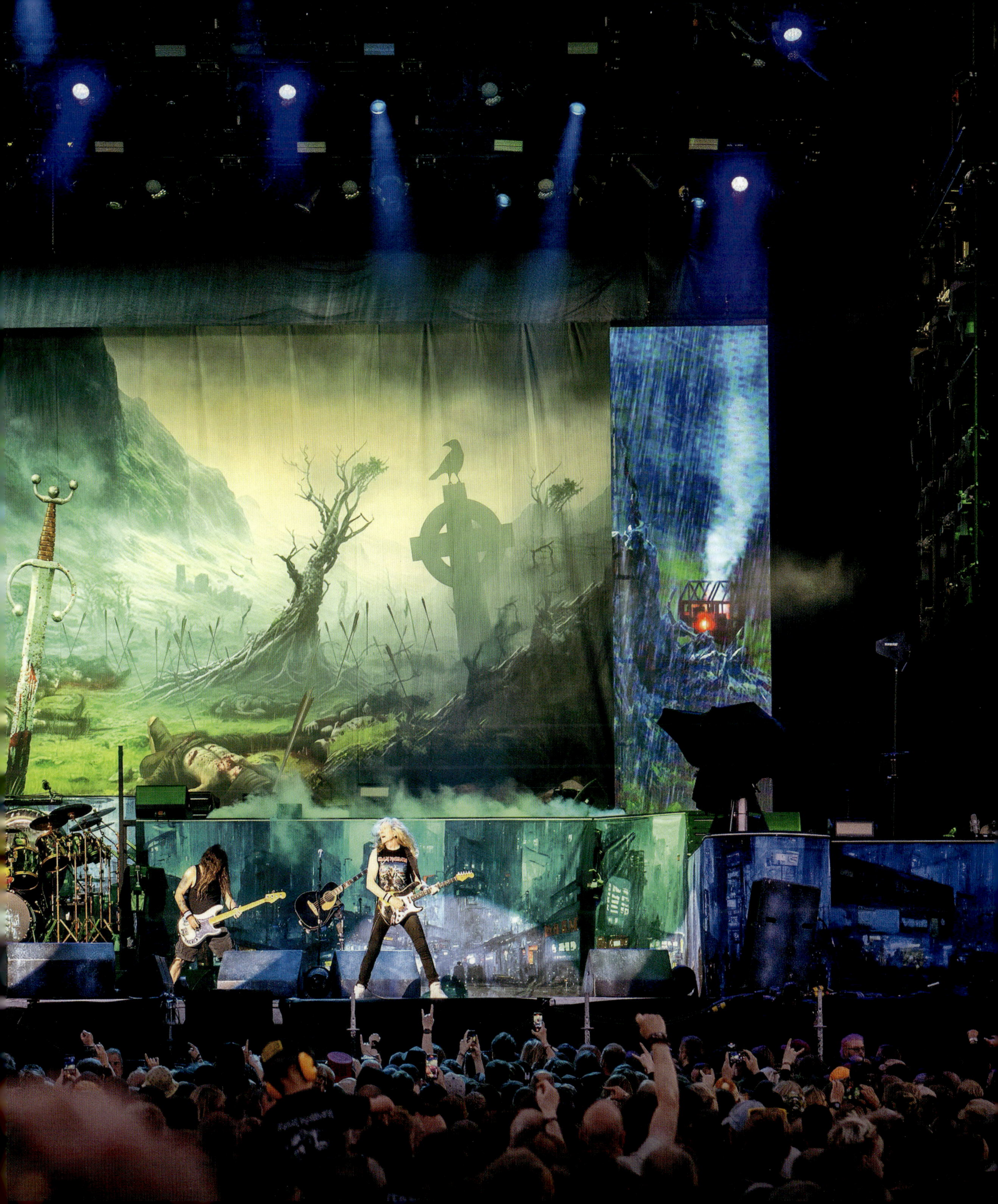

Quarto.com

© 2025 Quarto Publishing Group USA Inc.
Text © 2025 Daniel Bukszpan

First published in 2025 by Motorbooks, an imprint of The Quarto Group,
100 Cummings Center, Suite 265-D, Beverly, MA 01915, USA.
T (978) 282-9590 F (978) 283-2742

All rights reserved. No part of this book may be reproduced in any form without written permission of the copyright owners. All images in this book have been reproduced with the knowledge and prior consent of the artists concerned, and no responsibility is accepted by producer, publisher, or printer for any infringement of copyright or otherwise, arising from the contents of this publication. Every effort has been made to ensure that credits accurately comply with information supplied. We apologize for any inaccuracies that may have occurred and will resolve inaccurate or missing information in a subsequent reprinting of the book.

This book has not been prepared, approved, or licensed by Iron Maiden or any of its individual members, past or present. This is an unofficial publication.

Motorbooks titles are also available at discount for retail, wholesale, promotional, and bulk purchase. For details, contact the Special Sales Manager by email at specialsales@quarto.com or by mail at The Quarto Group, Attn: Special Sales Manager, 100 Cummings Center, Suite 265-D, Beverly, MA 01915, USA.

29 28 27 26 25   1 2 3 4 5

ISBN: 978-0-7603-9504-2

Digital edition published in 2025
eISBN: 978-0-7603-9505-9

Library of Congress Cataloging-in-Publication Data

Names: Bukszpan, Daniel, author.
Title: Iron Maiden at 50 / Daniel Bukszpan.
Other titles: Iron Maiden at fifty
Description: Beverly : Motorbooks, 2025. | Series: At 50 | Includes
   bibliographical references and index. | Summary: "Iron Maiden at 50
   takes fans on a journey through the legendary heavy metal band's
   half-century of performances, releases, personnel changes, and more"--
   Provided by publisher.
Identifiers: LCCN 2024060376 | ISBN 9780760395042 (hardcover) | ISBN
   9780760395059 (ebook)
Subjects: LCSH: Iron Maiden (Musical group) | Rock musicians--England. |
   Heavy metal (Music)--England--History and criticism.
Classification: LCC ML421.I76 B85 2025 | DDC
   782.42166092/2--dc23/eng/20250107
LC record available at https://lccn.loc.gov/2024060376

Design and layout: Burge Agency

Front cover image: Hans-Martin Issler/IconicPix
Back cover image: Paul Natkin

Printed in China